D0909846

# THE
# MORAL
# REVOLUTION

Also by Joseph N. Sorrentino
*Up from Never*

# THE MORAL REVOLUTION

BY
## JOSEPH N. SORRENTINO

NASH PUBLISHING
LOS ANGELES

HN 65
.S59
309.173
S7742

Copyright © 1972 by Joseph N. Sorrentino

All rights reserved. No part of this book
may be reproduced in any form or by any means
without permission in writing from the publisher.

Library of Congress Catalog Card Number: 74-186929
Standard Book Number: 8402-1269-0

Published simultaneously in the United States and
Canada by Nash Publishing Corporation,
9255 Sunset Boulevard, Los Angeles, California 90069.

Printed in the United States of America.

First Printing.

*To a creative, sensitive, and humane society.*

AUG 2 2 1973

# ACKNOWLEDGMENTS

This book was made possible by the efforts of my research assistants Mark Mahler and Paul Manof, and my students at UCLA, UCSB, UWLA, Valley State (special mention for Rhonda Ross), and the following speakers on my programs: George Latimer, Luke McKissack, Alfred Gitelson, Leonard Boudin, Charles Garry, Fay Stender, Yvonne W. Brathwaite, Joan Dempsey Klein, Vincent Bugliosi, Helen B. Andelin, Allen Charles, Dr. Leon Belous, Joseph R. Carter, Jr., Jeanne Cordova, Edward A. Germain, Stuart Goldfarb, Evelyn G. Hooker, Harold W. Horowitz, Barbara Ingle, Meldon E. Levine, James E. Miller, Troy D. Perry, Marvin Schachter, Thomas R. Sheridan, Alexander B. Taylor, Walter F. Trinkaus, Floyd L. Wakefield, Richard A. Wasserstrom.

# INTRODUCTION

This book evolved out of a public lecture series I created and coordinated for the University of California at Los Angeles, Social Sciences Extension. The series attracted the largest audience in the history of the university since Sputnik stampeded two thousand engineers to enroll in a course on space technology. Some fifteen hundred citizens came to the UCLA campus for ten sessions to gain some understanding of the profound and perplexing legal-moral issues of our day. Given the enormous response and sharp interest shown in the subjects of the lecture series, there seemed a need for this book.

For better or worse, we live in an era of revolutionary change. The abandonment of previously unquestioned philosophies and life-styles and the adoption of radical new convictions and guidelines in their place are the dominant characteristics of our time.

Some change is unquestionably good and long overdue. This book will explore many of the abuses that have plagued our criminal law system, wasting police time and energy and harassing conscientious citizens. But some elements of the moral revolution cannot be so easily endorsed. There are difficult questions that must be resolved if we are to convert our newly acquired technology and the energies of our youth into a better society. What of the specter of scientifically produced life? Should marijuana be legalized? What should the role of the modern woman be? These are problems that face all of us, and their answers must come from our collective wisdom. They are not merely the province of longhairs, scientists, and the "liberal press" as those of reactionary ilk would have us believe. If our democratic traditions are to mean anything, it is the duty of all American citizens to inform themselves on the issues of change that surround us. It is not enough to have an opinion, for a mere opinion can be born of stubborn ignorance and resistance. Informed rational opinions, whichever side they may fall on, are what our society needs. This book is dedicated to providing the kind of knowledge on which informed opinions are based. We can no longer afford to leave the decisions that will shape our society to a chosen, unchecked few. From penal reform to women's lib, from capital punishment to the sexual revolution, the controversies are essentially illuminated without preaching so that you, the reader, may effectively join the decision process.

# CONTENTS

# PART I
# REVOLUTION IN MARITAL PATTERNS

*Morals, which change so slowly, are changing today like clouds before the wind. Customs and institutions older than human memory melt under our eyes as if they were superficial habits, recently acquired and easily forgotten.*
*Will Durant*, The Pleasures of Philosophy
*(1953)*

# SPOUSE-SWAPPING

It could easily be the weekly session of the neighborhood bridge club. The four couples sit comfortably in the modest but tastefully decorated living room of Al and his wife Jean's San Fernando Valley home. Light conversation flows steadily. The weekend's football action and the upcoming election monopolize the talk. Sipping drinks and glancing occasionally at a television set in the corner, the hosts and their guests are a picture of Middle America. The wives are dressed stylishly, neither excessively mod nor behind the times. Their husbands, all moderately successful in their careers, embody genial middle-class sophistication. They might have been fraternity brothers ten years before.

But these couples are not out for a little relaxation away from the kids this particular evening. For as the night wears on, a subtle game of pairing develops. Each party present chooses a partner, some verbally, others by a visual kind of communication. Eventually the setting is right, and the newly formed couples proceed to waiting bedrooms for whatever brand of intimacy they choose. And when the festivities are over, husbands and wives reunite to drive back home to the baby-sitter. Another night of swinging was enjoyed.

This phenomenon goes by many names now—group sex, co-marital sex, wife-swapping, or, with increasing popularity, "swinging." More than two million predominantly middle-class Americans participate actively in it. It is tied together by a growing network of magazine listings, bars, and organized clubs dotting the entire face of this nation. It is the hidden face of outwardly conventional America, a silent but sometimes not so silent conspiracy of promiscuity. If you are not a participant, it may not seem so pervasive; but the odds are good that there are full-fledged swingers living nearby, most of whom are quite good in maintaining a straight facade.

## Reasons Given for "Swinging"

From what source did all this unfettered sexual activity spring? Why do husbands and wives not only consent to but actively encourage mutual infidelities by their partners? Dolly L. is a thirty-four-year-old mother of three with an uncalculating, straightforward air about her. Her response typifies swingers' feelings and suggests a number of reasons for the group sex trend:

"Look, I want you to understand right off the bat that I love my husband very much and I intend to stay with him for the rest of my life. He's been a warm and loving husband to me and a great father to our kids. The only thing about our relationship that's at all different from any other marriage is our attitude about sex.

"You see, Frank and I don't see sex as the ultra-serious, super-meaningful thing that you hear about in church. It's a wonderful thing, sure, and sometimes it's an act of love on a higher level. But other times, when you want it to be, it's just a damn good physical thing. No more and no less. I never get involved emotionally or personally with the men I make love to, and I never see them in any other context. In fact, after a few days, I can't even remember their names or faces.

"It wasn't always that way, believe me. When Frank first suggested it to me, I looked at him like he was kidding. I thought it was outrageous. I'd never cheated since we'd been married and the idea of climbing into the sack with some guy I'd never seen up to two hours ago, right in front of my husband, was just a total freak-out for me. Don't get me wrong or anything. I had my share of lovers before I got married, and I'd always enjoyed sex. But I'd always been into that whole scene where once you settle down with a husband, you cool it and stick with him. The ball game's over. I knew that Frank had a fling or two once in a while but I kind of accepted a double standard. It never really threatened our marriage.

"I refused at first. But when Frank insisted, I went along because I was afraid of losing him altogether. The first few times were bad because I felt a little guilty and I was too nervous to enjoy it. And I was jealous, too, to see the women who were sharing my husband. After a while, though, I kind of learned to detach my emotions from the physical side of sex and to enjoy lovemaking for its own sake.

"Let's face it. Even the married couples who really love each other tire of each other's bodies in time. The old magic begins to fade as the years go by. A new face and a new touch puts a lot of zest back into sex. It's an erotic stimulant that you can't supply any other way. Sex is an exciting adventure for me now, something I look forward to. It's not just doing the same old things with the same person over and over again. I turn on much better when I swing and when it's over, that's it. And when Frank and I make love now, it's a special event, with a lot of wonderful feeling—like it was when we first met.

"This way, I can still have my family. I like just regular middle-class life when you come right down to it. There's nothing very far-out or revolutionary about me. I like cooking, running the house, raising the kids and that sort of thing. It doesn't have anything to do with any women's liberation. Or maybe it does in a way because Frank and I have a great understanding, as equals, that we each need a certain amount of physical satisfaction. He knows that I have the same attitude about it that he does, and he respects that.

"We hide it from our kids. I don't think they could understand it yet. But we have the feeling that when they're older and can understand it, they'll feel the same way we do. We hide it from our straight friends too—not because we're ashamed or anything but just because their reaction would be too much of a disruption of our normal lives.

"I'm still a young woman, really. I don't see any reason why women in the prime of their lives should have to lock themselves up and wind up in oblivion just because they're married. I'm proud of my looks and my figure, and I like the reaction I get from men. All in all, it's sex. I love it and I don't have any hang-ups about it. I wouldn't want to live any other way without swinging now.".

Clearly, the style that Dolly L. describes is not by any means a rejection of traditional marriage but rather an adjustment to it—an accommodation of the greater sexual needs of the partners within the framework of a comfortable family relationship. When the couple succeeds in isolating their sexual behavior from their interpersonal and parental behavior, then swinging is least disruptive. It can also exert a positive marital influence, as opposed to being just a liability, in preventing many marriages from breaking up because of simple boredom and disinterest. This is the kind of slow and wearing process, often harmful to the children, which, in the swinger's mind, does not have to happen. For many people like Dolly, then, swinging is an adaptation to monogamous marriage, a way of preserving family life while satisfying one's sexual appetite. It is the ultimate separation of the romantic and the physical. In his article, "The Future of Marriage," Morton Hunt writes: "As long as the extra-marital sex is open, shared, and purely recreational, it is not considered divisive of marriage."

But if the swinging habit has improved or saved some marriages, it has proved disastrous for others. Not everyone is equipped with the psychological machinery to accept the attention and physical affection that his/her spouse is receiving. For some, the fears and jealousies that attend such continuous intimacy are never quite eroded. Equally stressful is the constant effort to shield their sex lives from the scrutiny of neighbors and children. It is a schizophrenic condition, not especially conducive to a peaceful, contented life. And even with successful camouflage, the swinging habit is often just plain tiring in ways that have nothing to do with increased expenditures of libidinal energy. Like any other hectic social schedule, swingers find themselves immersed in preparatory plans, making phone contacts, writing letters, constantly looking for new attractive couples. Because swingers eschew long-term relationships and the nonphysical attachments that tend to spring from them, the search is never-ending—not to mention the time and expense of consummating the actual meetings. For many, the life turns out to be so frantic and harried that all the sex loses its allure. It simply becomes no longer worth it, and they drop out.

Disillusionment weeds out countless others from the group sex crowd. One observer pinpoints the problem this way: "Finally able to act out adolescent fantasies, many swingers find that the fantasies were better than reality." If most swingers are trying to liberate themselves from sexual stereotypes, other disenchanted participants are learning something else—namely, that depersonalized, meaningless sex can get very boring very quickly. As is to be expected, a phalanx of psychologists, sociologists, and just plain analysts has descended on the swinging scene. Dr. David Reuben has suggested that co-marital sex is a basically self-damaging experience, "a direct outgrowth of hatred within the marital state." Chicago psychoanalyst Ner Littner contends that mate-swapping reveals an incapacity for true intimacy, a cover-up of overkill to hide personal shortcomings. Others assert that swinging is the product of various neuroses or a way to feed one's ego with a succession of new conquests.

On the other hand, there are a good number of observers willing to suggest nothing more in their interpretations than a lot of harmless, innocent fun-seeking. All of these interpretations contain some truth, and there are probably swingers abounding to fit every categorization.

### Scientific Study of Group Sex

The man who has done the most exhaustive work on the subject of group sex is Gilbert Bartell, whose book, *Group Sex: A Scientist's Eyewitness Report on the American Way of Swinging*, is the first full-length treatment of the phenomenon. An anthropology professor at Northern Illinois University, Bartell began his study by placing a number of typical ads in a Chicago area swinger's journal called *Kindred Spirits*. Generally, these ads contain special code words and phrases denoting preferred erotic activities, and run something like this: "Liberated couple, he—33, she—28, seek sophisticated adult fun. Enjoy good films, good food, and progressive experimentation. Forward address and photos with reply."

Finding the response to the ad overwhelming, Mr. Bartell and his wife plunged into the swinging world, attending a range of affairs from quiet encounters to large, raucous orgies, but maintaining always a scholarly detachment from the ultimate participation. Three years and 280 couples later, Professor Bartell documented his observations.

To Bartell, group sex is not so much the product of psychological aberrations, marital incompatibility, or extra-heavy sexual orientation, but rather an almost inevitable reaction to the boredom of modern, mechanized society. Drawing a parallel between the Eskimos, who have long practiced wife-swapping in their barren environment, and the swinging members of dreary, predictable suburbia, he counts the drive for excitement and stimulation as important as the lure of physical gratification. It is worth noting that the most prominent historical epoch of idle leisure, the latter stage of the Roman Empire, was also a time of unrestrained, bacchanalian indulgence. As the workdays and hours decrease, the demands of housework lighten, and the general quality of life becomes increasingly dull, comfortable Americans who do not take refuge in intellectual pursuits or other hobbies find themselves with an abundance of free time and excess energy. When you combine this kind of atmosphere with the climate of all-around sexual permissiveness in America, it is not especially surprising that couples everywhere are turning to the most instinctual way to enliven their existence. Not the most imaginative, perhaps, nor the most constructive or admirable, but the most logical for the times.

Bartell's "something to do" theory gains in plausibility in light of the identification of the average swinger. Spouse-sharing appears to be an almost exclusively white, middle-class pastime, a fact which seems to suggest an inherent contradiction because traditionally it has been the middle class which has safeguarded and sustained orthodox American morality. Dr. L. James Grold, Assistant Clinical Professor of Psychiatry at the University of Southern California, takes note of this development: "What is new is that respectable, middle-class people, who a few years back would have been horrified at the thought, are now indulging in activities historically coveted only by the wealthy leisure class."

It is *de rigueur* in the swinging scene to be excessively radical in style, an oddball or eccentric. The preferred image is to be hip or cool, a pose which in many cases turns out to be a superficially progressive, empty sort of sophistication. It is not a matter of consciously excluding the fringes because most of the new, revolutionary elements on the American scene find no need for the swinging world. Hippies or third-world people already have dubious regard for the prime admission ticket, marriage. Nor are they likely, with their relatively relaxed moral stance, to be as excited at the prospect of unlimited sex—certainly not to the point of marrying for it. While this may be a period of utter emotional lassitude for Middle America, it's a time of ferment and controversial politics for the radical youth. The swinger's brand of lazy, light-hearted debauchery is not in tune with their mentality, hungry for meaning and significance. And if the swingers' sex is radical, the rest of their life-style is decidedly establishment.

Steeped in escalating consumerism, class-consciousness, and intellectual complacency, the average swinger is probably the epitome of what the new left would characterize as status quo America. Rationalization or not, the increased sexuality of America's youth is one element of an overall drive to relate more closely with more people, in order to achieve deeper and more meaningful interpersonal relationships. Co-marital sex serves a totally antithetical end, partners sharing bodies and remaining ever-careful to avoid any other kind of contact. It is total depersonalization. In short, though both camps are mounting attacks on the bastion of conventional sexual behavior, they remain far apart in spirit and it is not likely that they will join forces.

## Attitude of Women's Lib

Nor are women liberationists likely to be especially enthused with swinging. Admittedly, group sex pays some deference toward the push for equality between the sexes in that it erases the double standard and opens the way for wives to enjoy the same freedom that they have always tacitly extended to their husbands. But for many feminists the price is too high. Germaine Greer sees it this way: ". . . wife-swapping is a bit like the shared sin of drunkenness. What I mean by that is, in America, drunkenness is a sort of social imperative, which means that no one can squeal on anyone else, because everyone gets sloshed and you all enjoy a special sort of anarchic behavior that your superiors are prepared to overlook. So, wife-swapping is like a form of incest in which nobody's more guilty than anybody else. You make sure that everybody's got the same; no one can say that the other sinned." Ms. Greer intimates that the swinging wife's equality is a deceptive one; other liberationists repudiate it more vehemently, claiming that swinging is just one more example of men exploiting women as marketable sexual commodities—and an especially degrading one at that. The men use their wives to gain access to other women in one big merry-go-round of flesh.

To women who are trying to force men to accept them as complete human beings and not inferior objects of lust, swinging must necessarily be anathema. For a liberationist, it combines the worst of both worlds—the drudgery of the stifling role of wife and mother and the indiscriminate promiscuity that relegates women to the status of sexual entity and sexual entity only. It offers a mirage of freedom and equality but actually changes nothing, simply making more victimized women available to more sexist men.

Of course, marriage is a dying institution anyway in the feminists' minds, a relic that will gradually wither away as more and more women shed their dependence on men. True liberation lies, the credo goes, in the courage and ability to control one's own life, and sexual freedom need not be tied to marriage. For these women, swinging is just a hopeless accommodation to an outmoded patriarchal institution—a kind of perverted equality that does women no good at all.

Clearly, then, swingers have little in common with the movements of radical youth and women's liberation. Nor does swinging involve the poor to any great extent, mostly because they lack the time and money to engage in such a luxury.

## Who and Where Are the Swingers?

Professor Bartell's study covers an age group ranging from eighteen to seventy, but his estimate of the average age of a swinger is twenty-nine for women and thirty-two for men. "However, it became obvious that almost all couples minimized their ages, except those in the group aged twenty-one to thirty. The point is that age plays an extremely important role in being accepted or rejected for swinging." This suggests that for many, swinging can be a vehicle for holding onto youth and its freedom, sometimes well past the point of reality.

Occupation-wise, Bartell found that a full 42 percent of the men he interviewed worked as salesmen, a correlation which might be traced to the generally extroverted, aggressive nature of those who make their living by selling. Doctors, dentists, university professors, and engineers were in evidence as well as truck drivers and factory workers. Of the professionals, lawyers were most numerous. All of this says nothing binding or mathematically certain concerning the various backgrounds of swingers, but much about the wide variety of representation.

Los Angeles can be fairly designated the modern capital of group sex, with San Francisco, New York, Boston, and Washington ranking close behind. But it is hardly an urban phenomenon; any neighborhood will do. The cities are prominent simply because they contain more people and more potential combinations. And with their size and anonymity, the chances of harmful detection are slim.

Becoming a "Swinger"

So how does a couple, convinced that the swinging life is for them, make entry into such a forbidden pasture? The process is no more difficult than joining the local party circuit, the required assets being merely a moderate degree of attractiveness and the willingness to give and take. For the neophyte, the plunge may come through an opportunity born of word of mouth or perhaps through reference to one of a host of slick advertising publications that have surfaced with the expansion of the movement. A number of these magazines circulate nationally, selling in "adult" bookstores for as much as seven dollars. Between the covers of *Swinger's Life*, *National Registry*, or *Suburban Swingers* will be found column after column of personal ads placed by swingers seeking new playmates. Local swingers' sheets with much the same purpose and content sell for less in the same places. If the beginners decide to answer an ad, the normal procedure calls for the arrangement of a casual encounter which enables a mutual feeling-out and inspection. Providing the chemistry is right (and for swingers, it usually is), a second date is set and intimacy begun.

Aspiring couples preferring a more direct approach can bypass the mail contact route and simply drop in at one of the increasingly numerous swinger's bars that have opened within the last few years. There, husbands and wives make their interchanges over drinks or on the dance floor. At The Swing, a popular Los Angeles hangout, face shots of available partners are projected on the walls for the sampling pleasure of the uncommitted. In New York, the heaviest action is at Captain Kidd's where old hands and nervous newcomers blend in new partnerships.

A third method of entree lies in membership in a formal swinger's club. Most of these clubs have sprung from the efforts of a few local swingers who see a golden opportunity to profit financially while simultaneously attracting new couples with whom to bed down. Typically, a weekly get-acquainted meeting will be held for interested newcomers. If they remain enthused, the owners conduct personal interviews to screen out undesirable or unsuitable applicants. If a new couple appears indiscreet, overly aggressive, or uninclined to swing in open fashion with enough people, chances are they will be turned down. But most pass and upon payment of a membership fee and regular dues, gain entrance to the regular round of weekend parties. "These are just like regular parties," says one member of the Los Angeles-based Club 101. "The only difference is at the point where a guy would usually ask a girl for her phone number; instead, he asks her if she wants to go to another room and have sex." Designed to create an appropriate and encouraging atmosphere for the kinky sex styles and combinations its members practice, Club 101 is filled with hidden passageways, bizarre lights and mirrors and, of course, an adequate supply of beds. More importantly, the club method offers the security of an understanding and like-minded society, an end to the sub rosa machinations that accompany the more individualized approaches to swinging.

What actually goes on at a swinging session depends on the people involved. Bartell claims that when couples meet to swing, tension is very high and heavy drinking is necessary to make things work. The situation is similar to "a high school prom where no couple wishes to be the first one on the dance floor." But if some swinging scenes suggest only partial liberation, others are emphatically decadent; orgies of food, drink, and carnival sex around the clock. *Esquire* magazine ran a piece a while back on the First National Swingers Convention held at a Chicago motel, and the theme was one of unrestrained, let-it-all-hang-out madness. Women parading in all forms of undress at all hours, public copulation, all conceivable permutations of bodies and genders in bed, and a whole list of canceled golf tournaments, tennis matches, and sightseeing tours—presumably, no one could be rousted from their lovemaking chores. Not a hint of sophistication or discrimination, and certainly no signs of reserve, were in evidence.

Oddly enough, while the male participants seem to be especially self-conscious about their virility and exhibit a complete disdain for homosexuality, mating of women is common. Apparently, it is a source of pleasure for both the females involved and the males watching.

What then is to be said for the group sex explosion? Can it rightfully be called part of a moral revolution? The answer is yes in the sense that swingers have discarded their puritanical inhibitions and societal taboos. Radically redefining the art of marriage, they have divorced sanctity from sex, leaving sex in the realm of simple physical pleasure. But the answer is no if moral revolution means a new philosophy for making some sense out of the universe. Swingers have abandoned a morality they no longer believe in but they have substituted only hedonism in its place—and hedonism is only by negative inference, morality.

Perhaps swinging is a transitional step in the moral revolution—away from stifling institutions and toward something else as yet undefined. But the ultimate irony at the moment is that swinging is just another celebration of the mechanical and routine—the same qualities from which it came. Like any other overuse, it smacks of staleness and emptiness. Hopefully, true sensuality will not be totally eclipsed in the future.

The significance of swinging as a radical experiment can be better appreciated when viewed against the full sweep of marital history. The next chapter will briefly explore the evolution of marriage.

# THE HISTORY OF MARRIAGE

## Primitive Cultures

*Promiscuous Relationships:* Dr. Bernhard Bauer, in his classic study *Woman and Love*, says he believes that "in the earliest period there was no such idea as marriage, or even anything faintly resembling it." Human beings were organized in hordes or tribes living in common, migrating from one area to another, subsisting on the land. It was the duty of the men to protect the tribe from enemies, to capture prey, and to keep order; and it was the duty of the women to look after hearth and home. Their first duty, however, was to bear and raise children so that the tribe should not die out. "It is only natural," says Bauer, "in this period of savage antiquity, that the idea of community of goods was extended to the sphere of sex. Complete promiscuity prevailed within the limits of each tribal group."

Anthropology presents evidence that out of this stage of unrestrained promiscuity, there developed gradually a system of groups within the horde; and from this the next step was to "group marriage." This form of sexual union did not consist of the union of single couples, but of whole groups of males and females of one tribal community with those of another. Among the aborigines of Australia there is the concept of blood kinship of the members of the group with a distinctive totem, i.e., the symbolical representation of an animal or plant. A sexual union within such a totem group was regarded as incest and was prohibited.

In promiscuous societies, since paternity could not be proved with any degree of certainty, the children were committed to the power of the mother, and there gradually developed that legal institution which we call the matriarchate or mother right. The mother had the power of life and death over the children. After her it was not the father but her nearest male relative who had supervision over the children. Among the primitive Congo tribes the husband is changed so frequently that it is difficult to decide who is the father of a particular child. Moreover, they do not regard intercourse between their women and other men as wrong and, in fact, encourage it when lucrative. For this reason children inherit name and rank not from the father but from the maternal uncle.

It is unknown when and how the relative positions of the man and woman were changed, but history shows the matriarchate giving way to the most absolute patriarchate, in which the father had power and authority not only over the children but also over the woman herself.

*Rape Marriage:* The earliest form of marriage, where a man takes the woman of his choice, was "rape marriage," or marriage by abduction. The legend of the rape of the Sabines provides an example of marriage by abduction. Among the tribes of the South American Indians the practice of rape marriage reached a high level of prestige. The Indians of Patagonia were in a chronic state of war, tribe against tribe, the issues of victory in every case being the capture of the women and the slaughter of the men.

The status of a wife by capture in aboriginal Australia is a slave in the strictest sense of the word; she is a beast of burden, a provider of food and a ready object on which to release pent-up passions. For those coveting such a luxury, expeditions are organized to go women stealing from other tribes. Sir John Lubbock, in *Origin of Civilization*, details abduction "courtship" in aboriginal Australia: "Stunning her by a blow from the 'dowak' they drag her by the hair to the nearest thicket to await recovery. When she comes to her senses they force her to accompany them. . . ."

The custom of rape marriage still existed at the turn of the 20th century. Among some of the Caucasian peoples, notably the Tcherkes, this form of marriage was usual. The abductor was required by custom to inform the girl's relatives of the robbery when he has fled a certain distance away. It usually took place at night. He placed the girl before him in the saddle, and his chance of getting away with her depended on the speed of his horse. If the couple were caught by the pursuers, the ravisher lost his prize and his horse and arms to boot; if, however, the flight was successful, the bride could not be taken away from him.

Rape marriage indicates the low esteem in which women were held in primitive times. She was treated as a chattel, and simply regarded as booty, which the man took in order to satisfy his sexual appetite. In this kind of conjugal union all spiritual elements were totally absent.

The tradition of marriage by abduction has passed out of existence, yet customs still survive which symbolize rape marriage. "Among the Southern Slavs, Magyars, and other Southern European peoples," Bauer tells us, "the bride, although she is betrothed with the full knowledge and consent of her parents, is abducted by the bridegroom from their home, amidst great festivities. The custom of the 'honeymoon journey' is also perhaps a survival of marriage by abduction. That custom of 'going away' after the wedding may be a symbol of the bridegroom's abducting the bride and wishing to liberate her completely from her parents and relations."

*Marriage by Purchase:* Out of marriage by abduction evolved marriage by purchase. The man chose a woman to be the mother of his children; and, as she was viewed as an inferior creature, a chattel, it was natural that he should purchase her from her parents. Women acquired a commercial value, since they could be bought at a definite price paid to the father. Among the Australian aborigines, the price for a wife was a knife, a glass bottle, or a nose ring. In India, reports Bauer, the price for a wife in the early 1900s varied "between a pig and twenty oxen, ten head of cattle or horse, according to the condition, appearance, and age of the woman." Among the Tartars, when a wife is purchased the transaction is like any other business deal. The men shake hands and take a drink together; the purchaser turns the girl around and inspects her carefully as he would any other merchandise. If he is not satisfied with this inspection, his female relatives take the girl to the bathroom and submit her to a more thorough examination. In Petrograd and Moscow at Easter, public marriage markets were held at which girls of marriageable age were displayed for sale. The youths inspected the girls from head to foot and selected their choices. The price was then settled upon and the marriage celebrated.

In cultures where a woman is only a chattel, polygamy is usually an acceptable practice. Provided the price is paid, nothing else matters. Polygamy was practiced by the patriarchs in Old Testament times, and we read that Solomon had "seven hundred wives and three hundred concubines." Eclipsing even Solomon, however, was the king of Uganda who was said to have had seven thousand wives. In Ashanti the law limited the royal harem to 3,333. Even in polygamous societies where marriage is purchase, monogamy is the rule for the majority of the population. Only the rich can afford to purchase and support more than one wife. In defense of polygamy a Zulu chief exclaimed: "If I have but one wife, who will cook for me when she is ill?" On a higher note, when a Moroccan shereef was asked why he wanted more than one wife, he replied, "One cannot always eat fish." Obviously these civilizations have no counterparts to Germaine Greer and Kate Millet.

In societies where marriage by purchase prevails, it is the husband's right to dispose of the wife again if he wishes to sell or trade her. These people see nothing strange or immoral in selling or trading wives. If a Tungusic man finds that his wife pleases his neighbor, he will willingly barter her for the other's wife, with a bag of grain in the bargain, and the women have no recourse. The custom of selling wives has been documented for past eras in China, Norway, Iceland, and England. English women were being sold publicly by their husbands as late as the nineteenth century London. If a woman provoked her husband's anger, she could be bound, taken to the cattle market in a halter, and there sold to either an old widower or a young bachelor. When sale was consummated the woman became the legitimate wife of her purchaser without further ceremony.

Among many primitive tribes premarital intercourse was common, but if offspring resulted marriage was mandatory. Hence, marriage was simply a binding force to ensure a conjugal unit for the survival of offspring. Early primitive societies emphasized the property value of a woman in marriage. The notion that a woman was owned by either her father or husband was common. Chastity was strictly enforced because a loss of virginity resulted in a lowering of the property value. After marriage the woman was encouraged to fornicate with her husband so that he could realize the full worth of his property.

Clearly missing from these primitive cultures is the idea of romantic love. Robert Briffault, author of *The Business Side of Marriage*, tells us:

> When an Australian black is asked why he marries . . . he answers that he requires a wife to fetch sticks for his fire, to cook his dinner, and to attend to household arrangements generally. He does not say that he marries her because he loves her or because his instincts demand it. Those reasons would be absurd.

## Marriage in Ancient Civilizations

*Greece:* Greek civilization exalted bodily beauty and excellence of mind. The fusion of body and mind so highly appreciated by the Greeks found expression in the term *kalokagathia*, meaning a harmonious and symmetrical development of body and soul. The emphasis on bodily beauty led to the idealization of the naked body and to its glorification in temple art. The gods themselves were portrayed as enjoying robust sexuality. Due to their sexual code and esteem for physical beauty, the Greeks accorded women a high position in society.

Women in Greek society were divided into two categories: wife and mother on the one hand, and courtesan on the other. Both were venerated in their proper spheres. Maternity was deemed a solemn responsibility, and the woman exercised dominion over home and children. Her behavior was expected to be sober and correct. Greek marriage was monogamous, and took place after a short betrothal. The bride was expected to be a virgin, and afterward remain faithful. Divorce was readily accessible for numerous causes. A husband could obtain a divorce on grounds of adultery, incompatibility, and infertility. Greek marriage took various forms. In some cases the woman was purchased by the husband from her father or guardian, and her consent was not required. While there was no law against polygamy, the practice appears to have been regarded as unworkable.

Although beauty was idealized, Greek marriage did not emphasize either sexual relations or love. The Greek wife was regarded as a friend, a housekeeper, a mother of lawful children—but not as a sexual partner. Chastity and fidelity in wives were regarded as family obligations, rather than as qualities in an ideal. The concept of such a virtue as chastity regarded as moral merit, and applicable to both sexes, was unthought of by the Greeks. Given the utilitarian foundation for marriage (in contrast to the sanctified state it assumed later in Christian civilization), divorce was an easy matter for the Greek husband. In early times only the husband could dissolve the marriage, but eventually this freedom was extended to the women as well.

The mores of Greek society did not prohibit men from extramarital relations as long as these did not involve the wife of another man. The women Greek husbands often rendezvoused with outside of marriage were the *hetaerae*. The term *hetaera* means "life partner" or "friend." Usually the hetaerae were highly educated and from the upper social strata. They lived in splendid houses and provided sexual and intellectual companionship for the leading philosophers, poets, and statesmen.

A refined sensuality was central to the Greek version of the good life. The pleasures of the senses were seen as essential to a balanced life and earthly happiness. Sensuality was conjoined with intellectual activity in a state of fruitful interaction. Seduction of a married woman was a serious offense, but Greek public opinion saw no wrong if a man sought relaxation in the caress of a courtesan, or in the embrace of another young man. The Greeks recognized and accepted the bisexual potential of man.

*Ancient Rome:* In the ancient Roman world there appear to have been three forms of marriage. The first form, called *usus*, was based upon one year's cohabitation; that is, if a man and a woman had lived together for a year they were considered to be legally married and their children could inherit property. *Usus* was the commonest form of marriage. Another form of marriage called the *confarreatio* was for the aristocracy. Being the most solemn and ceremonious, it required ten witnesses and could not be dissolved. An important aspect of this form lay in the fact that the guardianship of the woman passed from the father to the husband. It was the form of marriage for those of patrician status. A third form of marriage was called *coemptio*. This was a lesser version of *confarreatio* devised for the common people. Five Roman citizens were required as witnesses. It differed from *usus* in being recognized as legal from the outset.

*The Hebrews:* The Hebrew legal term for marriage is *kiddushin*, and is universally interpreted as "the state of holiness." Judaism has always recognized two purposes in marriage: procreation and companionship. Neither of these two ends outweighs the other in significance. The Halakah (the written Jewish law) justifies sexual pleasure, though intimate and private, even without the goal of procreation. Older people, even sterile elders, are encouraged to marry for the companionship they can share. The Bible and Talmud are candid and outspoken in dealing with sex. In the mystical treatise *Iggeret Ha-kodesh*, attributed to Nahmanides, the classic Jewish attitude on the subject of sex is set forth in clear and vigorous words: "We who are the descendants of those who received the sacred Torah believe that God, blessed be He, created nothing containing obscenity or ugliness. For if we were to say that intercourse is obscene, it would follow that the sexual organs are obscene. And how could God, blessed be He, create something containing a blemish or obscenity . . . before Him there is neither degradation nor obscenity; He created man and woman, fashioning all their organs and setting them in proper function, with nothing obscene in them." Any act of sex that is agreeable to both husband and wife is therefore perfectly acceptable. Sex on the Sabbath or holy days is considered a great blessing in the Jewish tradition. In contrast, avoidance of sex on the Sabbath or holy days in memory of the Crucifixion or of Mary's death is considered laudable according to the Catholic Church.

The same root word *ahav* in Hebrew is used to denote both physical and spiritual love. *Ahav* applies to the relationship of man to God, the love of one's fellow man, and the love of man and woman. Christian semantics, derived from the Greek language, has adopted two terms of love: *eros*, which denotes carnal love; and *agape*, which means spiritual love.

The Talmud is by no means free from opinions and interpretations that portray the sex drive as an "evil impulse." The prevailing mood of the Talmud, however, is to view sex as basically good. It acknowledges the capacity of sex for evil, but Jewish law and tradition have never made a blanket condemnation of sex in the unreserved manner of Christianity.

As an outgrowth of its views on marriage, Judaism does not consider divorce a sin. Divorce is more a tragedy than an immoral act. The Hebrew tradition permits divorce, but every effort is made to encourage a couple to strive for permanence in marriage. All the resources of the community are mustered to salvage a floundering marriage. The husband and wife are admonished to recognize the sanctity of their union. But once it becomes clear that the marriage has failed, without further recourse Judaism recognizes that the union has lost sanction and sanctity. When the conditions of love and mutual respect no longer exist society stultifies itself by trying to ignore the truth. The presence of children in the Hebrew tradition does not negate the possibility of divorce for a Jewish couple. The grounds for divorce under Jewish law may seem superficial to an outsider; for example, the wife burns the meals or the husband suffers from bad breath. The grounds for a divorce were really unimportant in the Talmudic view, since whatever the parties claimed, it was evidence of a deeper clash of personality between husband and wife. It was testimony that the community spirit, which is the essence of marriage, had ceased to exist.

### Early Christian Marriage

*"Better to Marry Than to Burn":* Christian morality displaced the traditional Greco-Roman patterns of sexuality. The Jewish Old Testament offered an excellent explanation of the origin of evil and a thorough justification of antifeminism and celibacy. The Bible said the primal violation of man against God was instigated by woman, who created the sense of sexual shame and brought about the permanent misery of mankind. Morton Hunt in *The Natural History of Love* comments that "God himself explicitly stated that a permanent antagonism would thenceforth exist between the sexes." God told Eve, "I will greatly multiply thy sorrow and thy conception. In sorrow shalt thou bring forth children; and thy desire shall be to thy husband, and he shall rule over thee."

The early Christians were obsessed with the connection between sex and the Fall. They misinterpreted, however, the attitude of the Jews. Though women were sometimes depicted as conniving and shrewish in the Old Testament, they were not said to have caused the pollution or corruption of man's soul. And though the Jews condemned fornication, adultery, homosexuality, harlotry, and all forms of sodomy, their view toward sex within marriage was by no means prudish. The Song of Songs contains numerous passages which refer to sex in love without any hint of sin or smut.

It was in the first century that Paul crusaded against the sins of the flesh. It was Paul who focused on Temptation, Original Sin, and F ll as the eternal tragedy of mankind. Because of Eve's guilt women were justifiably relegated to subordination in life. The Old Testament Jews had considered marriage and procreation a holy duty, scorned childlessness, and even ostracized eunuchs from their congregations (Deut. 23:1). In contradistinction, Christ, in his preachings, spoke praisefully of those "which have made themselves eunuchs for the kingdom of heaven's sake" (Matt. 19:12). This quote is generally agreed to mean that Christ favored voluntary abstinence. However, many early Christians construed it as a plea for castration, and thousands mutilated themselves for a number of centuries. Eventually the Church concluded that this was absolutely forbidden. Paul picked up the message of abstinence from Christ and riveted it into Christiandom. He urged all men to be abstinent. His statements in the New Testament concerning sex and marriage have shaped Christian doctrine on the subjects. "It is well for a man not to touch a woman." He said, "But because of the temptation to immorality, each man should have his own wife and each woman her own husband. I say this by way of concession, not of command. I wish all were as I myself am.... To the unmarried and the widows I say that it is well for them to remain single as I do. But if they cannot exercise self-control, they should marry. For it is better to marry than to be aflame with passion . . . so that he who marries his betrothed does well; and he who refrains from marriage will do better. A wife is bound to her husband as long as he lives. . . ."

These salient passages illustrate the traditional Christian view of sex as basically evil and marriage as a concession to man's baser instincts, which ought to be kept under control. Christian doctrine treats marriage as an institution to perpetuate the human race, and by Paul's tone, a rather grudging concession. One might infer that his preference would be for all mankind to go through life in a state of blessed purity.

Slightly more than a generation after Paul's death, the author of *Revelations* envisions a Utopian scene of 144,000 virginal men who had never been defiled by a woman standing next to the Lamb of Zion. Within the following two centuries Christianity developed a fanatical obsession with the glory of virginity, and the evilness of sex. So crucial did asceticism seem to the early church that a monk named Jovinian was excommunicated in A.D. 385 for arguing that marriage was superior to celibacy.

Christianity promulgated the subjection of women to men. The concept of the wife was that of an inferior and sinful creature who should be controlled, dominated, and chastised according to need.

"What cause have you for appearing in public excessive grandeur?" wrote Tertullian, reprimanding wives for putting on fine clothes and jewels. "You have no reason to appear in public except such as is serious. . . . Submit your heads to your husbands, and you will be enough adorned. Busy your hands with spinning; keep your feet at home; and you will please better than by arraying yourselves in gold." The Apostolic Constitutions of the fourth century epitomized the early Christian view of woman's place in marriage: "O wife next after the Almighty . . . and after His beloved Son, our Lord Jesus . . . do thou fear thy husband and reverence him, pleasing him alone, rendering thyself acceptable to him in the several affairs of life. . . . Ye wives, be subject to your own husbands, and have them in esteem, and serve them with love and fear, as holy Sarah honored Abraham. For she could not endure to call him by his name, but called him Lord."

The Christians criticized and attacked the wanton customs of marriage and divorce that had long existed in the Roman Empire. In the course of several centuries Christian dogma on marriage and divorce crystallized. The process was slow because of internal debate as to what Christ Himself had thought about divorce. In Matthew (19:9) He recognized "fornication"—the word means "adultery" in Biblical usage—as grounds for divorce, but in Mark (10:11-12) He recognized no grounds whatever. For centuries it was held by some Christians that a second marriage was equal to adultery; others would allow two but not three, others three but not four, and so on. After the conversion of the Emperor Constantine, civil divorce regulations became tighter and religious opinion stricter. Eventually marriage came under the domination and jurisdiction of the clergy. By the fifth century virtually every wedding included an ecclesiastical benediction, and by the Middle Ages marriage was held to be a sacrament, a holy act, not dissoluble by private or personal wish. The laws of Justinian, codified in the sixth century, made divorce almost impossible and cited adultery as a capital offense. Monogamy became the established pattern of marriage under Christianity, and it was regarded as a lifetime contract, not to be dissolved lightly, if at all.

### Personalized Marriage Ceremonies

Beginning in the 1960s and continuing through the 70s, there has been a flowering of personalized marriage ceremonies. Young couples write their own vows, design their own ceremonial dress, and plan new kinds of wedding receptions. These new rituals express a new attitude toward marriage. Under traditional Christianity, as we have seen, marriage has been a sacred covenant, evidenced by such terms as "holy estate" and "holy matrimony" in the services. At a Christian wedding, pledges are made in the name of the Father, and the Son, and the Holy Spirit. Today, the young are turning away from organized religion and either joining groups which look at religion from a different perspective, or are abandoning established creeds for new mystical sects. As a result, references to religious images are being omitted in many of the personalized marriage ceremonies. The following vows are an example:

> Family and friends, we are gathered together to unite_____ and_____ in marriage. This celebration is the outward token of an inward union of hearts, which the church may bless and the state make legal, but which neither state nor religious institution can create or annul: it is a union created by loving purpose and by abiding will. Into this estate_____ and_____ come to union.

Marriage laws vary from state to state, but all of them treat the marriage contract as a lifetime commitment. The traditional wedding ceremony also has a tone of irrevocability. The vows taken during the ceremony reflect an anticipation of permanence as in the phrase " 'til death do us part." With America's escalating divorce rate, many young couples writing their own vows are no longer making grandiose pledges for life. For example, one couple refusing to vow "to love each other as long as we both shall live," inserted instead, "to love each other as long as we both shall love."

The law requires certain basic steps which must be met for any marriage to be legal. Both parties must be of marriageable age or have parental consent. A medical examination is necessary before a marriage license will be granted. The ceremony must be performed by a licensed official or cleric, and two witnesses of legal age must be present. Only a minimal few phrases are dictated by law for the ceremony. The rest of the ceremony can be created by the couple themselves, and there is definitely a trend in this direction. Today's youth have decided that they want to take a more active role in planning their marriage ritual in order to give the event a more personal meaning. For some this has been accomplished by borrowing from the format of other cultures, as illustrated by the following Indian ritual.

Apache Indian Prayer
by Kenneth Patton

Now you will feel no rain, for each of you will be shelter to
    the other
Now you will feel no cold, for each of you will be warmth to
    the other
Now there is no loneliness for you.
Now you are two, but there is only one life before you
Go now to your dwelling place, to enter into the days of
    your togetherness
And may your days be long and good upon the earth.

The new personalized ceremonies incorporate the social consciousness of the new generation. A California minister, Reverend
Cecil Williams, has his couples recite the pledge, "I_____, take
thee_____, to be my woman, to work for the liberation of all
people, for frustrated, lonely people . . . to love, embrace, to
commit ourselves to do battle through the journey which is the
celebration of life." Phrases such as "to obey" and "man and
wife" are being replaced by "to mutually respect" and "husband
and wife" as part of the equalitarian treatment of the sexes. Along
with this trend, some fathers are not giving their daughters away.
One couple had their parents give them to each other. Other brides
are retaining their maiden names when they marry, although the
courts are not backing this movement.

Not only are the words used in marriage services changing but
so are the places where weddings are held, the dress that is worn
by the bridal party, the invited guests, and the mood of the
post-celebration. An attorney in San Francisco chose to be married on a foggy day, and the ceremony was held as the fog lifted to
symbolize a new beginning. In Oregon, a mini-skirted bride and
barefoot husband were married on a mountain trail on which they
had often hiked together. Two ski buffs took their vows on a
Canadian glacier accessible only by helicopter. Another couple was
united in holy matrimony while sitting on separate rocks in the
middle of the Potomac River. No wonder writer Anne Chamber
observed, "It no longer matters what you wear but whether you're
in shape to get where it's at."

The reception can now be a simple picnic with cheese and
crackers. An astrologically oriented couple had their wedding cake
decorated with signs of the zodiac. One bride served food that
symbolized her philosophical values. Bread was given for support,

wine for joy, cheese for poignancy, and an apple for love. Attire at these receptions ranges from elaborate costumes to total nudity. In a California ceremony a nude couple marched up to the altar to face a nude minister. This trend in personalized marriage ceremonies is not confined to counterculture people. A growing number of middle-class youth with conventional aspirations also follow it. Those who choose a personalized ceremony feel that they are giving more uniqueness to their lives. In this mass society of mass production and mass conformity, the unique is welcome.

With this historical overview in mind, it is clear that the concept of marriage is by no means a static phenomenon. And the fact that most of us have become accustomed to the conventional modern marriage often eclipses the unmistakable reality of further change in the present.

One might say that marriage is in a state of rejection, as more and more couples live together without ceremony. But an equally valid interpretation of these developments is simply that new, flexible forms of marriage are evolving. An examination of them will perhaps mirror the shape of the future family.

# FUTURE FORMS OF THE FAMILY

### Interracial Marriage

Most of the aspects of the sexual revolution are nationwide phenomena. There are those who will still rail against premarital sex, the divorce proliferation, and birth control, and warn about the disastrous results of moral decay; but for the most part the new attitudes reflect a national consensus. One development, however, far from being commonly accepted, is the subject of bitter controversy in America: interracial sex and marriage.

There is perhaps no subject that raises more acrimonious and heated reaction from conservative America than interracial marriage. Many authorities have suggested that the fear of black sexual superiority lies at the core of white racism. Many whites who approve of economic and educational progress for blacks stop well short of endorsing "race-mixing." It would be difficult to think of a more deep-seated taboo in this country. In fact, interracial marriage was once a felony under federal law before the U.S. Supreme Court abolished miscegenation statutes as unconstitutional.

But in 1971, the Merit Publishing Company solicited responses from 23,000 student leaders in 18,000 of the nation's public, private, and parochial high schools, and the results are revealing. Those questioned were outstanding achievers who were recommended by their principals and counselors for high intelligence and leadership qualities. Seventy-three percent of those polled said they would accept or make a date with someone of a different race. Fifty-three percent said they would be amenable to interracial marriage.

Clearly, there is a new consensus emerging among the nation's youth. In the major cities mixed couples are not an uncommon sight, and the social pressures that formerly attended these relationships in the past seems to be relaxing. It is all part of the effort to see beyond a person's "category" and to find out who he really is. And the youth of America is leading the way.

## Mating Without Matrimony

Informal, nonlegal unions have long been common among poor people. In 1971 *Look* magazine reported that it was becoming a universally recognized social trend. For white middle-class couples choosing this arrangement, it has been an avenue for a more honest and vital relationship than conventional marriage. One middle-aged couple living together in Beverly Hills explained their philosophy in *The Futurist* (April 1970):

> Personhood is central to the living-together relationship; sex roles are central to the marriage relationship. Our experience strongly suggests that personhood excites growth, stimulates openness, increases joyful satisfactions in achieving, encompasses rich, full sexuality peaking in romance. Marriage may have the appearance of this in its romantic phase, but it settles down to prosaic routine. . . . The wife role is diametrically opposed to the personhood I want. . . .

In effect she resents cooking and washing dishes full time and prefers to pursue a career and fears that if she became a legal wife, she would be relegated to the traditional female roles. She has rejected marriage and chosen nonlegal union so she can escape the restrictive role of homemaker.

Couples are living together openly now on many college campuses, in some instances at risk of punishment by college authorities (but the risk is diminishing every day), and defying their parents' outraged objections (but getting resigned acceptance more and more). In most of these relationships, the couple lives together in close, warm, and committed fashion, very much like traditional monogamy. They pledge not to have sex with anyone else, and refuse dates with others. Living together appears to be more a form of apprentice marriage than a true rebellion against it. Margaret Mead and others have suggested a revision of our law to legalize these arrangements. The young consider the idea unnecessary. They are already creating their own form of informal marriage. The only thing gained by a stamp of legality would be social approval which has become of minor relevance from their point of view.

### Companionate Marriage

The chief argument for the indissolubility of marriage is the necessity of providing a stable home for children. Without birth control, children are a definite probability; therefore, the institution of marriage must be designed on the assumption that there will be children. With birth control, it becomes probable to assume that some marriages, at least for some period, will be without offspring. In this case what interest does society have in opposing divorce?

Judge Ben B. Linsey over a quarter of a century ago proposed that there be two kinds of marriage, or two stages of one marriage. The first stage would be a "companionate marriage," in which the expressed intention of the couple would be companionship without children. So long as they were able to remain childless through contraception, divorce would be easy. If they desired children they should go through a second, more solemn ceremony. Stringent conditions would be set by society for admission to this second stage of marriage. Once a couple was joined in a procreative marriage, divorce would be difficult to obtain.

### Legalized Bigamy

Some commentators, admittedly a minority, suggest that bigamy is the sensible way to correct imbalances in the ratio between men and women and to legalize the relationships that many people engage in anyway—extra-marital affairs. In most instances, the need for sexual variety does not extend beyond one or two other partners outside of marriage, so why not incorporate that variety within the legal institution and eliminate sham? For those who feel the need for an affair but who do not wish to dissolve the other benefits of marriage, this would seem to be a pragmatic solution. One major problem, however, is that when a wife finds out about her husband's other woman, she is not likely to welcome her into the household.

### Right to Children Outside of Marriage

In 1965 a thirty-eight-year-old musician Tony Piazza became the first unmarried man in his state, and probably the nation, to be granted the right to adopt a baby. Alvin Toffler in *Future Shock* says, "We shall, however, also see many more 'family' units consisting of a single unmarried adult and one or more children." Courts are granting custody to divorced fathers with greater frequency. One factor influencing the culture's growing acceptance of child rearing by men is the fact that adoptable children are in oversupply in some places. Toffler quotes California disc jockeys' blaring commercials: "We have many wonderful babies of all races and nationalities waiting to bring love and happiness to the right families. . . . Call the Los Angeles County Bureau of Adoptions." At the same time, the mass media have glamorized womanless households as exemplified by "The Courtship of Eddie's Father." With the legalization of homosexual conduct in five states since 1961, and homosexuals solemnizing their relationships with religious contracts of marriage, we can expect to see homosexual couples adopting children. Another reflection of the new moral temper, an increasing number of unwed mothers are raising their own children. It is quite common these days to find unwed pregnant girls attending natural childbirth classes. These girls exhibit an attitude of enthusiasm for their expected child, which is a radical contrast to the traumatically shameful attitudes toward illegitimate children in the past.

### Rise of Singledom

Traditionally our culture has fostered the idea that it is better to be married than single, that one will be happier if he is married, that everyone wants to be married, and that it is a little sinful to remain single after an acceptable age. Marriage and divorce laws (and even tax laws) reflected this bias in favor of marriage. Marriage was a matter of record: all that was required was a license and authorized ceremony. Divorce was a matter of law, necessitating a court trial and a mandatory waiting period. The married state was very easy to enter, but extremely difficult to exit.

In recent years single life has been gaining stature. Increased mobility among the population makes it easier for social groups to tolerate a single person amidst married couples. He may not be as much of a threat when social lines change rapidly. Also, a rapidly changing society causes an individual to grow and change more throughout his lifetime, making compatibility with the same partner for life extremely difficult. Further, an affluent society makes it possible for women to support themselves to a degree that was never possible before.

In short, bachelorhood is no longer suspect. People are taking more time and exercising more caution both in the decision on whether to marry at all and in the selection of a partner. Marriage is becoming a status in life that develops naturally, not necessarily something which must be prodded or manufactured merely because an individual reaches a certain age.

Yet for all the innovations and pragmatic adjustments to marriage, there remains one very reliable indicator which points to the lasting vitality of traditional marriage: the divorce rate. But, as we shall see, even the area of divorce is feeling the effect of the new marital morality.

# THE DIVORCE EXPLOSION

## Religious Implications

As has been seen, marriage has been traditionally viewed in the Western world as an inviolable, God-created state. The Judeo-Christian ethic elevated the institution to a sanctified position. Consequently, the notion of divorce has historically encountered stiff opposition. Theological justification for the irrevocability of marriage comes from Scripture: "Wherefore they are no more twain, but one flesh. What therefore God hath joined together, let no man put asunder." (Matt. 19:6).

And while the church has played its part, the state as well has sought the stability inherent in indissoluble family bonds and has done much to discourage the breakup of the family unit. But even in civil divorce, church influence prevailed in the basis for divorce. Originally, the only permissible cause was adultery. In the Old Testament there is reference to adultery as justification for divorce: "When a man hath taken a wife, and married her, and it comes to pass that she find no favor in his eyes, because he hath found some uncleanness in her: then let him write her a bill of divorcement and give it in her hand, and send her out of his house.

And when she is departed out of his house, she may go and be another man's wife." (Deut. 24:1-2). The New Testament is rather ambiguous and has been subject to diverse interpretations. Though Jesus is quoted in Matthew as saying: ". . . Let no man put asunder," he also says later in the same gospel (Matt. 19:9), "But I say unto you, that whosoever shall put away his wife, saving for the cause of fornication . . ." These and other Biblical pronouncements have provided grist for the argument that Jesus may have tolerated divorce under certain conditions.

## Legal Implications

Under English common law the power to grant divorce was vested in Parliament and the new United States followed this example. During the early days of our country, no general divorce laws existed. Each divorce required an act by the legislature of the state in which the petitioner resided, and divorces were, as a rule, available only to the wealthy and influential. Since adultery and insanity were still the only bases for divorce, a social stigma with deterrent effect operated to discourage the practice. Divorce was frowned upon in the public eye and regarded as scandalous—akin to alcoholism and conjuring up visions of fallen women, brutish men, and unseemly conduct. In 1816, when President Timothy Dwight of Yale thundered against the "alarming and terrible" divorce rate in Connecticut; about one of every 100 marriages was being legally dissolved.

As divorce laws did evolve, it was through the several states and their separate legal systems. Regulations governing divorce were contained in state constitutions or state statutes enacted by state legislatures. This created considerable variation in the requirements for divorce in different states, but the prevailing basis for divorce action remained adultery. But as women began achieving a certain degree of emancipation during the nineteenth century and as the purposes of marriage changed, divorce laws were liberalized and the rates began climbing.

In the 1970s, the solutions to the divorce problem have become simpler. For one thing, people are marrying less. Fewer people marry for sexual reasons in this era of sexual freedom. It is commonplace for couples to live together under experimental conditions before marriage, eliminating those hasty, ill-conceived marriages that so often end in divorce. Others are rejecting the institution outright, preferring less rigorous relationships or a series of mates. Similarly, the feminist movement has done much to erase the notion in young girls' minds that marriage is an imperative. As women become more and more independent, and the relationship between man and woman changes, marriages and all the mutual interdependencies that they suggest decrease. In short, marriage is not the central theme that it once was. And the smaller the marriage rate, the smaller the divorce rate.

The legal institutions reflect this philosophical switch. In California, it is no longer necessary to allege a reason to obtain a divorce. The notion of blame has been removed from divorce litigation, as the courts recognize the futility of chaining people to mutual incompatibility and unhappiness. The prospect of complete divorce is not a concession to moral laxity. Rather, divorce is a concession to the realities of human existence.

Professor Joseph Goldstein of the Yale Law School believes we should abolish all grounds for divorce, whether based on fault or not. Under the reform law he proposes, divorce would be available as a matter of right. In his view the judicial inquiry required by any ground for divorce, even by nonfault grounds, is an unjustifiable state intrusion into the privacy of the marital relationship. The fault-concept ruling of most of American jurisdictions requires an adversary contest. No degree of kindness or civility or generosity on the part of the spouse can avoid their assuming the posture of combatants. The process of battle for those who seek it, because of the fault concept, can traumatize, impoverish and enrage spouses; it can delay decisions and cripple children; and, if used to the most disgusting limits, it can defeat the divorce and thus maintain in law marriages which are dead in reality. The model statute Professor Goldstein offers provides that husband or wife, or both, may begin a divorce action by filing a simple application for divorce with the appropriate court. A statutory waiting period follows, during which the parties may reconsider their decision to divorce. If they have not changed their minds by the end of the "cooling-off" or "warming-up" period, they may file a petition for a Decree of Divorce.

## Historical Trends

The historical trend appears to be moving toward recognizing divorce as a matter of right. Several nations have recently liberalized their divorce laws. The English law was revised in 1969 making "irretrievable breakdown of marriage" the sole grounds for divorce. Italy, the home of the Papacy, after countless centuries of prohibition has finally permitted divorce. Two American states have eliminated the fault grounds. The increasing incidence of divorce adds pressure for recognizing divorce as a matter of right. After the close of the Civil War, ten thousand divorces were granted annually in this country. In 1971 over 1.4 million divorces were granted. For the last half century this nation has led the world in divorce.

In the twentieth century, as society has become more industrialized, educated, and mobile, pressures mount for easier divorce. Also, at one time, when a couple vowed "till death us do part" the average life expectancy was thirty-five. Today it is about seventy-two years old, a long time to remain with one partner. Critics of lifetime monogamy compare it to a one-book library. However fascinating that one book might be, a person's life is further enriched if he has also had occasion to read other books.

According to treasured folk belief children hold marriages together, but contemporary statistics prove otherwise. In 1948 only 42 percent of divorcing people had children. In 1962 the figure leaped up to 60 percent. People no longer feel they should endure their miseries and stay together for the sake of the children. They are giving greater weight to their own happiness and coming to think that it is no favor to the children to maintain an unhappy marriage.

Since adultery has traditionally been the predominant legal basis for divorce, it follows that an adjustment of public opinion concerning adultery could significantly affect the divorce rate. For centuries adultery stood as the most diabolical matrimonial offense, and at one time merited death. It was more heinous than cruelty or the most immature selfishness. Not only did the law visit punishment upon the adulterer's head, it meant disgrace and social ruin. Christianity condemned it as absolutely wrong under all circumstances.

## Modern Trends

In the past few decades, though, a body of opinion has emerged which accepts and respects adultery in certain situations. The Society of Friends in England published a report in 1963 placing a radical new light on the subject. The report is cautiously worded, but the implication in the advice given to marriage counselors is clear.

We have been unable to avoid the continued challenge of this question, "When is it right to have intercourse if it is not to be confined wholly to marriage?" At one time or another every counselor has to face it. He may himself believe it should be confined to marriage: if so, he must say so quietly and humbly while entering with the understanding into the problem of his questioner who is less sure that one rule meets all cases. Counselors and parents do well to hesitate before passing judgment: it will be wiser to ask how deep a relationship is, how much personal intimacy there is to express in coitus. Such questioning will throw the onus on the persons concerned to make their own moral judgments.

This is a definite departure from established Christian attitude on adultery. To place the onus on the individual suggests that the convention forbidding adultery is not absolute and may therefore be broken. By emphasizing the importance of individual conscience the report approves a redefinition of chastity as "emotional sincerity." In his view, it is not the act of adultery that is wrong, but the deception and insincerity with which it is usually accompanied.

The British Council of Churches has come out with its own report on adultery equally tolerant in its implications: "We have tried to show that rules by themselves are an inadequate basis for morality. No rule can cover all the varied and complex situations in which men and women find themselves." Dr. Eustace Chesser urges that "extramarital relations be judged according to individual needs and circumstances, not by regulations handed down from a remote past." She also observes, "The tide of opinion has changed so rapidly in the last few years that what was once denounced as outrageous is now accepted as common sense." Dr. Alex Comfort approves of adulterous sex as long as two cardinal rules are followed: (1) never exploit other persons' feelings and wantonly expose them to an experience of rejection; (2) never under any circumstances negligently risk producing an unwanted child. Commenting on the rise of adultery, Dr. Hyman Spotnitz says: "It would seem that the married man who has never had an affair in this year of 1965 is a rara avis (rare bird) in America."

The message is clear: Adultery, far from being an automatic cause for divorce as it often was in the past, is now considered by more and more Americans as a healthy outlet in otherwise healthy marriages. Instead of resorting to divorce for renewed sexual freedom, partners are granting each other sexual freedoms and maintaining their marriages. For many, as adultery and affairs increase, divorces decrease.

Our legal system reflects the growing nonchalance over adultery. While it remains a criminal offense on the books, prosecutions are unheard of. The conclusion one may reach is that society is taking a more tolerant attitude toward this form of immorality. As in the case of premarital sex there appears to be growing professional psychiatric opinion giving institutional support to this behavior for mental health objectives. Whereas religion unreservedly condemned adultery, modern psychiatry is beginning to recognize some value for the marital couple in allowing and accepting it.

These notions may be hard to swallow for those of us who have been raised in a strongly orthodox Christian family, but future generations may accept them as casually as young collegians now accept interracial dating.

# PART II
# THE
# BIOLOGICAL
# REVOLUTION

*The air now clearly swarms with unsettling new spirits.*
*Even the most myopic Americans are becoming steadily more*
*conscious of what H. G. Wells called the 'shrinking and*
*fugitive sense that something is happening so that life will*
*never be quite the same again.'*

William Hedgepeth and Dennis Stock, The Alternative
*(1970)*

# THE BIOLOGICAL REVOLUTION

It is becoming increasingly clear that mankind will have to harness the new biological technology which promises to change man's relation to the universe. As our scientific sophistication grows, so too grows the danger of scientific abuse. Our fundamental notions of life and death and how they ought to be controlled stand ready to be shaken. More and more citizens are realizing that merely because something is scientifically attainable does not necessarily mean that it is desirable.

The problem is that those who are endowed with most of this knowledge enjoy an insularity that makes popular control of that knowledge somewhat less effective than it ought to be. Everyone has a stake in these things for everybody's life promises to be affected. This chapter will touch upon some of those current and anticipated developments in the field of biology which have serious moral and legal implications. Its contents should surprise those who have been oblivious to the biological revolution.

Two hundred years ago the French encyclopedist Diderot, in a visionary look at the future which he called *The Dream of d'Alembert*, described how one day human embryos would be artifically cultivated and their hereditary endowment predetermined. Today his vision no longer seems entirely fanciful, and some biologists believe that before the end of the century it may be realized. Other men of imagination, among them H. G. Wells and Bernard Shaw, have conjured up visions of control of growth, of tampering with memory, of raising intelligence, and of stretching human life span into centuries. Even these no longer seem far-fetched. In 1966 California biochemist Joshua Lederberg, Professor of Genetics at Stanford University, declared in the *Bulletin of the Atomic Scientists*, that "a very consequential danger in life-span and the whole pattern of life are in the offing, providing that the momentum of existing scientific effort is maintained." Similarly, Professor Bentley Glass, president of the American Society of Naturalists and one of the world's best-known authorities in the field of human genetics, has admonished society on what he calls "the stupendous ethical problems which will face mankind in the very near future, as man begins to apply his knowledge to the control of his own reproduction and future evolution." At the same time the British Nobelist Francis Crick has pointed out that "the development of biology is going to destroy to some extent our traditional grounds for ethical beliefs, and it is not easy to see what to put in their place."

# AMNIOCENTESIS

## Genetic Research

In 1959 the French geneticist Jerome Lejeune discovered that patients with mongolism (now usually called Down's syndrome) do not have a mutant or defective gene, but rather, carry an extra chromosome that in itself is probably normal. Shortly afterward, it was discovered that this condition could be detected by examining viable cells suspended in amniotic fluid within the amniotic sac that surrounds the developing fetus. Amniocentesis, the removal of fluid from the amniotic cavity by needle puncture, became useful in the early 1960s for detection of unborn infants who ran the risk of Rh incompatibility. These "Rhesus Babies," if they survived, could be born with severe anemia or brain damage.

Genetic research in the 1960s continued to identify diseases and "birth defects" caused by defects in human genetic components. More than 1,600 such diseases have thus far been recognized, among them, cystic fibrosis, sickle-cell anemia, hemophilia, and Down's syndrome. Through amniocentesis, at least forty serious genetic diseases can be positively detected, and researchers predict that new tests will be developed to detect both the carriers and the unborn victims of many more genetic conditions.

At present, genetic screening through amniocentesis is recommended in cases where the families of either parent have a history of congenital birth defects or disease, and in cases of potential Rh incompatibility. On the horizon, amniocentesis is expected to become a routine part of prenatal care—similar to tests on the mother for syphilis, diabetes, and high blood pressure—as an effort to detect fetal diseases and malformations before birth. Obviously, the main purpose of such procedures is to reduce or eliminate the incidence of genetic diseases which places a tremendous emotional burden on parents and often causes suffering and death in affected children.

## Ethical, Legal and Economic Considerations

The moral and ethical implications of prenatal genetic screening was studied at a recent conference, cosponsored by the Institute of Society, Ethics and Life Sciences and the James Fogarty Center of the National Institute of Health. Dr. Daniel Callahan, director of the Institute of Society, spoke of the high cost of caring for defective children. "We can now, quite literally, put a price on everyone's head, working out the long-term financial costs to individuals and societies of caring for a defective child." Mass screening tests to identify carriers of genetic diseases would make it possible to keep records of genetic characteristics of millions of persons. With widespread genetic screening, the staggering costs of caring for congenitally deformed or diseased children could be almost eliminated if the diagnosis was followed by therapeutic abortion.

Because of this inexorable relationship of amniocentesis to abortion, the procedure is one of the most controversial in medicine—not from the medical standpoint, but because of the moral, ethical, and legal questions that its use raises. Once amniocentesis determines whether an unborn baby conceived by known carriers will become a victim of the disease, someone must decide whether the fetus should live or be aborted. The decision to abort the defective fetus could eliminate the suffering and pain of parents and victims alike. In addition, some geneticists argue that preventing a defective child from being born will lessen the "pollution" of future generations by those defects.

At the conference cosponsored by Dr. Callahan's institute, counselors emphasized that parents must have the choice of deciding how they will use the genetic information provided by amniocentesis. They have the freedom to decide—at least in the seventeen states that allow therapeutic abortions—whether to have an abortion or not. During the conference, however, Dr. Callahan said he detected a change of views that could eventually deprive people of their choice and "blame" them for the defective children they bring into the world. Common practice at present is for parents to be reassured by genetic counselors that the defective fetus or child is "not their fault."

Already there is an undercurrent of opinion among genetic counselors that would in effect brand as irresponsible any decision to allow a mongoloid child to be born. If we begin blaming those who make what we term "irresponsible" choices, they say, then the freedom of choice now extolled in genetic counseling would become a mockery. A University of Colorado pediatrician, Dr. Herbert Lubs, suggested that pressures might be exerted on the public by the government and private health insurance companies.

Because of the costs to the government and private insurance companies of caring for defective children and adults, it is not inconceivable that amniocentesis could become a required part of regular prenatal care. It is not inconceivable that prenatal diagnosis of genetic diseases through amniocentesis and the subsequent recommendation of therapeutic abortion would emerge as a major method of preventing many defective children from being born.

Presuming that the restrictions against abortion were eliminated, the procedure would still not be without its own moral and ethical dilemmas. Would parents who decide to have a child despite a prenatal diagnosis of congenital disease be subject to some sort of penalty? What would be the attitude of the rest of society toward such a child? A possible legal complication revolves around the question of whether a child can successfully sue his parents for failing to have him aborted when amniocentesis revealed that he would be born with defects.

In the past ten years there have been attempts on behalf of children to sue various parties for their part in giving the child "wrongful life." It was thought at the time that the "thalidomide babies" might have such a claim. In each case the courts have denied the claims, but some lawyers at the conference felt that amniocentesis may give such suits a new potential.

The implications of amniocentesis and prenatal diagnosis of genetic disease may soon involve the rights of society itself. Cost-benefit analyses have shown that detection programs for Tay-Sachs disease (a genetic disorder that causes blindness, mental retardation, and death within a few years) and Down's syndrome alone would result in very large savings for individual families and for society as a whole if affected fetuses were aborted instead of being born and ultimately institutionalized at state expense. Four thousand infants with Down's syndrome are born each year in the United States, and lifetime institutional care for each one costs approximately a quarter of a million dollars. Add a billion dollars each year to the already burgeoning costs of caring for the still living mongoloids born in prior years, and the enormous economic burden they represent becomes apparent.

In considering the rights of society, economic considerations like this one are undeniably important, but it seems a dangerous precedent to justify prenatal screening and abortion programs solely on the basis that they could eliminate an economic burden on families and society. One could argue cogently that society has a greater right to the elimination of disease than to the removal of an economic burden. There are certain to be legal tests of the liability of parents and others for offspring born with genetically determined handicaps that are predictable. Suits involving genetic diseases will soon test the concept that we—as parents, physicians, and human beings—have obligations to the unborn to protect them from the likelihood of genetically determined defects.

As amniocentesis becomes known to the general public, and its implications are realized, a new moral and ethical dilemma will confront those who argue against the reform of restrictive abortion laws. Amniocentesis and similar methods of detecting genetic anomalies may end up becoming an important new weapon in the battle for abortion reform. Selective abortion appears to be the logical method for eliminating many congenital diseases from our society.

In the controversy surrounding liberalization of abortion laws, some of society's basic attitudes toward life are laid bare. Through recent upheavals in our social, legal, and religious institutions we are faced with the dilemma of assigning to the fetus certain rights. In several instances, damages have been awarded on behalf of fetuses in criminal and tort suits. At the same time, abortion laws (in seventeen states) have been liberalized to the point of suggesting that early fetuses do not have the right to life if the mother wants to abort a pregnancy.

In the final analysis, amniocentesis and its implications of eliminating genetic diseases will confront society with the ultimate choice: strict abortion laws, or a better quality of human life. Dr. James V. Neel, a geneticist from the University of Michigan, has pointed out that condemning many of today's infants to famine or inadequate development does not display greater respect for the quality of human life than is found in primitive societies that practice infanticide with undesired or defective newborn infants. Others have questioned the moral and legal justification for making these life-death decisions.

Until now, the life-death decision, and the right to make it, has been the basic issue. The moral and ethical dilemma is compounded by the ability to detect and diagnose birth defects and genetic diseases in early pregnancy. Now we see that we are faced with problems of assigning values to individuals with given genetic characteristics and designing programs against them.

These problems will undoubtedly accentuate the conflict in our society between personal choice and governmental control, which could possibly come in the form of programs of compulsory screening and mandatory abortion for some conditions that are deemed socially intolerable.

Once abortion reform has become universal, and the legal barriers against abortion are lifted, it still does not seem likely that the dilemma will be resolved. There are some obviously dangerous extensions of the practice of compulsory screening and mandatory abortion. These extensions would impinge so drastically on our individual liberties as to make them unacceptable and morally unjustifiable. All the answers are not in yet. The conflict is not over yet—in fact, it is just beginning.

# ARTIFICIAL INSEMINATION AND ARTIFICIAL OVULATION

In February 1966, a New York physician sued for divorce on the grounds of adultery. His suit posed a curious legal question: Does artificial insemination constitute adultery?

**What Is Artificial Insemination?**

Artificial insemination (A.I.) is a method of fertilizing a woman by a means which is a substitution for natural intercourse. With the aid of instruments, semen is deposited in a woman's vagina, cervical canal or uterus, in order to induce pregnancy. There are two kinds of artificial insemination: A.I.H.—in which the "H" stands for use of the semen of the husband; and A.I.D.—in which the semen is provided by a donor, a fertile male, other than the husband. The identity of the donor is ordinarily known only to the physician. Sometimes, these two types of insemination are combined, and a mixture of the husband's and donor's semen employed (A.I.H.D.). A.I.H. is used in cases of impotence, vaginal spasm, and failure to ejaculate. A.I.D. may be employed where the husband is sterile or suffers from a hereditary disease, or for eugenic reasons.

## History of A.I.

The first mention of artificial insemination is found in the Babylonian Talmud (sixth century A.D.). A Talmudic student, so the tale goes, presents to his rabbi-teacher the hypothetical case of a woman who became pregnant after bathing in water, which unaware to her, had contained seminal fluid. The rabbi decided that the woman was morally innocent. There had been no intercourse and the insemination was an accidental result. Stories of A.I.D. with animals are found in Arabic writings dating back to the fourteenth century. It is said that as a war stratagem hostile Arabic tribes secretly inseminated their enemies' stock of thoroughbred mares with sperm from inferior stallions.

A "serious" document was written a century ago depicting a pregnancy supposedly caused when a rifle shot fired in the Civil War passed through the testes of a soldier and then lodged, with its film of semen, in the abdomen of a nearby young woman. Dr. Alan Guttmacher, looking back in jest, says that "a fitting denouement for this incident would have been a shotgun marriage."

The first scientific paper on artificial insemination in dogs was published in 1780 by Lazzaro Spallanzani of Italy. Ten years later, John Hunter, a British surgeon, carried out the first successful human insemination, his subject being the wife of a linen merchant suffering from hypospadias, which means he was unable to ejaculate semen into his wife's vagina. To solve the problem, Hunter injected the man's sperm with a syringe into his wife's vagina, and she conceived.

The first recognized artificial insemination in the United States was effected in 1866 by the New York gynecologist Dr. J. Marion Sims, who did a series of fifty-five intrauterine inseminations with husbands' sperms. Only one woman successfully conceived, and in her case only after the tenth A.I.H. Dr. Sims attributed his failures to faulty techniques.

The Russian physiologist A. V. Ivanov published a book in 1907 on A.I. in animals. The methods he prescribed have been widely followed for breeding horses, cattle, and other species. With A.I., one thoroughbred can sire numerous mares, and the threat of injury during the mating act is avoided. Animal semen can be refrigerated and shipped long distances. In 1960, two-thirds of the calves born to dairy cattle in America were sired artificially

In 1909, an American doctor, A. Hard, reported the use of a donor's semen to fertilize a woman whose husband was sterile. Since the turn of the century the employment of artificial insemination for human purposes has steadily increased. The *New York Post* ventured an estimate of 50,000 A.I. pregnancies in 1955 for the United States. This figure rose to 100,000 in 1958. A decade later *Time* reported twice this number of A.I.D. children. Sperm banks are now located in Los Angeles, New York, and several other cities.

### Medical Procedures for A.I.

The medical procedures for A.I.H. and A.I.D. are essentially the same. The husband or donor is required to masturbate for his semen specimen. Insemination should be completed by the physician within a few hours after the specimen has been ejaculated, since timing of insemination is critical. It must be carried out at about the time of ovulation to accomplish its purpose. Some physicians attempt artificial insemination on a patient only once each menstrual cycle—trying to arrive as close as possible to the day of ovulation.

No special preparations on the patient's part are necessary. She and her husband may or may not have had intercourse immediately prior to insemination. Preliminary coitus does not enhance the chance of successful A.I.D., but physicians indicate that for some couples it has psychic benefit. With the patient lying on the examination table, the physician introduces semen into the vagina by use of a syringe with a blunt needle attached to it. After insemination the patient is left on the tilted table, shoulders lowered and pelvis elevated for twenty to thirty minutes, sometimes as long as an hour.

The selection of a donor for A.I.D. is an important responsibility. A donor must be free of venereal disease, his hereditary background must be free of lethal genes, he should be of the same physical characteristics as the husband, and should have a high degree of fertility (preferably be a father himself). If the prospective mother is Rh negative, the donor must also be Rh negative. The donor's identity must remain anonymous to the prospective parents. In 1947, an amendment to the Sanitary Code of New York City, imposed certain restrictions on the use of donors. Clinics such as the Tyler Clinic in Los Angeles, which have established sperm banks, screen their prospective donors extensively. Emphasis is on eugenic considerations in donor selection. For this reason there has been severe criticism of sperm banks. Father Filas says in *Today's Health:*

The sperm bank is the scientist gone mad and the scientist gone mad plays God. A wider application of the immorality of donor insemination will make us more and more creatures of the state and like animals. It will take away human dignity and privacy and put the doctor/scientist in the place of God. I think this is an area that God does not intend to be in our power.

Dr. Aguiles J. Sobrero of the Margaret Sanger Research Bureau shares this point of view: "I approve of using sperm banks to protect human germ plasm from genetic defect or disaster—but not to make a generation of robots or a super race of Nobel Prize winners."

Physical attractiveness is one attribute given importance in a western sperm bank. By this criterion, Abraham Lincoln would be rejected as a possible donor.

## Legal and Religious Attitudes on Artificial Insemination

*A.I.H.* From the legal standpoint, A.I.H. is of minor significance. The child is clearly legitimate and a legal problem only arises if one party seeks to dissolve the marriage on the grounds of non-consummation. Does A.I.H. and the resultant birth of a child bar a dissolution? An English court has held that it does not constitute such an impediment and of itself does not ratify the marriage. The Royal Commission on Marriage and Divorce recommended that the rule should be changed. "Consent to an act which is likely to produce a child of the wife is in our view so fundamental a step that it must be taken to mean that the parties acquiesce in the marriage." At one time such a decree would have bastardized the child, but laws have been passed in many American jurisdictions which now prevent this result.

Since all Christian theologians agree that procreation is a fundamental purpose of marriage, one would not expect to hear opposition to A.I.H. The Church of England Commission appointed in 1945 cautiously commends A.I.H. where a substantially grave cause exists for its use. Thus, its employment would be lawful if the husband suffered from a permanent physical disability rendering him impotent, and would only be used after diligent inquiry and with the most extreme caution. This view represents that generally held among non-Roman Catholic Christians.

Theological difficulties arise when the methods of obtaining semen are considered. The chief method, masturbation, caused

Roman Catholic theologians to condemn A.I.H. Masturbation in the Catholic view is an act of self-pollution, intrinsically evil, and is irredeemable becau·· it is not directed toward procreation. The Church of England Commission takes issue with the Catholic position. "The act which produces the seminal fluid, being in this instance directed towards the completion of the procreative end of the marriage, loses its character of self-abuse. It cannot, in this view, be the will of God that a husband and wife should remain childless merely because an act of this kind is required to promote conception."

When other methods of obtaining semen became feasible, such as by puncturing a testicle and the epididymis, the morality of A.I.H. was again debated. Father Kelly in *The Ecclesiastical Review* writes: "But the puncture of the epididymis involves no use of the sexual act. Of itself, its intrinsic morality might partake of the nature of a minor mutilation, somewhat similar to that involved in a blood transfusion."

Catholic theologians reply that the pleasure obtained from the act of masturbation does not constitute its evil, but that the act is evil in itself and so renders the pleasure illegitimate. With respect to the method of puncturing the epididymis, they argue that the removal of semen from the male organs is intrinsically evil as this destroys the ordination of semen to generation as required by the natural order. In order that the semen be physically ordained to generation, it must remain within the generative organs of either the male or female. By this view, man does not have full dominion over his semen, but merely a right to its use and then only in connection with generation which is brought about by natural intercourse. One cannot help but feel that the doctrinaire opposition to A.I.H. sperm production is the worst kind of religious hair-splitting.

*A.I.D.* Does A.I.D. constitute adultery at civil law and thus provide a ground for divorce? Adultery gives rise to divorce on two grounds: it violates the exclusive right to sexual intercourse granted to the spouses by the marital pact, and it may introduce a foreign strain of blood into the family. Until 1921 there had been no case on the issue, but in that year in *Orford* v. *Orford* a Canadian court held that by submitting to A.I.D. the wife had committed adultery. "The essence of the offence of adultery consists not in the moral turpitude of the act of sexual intercourse, but in the voluntary surrender to another person of the reproductive powers or faculties of the guilty person; and any submission of those powers or faculties to the service or enjoyment of any person other than the husband or wife comes within the definition of adultery." Judge Orde's view that A.I.D. constitutes adultery has been followed in one United States case, *Doornbos* v. *Doornbos*, an Illinois decision of 1954, but in other jurisdictions it has been severely criticized.

In a 1959 Scottish decision, Lord Wheatley maintained that the test of adultery must be sexual intercourse, declaring that "just as artificial insemination extracts procreation from the nexus of human relationships in or outside of marriage, so does the extraction of the nexus of human relationship from the act of procreation remove artificial insemination from the classification of sexual intercourse." The notion that adultery might be committed by a woman alone in the privacy of her bedroom aided and abetted only by a syringe containing semen made no sense whatever to Lord Wheatley, but it does to Father Francis F. Filas. He rejects Wheatley's argument:

> Some writers argue that it is not adultery because there is no physical contact between the woman and donor. Adultery is not mere physical contact. It is the violation of the marriage bond which is oriented to new life and in which the husband and wife have a right to each other's life-giving powers. The husband's right to his wife's procreative power is a gift from God which he cannot give away. He can no more tell his wife to receive semen from a donor than he can tell her to have intercourse with another man.

## Medical Attitudes Toward A.I.

Even though the practice of A.I. is increasing, general acceptance by the medical profession is still lacking. A prominent physician, Dr. T. J. Gold, expresses his reservations. "Carrying a baby for nine months doesn't make a woman a mother any more than fertilizing an egg makes a man a father. Parenthood is in the joys and problems of raising a child. A couple can adopt a newborn child and become parents in every way except the physical sense. I don't think A.I.D. is all that important." In 1955 the French Society of Gynecologists and Obstetricians almost unanimously denounced A.I. as a social experiment fraught with medical, legal, and moral hazards. A German textbook on forensic medicine, published in 1957, accepted A.I.H. as permissible, but roundly condemned A.I.D. The German Commission on Penal Law recommended that its new criminal code should prohibit A.I.D. but permit A.I.H.

To protect themselves as well as their patients, most physicians require written consent from husband and wife before starting A.I. As we have seen, the wife may be sued for adultery after insemination with a donor's sperm, and there is a prospect the doctor who performed the A.I.D. may be subject to prosecution. Cases have been reported where a physician will refuse to deliver the child after having successfully performed the A.I.D. Aware that the patient's husband is not the father of the child, there is a fear that signing the birth certificate may bring legal consequences. The fear is unfounded since this signature merely certifies the date and hour of birth and that the doctor was in attendance.

In 1958, the American Medical Association issued the following statement: "When the physician uses semen from a donor other than the husband, there is a possibility that legal complications may arise. Certainly the physician assumes a certain degree of responsibility as to the suitability of the donor."

## Future Horizons of Artificial Insemination

*Mixture of Penicillin with Sperm:* By mixing penicillin with sperm it is believed that the span of survival of semen in the cervical mucus will be longer, and it will also remove the danger of infection. Given the fact that many people have become allergic to penicillin, its addition to sperm in A.I. could be dangerous.

*Frozen Semen:* In animal husbandry use of frozen semen is a common practice and produces superb results. Use of frozen semen in human insemination, however, is still in the experimental stages. Over two dozen normal children have been produced with frozen sperm, but fear of fetal abnormalities or genetic mutations still inhibits wider application. A.I. with frozen semen has definite advantages. It would decrease waste of seminal fluid to a minimum. The cost of sperm would be less and more would be available. Human ova banks comparable to sperm banks may be possible in the future. Human ova appear morphologically unaltered and fertilizable after frozen storage.

*Mixture of Husband's Sperm with Donor's Seminal Plasm:* When the husband's sperm count is low or the mobility of his sperm poor, the sperm is mixed with a donor's seminal fluid from which the spermatozoa have been removed. This method is intended to carry out A.I.H. pregnancies instead of A.I.D. as a matter of record, but there is danger that donor spermatozoa might find its way into the compound. The upshot is that it might be difficult to prove that conception was effectuated with husband's sperm.

*Sex Regulation Through A.I.:* While statistical data is scant, it is contended by some physicians that A.I., with either husband's or donor's sperm produces more male than female offspring. A.I. has been effectively used for sex regulation in rabbits. It was done by electrophoretic separation of rabbit sperm and subsequent insemination. Human semen can also be separated electrophoretically, but the potential danger of damage to the sperm, and resulting genetic changes makes the method unpracticable.

### Artificial Ovulation

In 1962 two South African Dorper ewes gave birth to two healthy Border Leicester lambs. Moreover, the fathers of these lambs had never left England. As written up in the *Journal of Reproduction and Fertility*, the eggs had been flown to South Africa nestling in the oviduct of a living rabbit, which had maintained them in the vital physiological conditions. L. E. Rowson of Cambridge has pioneered in the field of artificial ovulation—the transfer of eggs from one animal to another. His research promises to provide a valuable way of improving breeds of livestock, since it would enable a high-grade female animal to produce more of her own offspring than is normally possible. All animals are capable of producing far more eggs than they will ever need. Nature engenders a large surplus of immature eggs, just as it does in human beings. By injecting FSH, the hormone which normally releases eggs from the ovary, cows can be induced to release forty or more eggs in a single cycle. If these can be placed in the womb of other animals, to be brought to term, the blue-ribbon sheep can be made to produce offspring at the rate of hundreds a year.

In his initial experiment, Rowson used the same strain of animal; however, he has since successfully transferred eggs between different strains of animal. Thus, a Friesian cow gave birth to a Hereford calf. It was necessary at first to perform a surgical operation to recover the eggs and another to reimplant them. However, in 1964 the Japanese Livestock Industry Experimental Station succeeded in making a transfer without surgical methods, and produced a healthy calf. The eggs were washed out of the donor cow, and one was injected into a cow's uterus with a special double syringe.

Professor A. J. Parkes, Marshall Professor of the Physiology of Reproduction at Cambridge University, predicts "the transference of eggs of the required sex will be possible in man in the course of time." At the present time, there is no danger involved in attempting such an experiment with a human. The risk to health involved is minimal, and biologists say there is little reason to assume that the child produced would not be fully healthy and normal. When attempted, it will doubtless provoke a storm of moral and legal debate. A troublesome situation could arise, at least in some bigoted regions, if a white woman gave birth to a black child, or vice versa.

Albert Rosenfeld, *Life* science editor, paints the shocking picture of future women going into a kind of supermarket containing day-old frozen embryos and shopping around for the one they want. Presumably there will be a glamorized photograph of the adult expected on the pack, as when one buys a package of garden seeds. Though this is possible, it is highly improbable. Frozen semen is now available but it can only be obtained through a physician. Anyone who wants an implanted embryo will likely have to take a similar course and persuade her doctor. However, as the process becomes common, little persuasion may be required; it may be more like asking for a smallpox injection.

# ORGAN TRANSPLANTATION

## Historical Summary

Organ transplants involve the use of one person's parts in another. An easy example is the use of a person's kidney in another person. However, the general area of organ transplants can encompass any type of transplants: legs, arms, torsos, brains or hearts, whatever the mind can imagine, the same legal and ethical problems arise.

Organ transplants are not new—skin grafts outdate the birth of Christ, and blood transfusions have been performed for over 150 years. What is new, however, are the parts of the human body that can be transplanted—basic life-giving organs such as hearts, lungs and kidneys.

As long ago as the sixteenth century, surgeons conceived the idea of transplantation of organs. An Italian, Gaspare Tagliacozzi, attempted to replace noses, lips and ears. His replacements however were short-lived and sloughed off. In the mid-1890s Alexis Carrel perfected techniques of joining blood vessels, believing that, since antiseptic methods were available, the permanent transplantation of tissues and organs could be achieved. When he found his implants were rejected he abandoned the effort in deep disappointment.

In 1950 French doctors removed kidneys from executed criminals and implanted them into uraemic patients. The following year American and British surgeons experimented with kidneys taken from hydrocephalic children. The surgery was satisfactory, and for several days the implanted kidney would work well. Then there would be a "rejection crisis." The body's defense mechanisms, which exist to combat invaders, would seek to expel the foreign kidney. As a result the survival time for an implanted kidney was usually only a few days.

Undiscouraged, the surgical profession continued to study the problem. The next phase was to attempt kidney transplantation with identical twins. It was known that skin grafts could be exchanged successfully between identical twins. On December 23, 1954, a team of surgeons removed the left kidney from a man identified as Mr. R. H. who was suffering from a chronic renal failure, and replaced it with a healthy kidney donated by his identical twin brother. After the operation Mr. R. H. made a complete recovery and eventually married the nurse who had looked after him in the hospital.

This was a historic event. For the first time, real hope of aiding sufferers from kidney disease had crystalized. By the fall of 1963 some 30 transplants in twins had been performed throughout the world. Not all were as successful as the case of Mr. R. H. Various snags have been encountered. For example, some people's kidneys are supplied with blood by two small arteries of unequal length, instead of one large one. But the main apprehension—the fear of infection—has been surmounted. Unfortunately, however, it also emerged that the implanted kidney was susceptible to the original disease. Mr. R. H. died of nephritis eight years after his operation.

But the operation marked the dawn of a new era in surgery, the age of organ transplants. After centuries of speculation, it suddenly became possible to seriously consider transplantation of not only kidneys, but arms, legs, lungs, livers, and even hearts. In 1968 transplant surgery took a major step forward with the achievement of the world's first successful heart transplant operation. In March of that year, Philip Blaiberg left a South African hospital on the power of an implanted heart. Perhaps even more significant, today 70 percent of kidney transplant donees are still doing well after two years. Sir Peter Medawar, director of Britain's National Institute of Medical Research, predicts that transplantation of liver and lungs may become routine practice within five years.

## Medical Problems in Organ Transplantation

As has been noted before, among the chief problems in organ transplantation is the problem of rejection. When the body is being formed in the embryonic stage, cells of different types seem to recognize one another and to join with their own kind, thus forming tissues. Recognition has been explained in terms of a pattern of electric charges, but the theory remains to be proved. It is probably the same power of recognition which enables the body to identify invading bacteria or foreign tissue and set in operation the scavenging systems which destroy the strange cells. Tremendous research is being done in the area of immunology, as the study of these processes is called.

Various methods have been offered to solve the problem of rejection. One method is to use X-rays or special drugs which will knock the immunizing mechanisms out of action. The obvious drawback of this approach is that it will also leave the patient vulnerable to infection by bacteria, and costly germ-free surgical units are required if the risk of the patient dying of some common infectious disease is to be avoided. Moreover, the X-ray can do damage to other body processes.

The first operation using X-rays to knock out the defense system was attempted in 1958; the first using an immunosuppressive drug (azathioprene) in 1961. In the latter case, the kidney took despite two "rejection crises," but the patient survived only 36 days due to the toxic effects of the drug. In the case of the X-rays the margin between a lethal dose and one which will knock out the defences long enough for the kidney to "take" is also an extremely narrow one.

A more promising approach has been developed recently known as tissue typing. This is based on the premise that people cannot accept transfusions of blood from any donor, but can only accept compatible types. Experience with blood types has led to the thought that perhaps there are also tissue types, so that people could accept a graft from a donor of the same type, but would reject one from a donor of a different type. According to Dr. J. W. Streilin of the School of Medicine at Pennsylvania University, we are on the verge of success in this area, while at least an interim solution of the problem will soon be available. There are also other paths to pursue. For example, it has recently been shown that the thymus gland in the base of the neck is responsible for manufacturing the antibodies which bring about graft rejection. Animal experiments show that removal of the thymus eliminates the immune response.

## Legal Ramifications of Organ Transplantation

In British law, and thus, generally speaking, in American law it is an offense to do anything which makes one unable to serve one's country, to consent to such a thing being done to one, or to do it to another. The law was established in medieval times and such an act is known as maim. The law forbid one to remove a front tooth, although it was permissible to remove a molar. As to why the distinction between teeth, it has been theorized that a front tooth could be used to bite one's enemy. National defense played an influential role in the law of maim. Castration was outlawed by the law of maim because it was believed that it reduced one's courage and aggressiveness. The law of maim, generally speaking, governs transplantation.

However, today the law is very broadly interpreted and exceptions have been made for health reasons. But surgeons have still been careful to obtain consent from potential organ donors and have sometimes consulted the coroner as well. After a person has given his consent, he is prohibited from bringing a lawsuit. The courts demand that the consent be based on a genuine understanding of the issues. Problems arise when there is an element of subtle duress involved as in the case of prisoners, or where the donor is of low intelligence. The problem becomes acute when donors under the age of consent are in question. In 1956, one of a pair of identical twins, whose age was under twenty-one, came to the hospital with advanced kidney disease; his brother was in excellent health. With the approval of the donor twin and the parents, a psychological study was made. The psychiatrist reported that in view of the close attachment between the boys, the knowledge that he had failed to help his brother when he might have done so would have a "grave emotional impact" on the healthy twin. In the light of this report, the Massachusetts Supreme Court ruled that the hospital and the surgeons could proceed, given the consent of the parents and the donor, without incurring liability, civil or criminal, for their action. The same court later allowed operations on twins aged fourteen. Similar judgments were made subsequently in other courts.

The line was drawn at age twelve by the hospital staff on the grounds that the donor was not old enough to understand the possible harm to himself, and so could not give meaningful consent. Also, it was thought that since he was so young, he would not suffer enduring emotional trauma from not being permitted to help.

While it is legal to remove an organ from a living person with his consent, one cannot legally consent to a public mischief. In an English case, a man had himself sterilized and was subsequently sued by his wife for cruelty. Since his motive was not one of health, one judge held that he had no legal right to have had the operation.

Surgeons and doctors have to face the moral and ethical question: is it right to take an organ from a normal person to rescue another who was ill and likely to die? Some surgeons maintain that it is wrong to take organs from a living person. They hold that it is wrong under the Hippocratic Oath to inflict any damage on the healthy. Another moral problem arises in the form of pressures put upon the donor and the possibility of moral blackmail. One doctor tells of a case when, after he told a possible donor that he was medically unsuitable, he was heard to mutter: "Now the family can't say I didn't try." Another problem is when a donor is motivated by a neurotic need for self-sacrifice.

Apart from what the law dictates with respect to consent, an ethical difficulty also resides in cases of those under duress. Dr. Alex Comfort believes that criminals might be asked to give up half their liver against a commuted sentence. In 1963, a murderer serving a life sentence was allowed to volunteer to receive a lung in the first lung transplantation ever attempted, at the University of Mississippi Medical Center. The governor indicated that he would commute the prisoner's sentence and grant a full pardon, but after 18 days the prisoner died. In this case the man volunteered prior to the governor's proposal, and hence it was not an inducement, but the prospect of prisoners being induced is a real possibility and a real moral problem.

Some authorities have made it clear that the solution to this problem is to not ask criminals to donate organs. They say that even if no reward is offered the criminal is bound to feel some sense of pressure and to feel that, if he refuses, it will be some kind of black mark against him. Moreover, while in constitutional countries the recourse might be employed with extreme care, there is a grave risk in despotic nations that such practices will be grossly and unconscionably abused.

In addition to the problems raised by moral considerations, there are the social problems created by irrational prejudice. For example, in six Southern states today the blood banks keep separate supplies of "whites" and "colored" blood, and there are many whites who would refuse a transfusion of the latter. Hence it is likely that such bigots would also decline the implantation of a "colored" kidney and one can expect a vehement refusal of a "colored" heart.

As the technical decisions become easier, the moral and social decisions become more significant. A new era is dawning with a new set of problems. As Gordon Taylor points out, "One thing is quite clear: these new technical powers demand more of the doctor as a man, as well as a surgeon. Superhuman wisdom and patience, insight and sympathy are needed by him who would wield superhuman powers."

The most perplexing question in the area of transplants is the question of when death actually occurs. Theological definition focuses in on the heart, that is, a man is dead when his heart stops beating. The medical definition is not a function of state law, but of local hospital administrative policy, and the best definition was given by a young intern who said, "I don't know how to define it, but I know a dead man when I see him." However, even the most experienced medical eye can be deluded as numerous cases of rising "dead men" attest.

# STERILIZATION

## Permanent Prevention of Conception

Temporary methods to prevent conception are usually lumped together under the term "birth control." They are employed by millions of couples with a high degree of effectiveness. For some couples, however, even the slightest risk of pregnancy represents too great a risk, since another pregnancy would be a disaster medically, economically, or emotionally. Under these circumstances, absolute protection against pregnancy is sought, and there are available safe surgical operations which render either the husband or the wife incapable of further reproduction. This is called sterilization. When a man or woman seeks out and consents to such an operation, it is designated by law as *voluntary sterilization*. If such an operation is ordered by an agency of the state against the wishes of the party, it is deemed *compulsory sterilization*.

## Extent of Voluntary Sterilization

Voluntary sterilization is on the rise in the United States and all over the world. In Puerto Rico, doctors estimate that in the past few years 60 percent of all the women who have their children delivered in hospitals request that sterilization follow the birth. Sterilization has been encouraged by the government of India and is now being done in railroad stations. A West German law passed in 1970 officially permits castration on a voluntary basis as a treatment of sex offenders. A recent Gallup poll in the United States revealed that two-thirds of the American people now approve of sterilization as a method of birth control. In 1970, the Association for Voluntary Sterilization reported that more than 750,000 sterilizations were performed in the United States. Three out of four operations were performed on men. Prominent advocates of Zero Population Growth like Dr. Paul Ehrlich of Stanford University and TV personality Arthur Godfrey have publicized their own sterilizations to encourage others to follow their example. The number of American women requesting sterilization is also increasing. Dr. Alan Guttmacher, president of Planned Parenthood-World Population, reported that in 1970 about one out of five women delivering in New York City's Municipal Hospital sought and obtained sterilization after giving birth. Most major medical plans such as Blue Cross and Blue Shield now include voluntary sterilization in their schedules of covered services. The federal Medicaid program will pay for it in about thirty-five states. Until 1970, the American College of Obstetricians had strict rules against sterilization, but in that year it said, "A sterilization can be performed on anyone who is legally capable of giving the obstetrician-gynecologist permission to operate upon her." About the same time, the Department of Defense announced that it had revised its regulations to permit sterilization for servicemen at all military hospitals.

There appears to be a definite geographic variation in the incidence of sterilization, ranging from a low of 2 percent of couples in the Northeast to 7 percent in the South and 10 percent in the West. The higher rate in the West is due to a higher proportion of operations on husbands—7 percent compared to 1 and 2 percent in other regions. The incidence of male operations, however, is on the increase throughout the country. The number of male operations more than doubled between 1955 and 1960.

## Methods of Sterilization

*Male:* A man can be castrated (have both testicles removed), an act which will render him sterile. This method is never used on normal individuals because it produces impotence and many other totally unacceptable effects. Castration not only eliminates sexual desire and potency, it alters the voice, causes fat to store up at various parts of the body, brings on loss of beard, etc. Castration is only advisable in cases of medical emergency as in cases where the patient is suffering from cancer or tuberculosis of the testicles. In some states, the court may order castration of a repeated sex offender before allowing him to go at large.

Today, sterilization of the male for purposes of birth control is carried out by a simple operation known as vasectomy. Vasectomy consists of uncoupling the duct which leads up from the testicle, where sperm are manufactured, to their point of exit, the penis. This uncoupling is achieved by cutting out an inch from the middle of this passageway known as the vas deferens, the duct which carries sperm from the testicles to the urethra, from which they are ejaculated during intercourse. This operation is extremely simple and entails no appreciable risk. In ninety-nine cases out of a hundred the operation is completely successful. By cutting the vas deferens, the flow of sperm to the urethra is stopped. Naturally, without sperm, a man cannot impregnate a woman. This simple procedure does not affect a man's sexual performance. After a vasectomy he still has normal sexual desire and potency. Since sperm cells make up a minuscule proportion of the semen, there is no decrease in the actual volume of semen produced at each ejaculation. Apart from the absence of sperm in the semen, there are no other physiological effects. Moreover, sperm continues to be produced after vasectomy, but with their exit blocked they simply disintegrate and are reabsorbed by the body.

Dr. Alan Guttmacher in his book *Birth Control and Love* (1969) states: "There should be no effect on the man's virility—except perhaps a subconscious one. Some men are so fearful of impregnating their wives that this fear diminishes sexual enjoyment and enthusiasm. The fact that after vasectomy they can have intercourse without the chance of impregnation may greatly revivify the sexual activity of such worriers. This is not because of any hormonal action but is simply a matter of emotions and attitudes."

A number of studies have been made of the end results of sterilization. A Japanese study of 101 vasectomized men showed ninety-seven favorable and four unfavorable. Careful studies were carried out by Dr. Frederick Ziegler, when he was psychiatrist at the Scripps Clinic, involving a battery of six psychological tests before and after vasectomy as well as interviews. He compares twenty-two couples in which the husband was vasectomized with twenty-two couples "who had been given prescriptions for ovulation-suppression pills."

One to two years after surgery, the subjects regarded the vasectomy as highly successful in accomplishing its primary objective—that of insuring contraception. They showed general enthusiasm about the operation and denied any association between the vasectomy and changes in life situation. Nevertheless, they concurrently manifested evidence of adverse emotional changes which exceeded those found in the comparison group (couples on the pill). The data suggest that the operation is responded to as though it had demasculinizing potential.

In 1967 a United States study of the results of male sterilization was completed by Ferber, Tietze, and Lewit. The investigation involved seventy-three male subjects and utilized an in-depth interview. More than two-thirds of the men stated that they felt freer and less inhibited sexually than before vasectomy, and three-fourths of the husbands reported that their wives felt less inhibited and freer sexually. Half claimed their wives "reached climax more easily."

Vasectomy is reversible about half the time, that is, one out of two vasectomized men can be restored to fertility. The reversal procedure is accomplished by sewing the two cut ends of the vas deferens together again. This operation is not considered reliable, and so those undergoing vasectomy are advised to view it as probably permanent. Theoretically it is possible to reverse vasectomy in 100 percent of the cases, but the technique remains to be perfected.

Dr. Hans Zinsser and his group at the College of Physicians and Surgeons of Columbia University has advanced a promising technique. He injects a semiliquid silicon rubber solution through an injection needle into the lumen of the vas deferens of a bear, which, after the introduction of a hardening agent, forms a rubbery plug that occludes the duct and blocks upward passage of sperm cells from the testes. After several months the plug can be removed by minor surgery, and the animal's fertility is restored. The chief defect with this method is that, after a year, the spermatic juices fragment the plug. Dr. Zinsser is in search of a more durable plastic from which to make the plug.

*Female:* Before a woman can become pregnant she must have at least one functional ovary, one Fallopian tube open throughout its five-inch course, and, naturally, she must also have a uterus. Therefore, pregnancy can be prevented if both ovaries are removed, or if both tubes are removed, or the canal in each is interrupted so the egg cannot pass down and the sperm cannot pass up, or if the uterus is removed.

## The Law and Sterilization

*Therapeutic Sterilization:* Where the patient is of sound mind and consents to sterilization, which is undertaken to preserve the patient's life or to protect his physical or mental health, the operation is legally permissible. In 1934 the Supreme Court of Minnesota indicated that such an operation is not against public policy and that medical necessity constituted valid grounds for its performance. In 1952, a California case reaffirmed this position where a doctor in the course of an operation discovered that his patient's Fallopian tubes were infected and removed the diseased portions. Judgment for the doctor was upheld on appeal.

*Eugenic Sterilization:* There are no federal laws on sterilization, but in twenty-eight of the states sterilization statutes are in force. All these statutes are aimed at eugenic objectives. They are intended to curtail the incidence of insanity, mental deficiency, feeble mindedness, sexual perversity, epilepsy, etc., by preventing the birth of children from parents suffering these afflictions. In most instances eugenic sterilization is compulsory. Vasectomy for males and salpingectomy for females are the operations usually designated, although other methods such as the irradiation of gonads or castration may be employed. In Nebraska castration is authorized by statute for male offenders who have committed rape, incest, and crimes against nature. Typically the sterilization procedure is recommended by the head of a prison rather than a judge. In several states special eugenic boards have been set up to make these decisions.

Most of the statutes (no doubt an attempt to anticipate the charge of "cruel and unusual punishment") specifically deny any punitive intent and are expressly for eugenic purposes for the protection of society. Yet a closer look at some of them belies such a function. Some are so lacking in scientific support that they can only be explained as an additional punishment for criminal offenders. For example, a Southern state once introduced a bill which would have compelled sterilization of people convicted of various crimes including chicken stealing. This bill, which fortunately failed of passage, could scarcely be supported on eugenic grounds.

Habitual criminals (often defined as people convicted of three or more felonies) are subject to sterilization in Delaware, Idaho, Nebraska, North Dakota, Oklahoma, and Oregon. In Wisconsin they do not even have to be "habitual" to come within the scope of the statute. In the light of scientific knowledge that environmental factors rather than hereditary ones mold criminals, these statutes are being challenged as having questionable eugenic value. It is argued that habitual criminals should be sterilized anyway, even if no eugenic purpose is served, simply because they are incapable of giving their children a good environment.

Sex offenders and sex perverts are subject to sterilization in California. The entire question of sex offenses is being reviewed and redefined by psychologists, psychiatrists, sociologists, and the like. It is known that many cases of shoplifting are the result of sexual aberrations. On the other hand, even indecent exposure can reflect a temporary lapse caused by alcohol or drugs, and the person thereafter will be sexually normal. The researches of Dr. Alfred C. Kinsey and his associates in the Institute for Sex Research, and the probes of other scientific investigators such as the Group for the Advancement of Psychiatry will hopefully provide the knowledge on which a more rational system of sex laws than now exists can be based. Several states have declared sterilization statutes unconstitutional and have been wiped off the books by court action. New Jersey and New York courts took this position, reasoning that the law was a denial of equal protection because, for example, Mary, a poor feeble-minded girl in a state asylum could be sterilized under the law, while Margaret, daughter of a wealthy family and in the same mental condition, would not be covered by the law because her family could afford to keep her under care at home or in a private institution. However, when this issue reached the Supreme Court in 1927, the Court upheld the validity of such statutes, explaining that a state has the power to pass a law which attempts a partial solution of a problem even though other parts of the problem are left untouched.

In the same case, the Supreme Court established the constitutionality of sterilization statutes in general. The suit was brought on behalf of Carrie Buck, an eighteen-year-old feeble-minded girl, who was a patient in a Virginia asylum. Carrie had given birth to a feeble-minded child out of wedlock. Her mother was also feeble-minded. It was in this case that Justice Oliver Wendell Holmes delivered his memorable epigram: "Three generations of imbeciles are enough." The court reasoned that the public welfare sometimes necessitates asking the nation's best citizens for their lives in war; concern for the welfare of the nation could require the lesser sacrifice of imposed sterility from people who were already draining the nation's strength. The Court said: "It is better for all the world if instead of waiting to execute degenerate offspring for crime, or to let them starve for their imbecility, society can prevent those who are manifestly unfit from continuing their kind."

Until 1942 the Supreme Court continued to uphold sterilization statutes, but in that year in the case of *Skinner* v. *Oklahoma* the Court unanimously struck down an Oklahoma sterilization law as unconstitutional. The statute authorized the compulsory sterilization of habitual criminals convicted of "felonies involving moral turpitude." Skinner, a criminal who had been convicted of three felonies, two armed robberies and one offense for chicken stealing, was ordered to be sterilized by the Supreme Court of Oklahoma. The United States Supreme Court, in invalidating the statute, declared that it failed to meet the equal protection clause. Justice Douglas pointed out that embezzlement could not be visited with sterilization but larceny could. "When the law lays an unequal hand on those who have committed intrinsically the same quality of offense and sterilizes one and not the other, it has made as invidious a discrimination as if it had selected a particular race or nationality for oppressive treatment." Since the Oklahoma decision, the constitutionality of all the sterilization statutes have been in some doubt.

# BRAIN PRESERVATION AND CRYOGENICS

### Keeping the Brain Alive

In 1963, after five years' work, a medical team at the Cleveland Metropolitan General Hospital surgically removed a monkey's brain from its skull and kept it alive on an artificial circulation system for seven hours. Various instruments recorded the electrical waves of this isolated brain which appeared normal; it consumed oxygen and released carbon dioxide into the circulating blood. All of these indicators seemed to prove the brain was still alive.

Not long after, Wisconsin surgeons reported similar experiments with dogs. Fifteen dogs were decapitated and their brains kept alive. These experiments provoked a great deal of moral concern. The *New Scientist* questioned the ethics of subjecting an animal to such pain. The surgeons had applied a local anaesthetic to the exposed tissues of the neck, but the *New Scientist* indicated "physical pain is not the only agony a disembodied brain could suffer."

By 1966, the Cleveland team was able to keep heads "alive" for a period of two days as a result of a new cooling technique. The entire head was maintained in the second state of experiments. When light was shone on them, the pupils of the eyes contracted.

Dr. Robert White, director of the Cleveland research, in a television interview has said that it is within the capability of science today to maintain a detached human brain. In fact, he thought it would be easier than maintaining monkey or dog brains since fully developed heart-lung apparatus for human beings was already in existence. Asked whether this was not a horrifying idea, he said: "Having talked to religious groups about this, I have been surprised that they were not more condemning. By the nineties or the end of the century the idea won't seem so overwhelming."

Dr. White added that at the present time he would not attempt such a human experiment because of the "social implications."

## Preservation by Freezing

The prospect of human beings being preserved alive by freezing for long stretches of time seems an idea only science fiction writers would concoct, but the prospect is being taken seriously in the United States. A number of societies have been formed to accelerate progress, notably the Life Extension Society of Washington, the Immortality Research and Compilation Association of California, and the Anabiosis and Prolongevity Institute of New York. Moreover, a number of people have paid sums to insure that, at death, their bodies will be preserved by freezing, in the conviction that the methods will soon be discovered to revive them. Dr. James H. Bedford, a retired professor of psychology, set aside $4,200 for this purpose before his death of cancer, at the age of seventy-three, in California last year. The Cryogenic Society of California performed the freezing operation. The initial step was the injection of an anticlotting agent, heparin. His chest was then opened and heart massage applied, so that the brain's supply of blood would be maintained. Immediately after, Dr. Bedford was transferred to a heart-lung machine and his body temperature lowered by packing with ice to 8°C. Most of the blood in the circulatory system was extracted and replaced by a solution of salts. The temperature of the body was then lowered to -79°C, and it was placed in storage at -190°C in liquid nitrogen. Aware that the freezing would do damage to his body, Dr. Bedford left $200,000 for Cryobiological research in the hope that before too long scientists would find a way of repairing such damage and reviving stored bodies.

If science does succeed someday in preserving life by freeza-toriums, it would create amazing opportunities for the living. It would offer the possibility to people suffering from an incurable disease of waiting around until a cure was discovered. If a person who died of pneumonia in 1920 had been preserved until today, he probably could have been saved. If the technique proved safe, others might wish to store themselves until interplanetary space travel was possible or until world peace was assured. And if they did not like the world they found, they could no doubt return to the freezer for a second period.

The legal, economic, and social consequences of such a fantastic notion are overwhelming. Among the problems one can anticipate arising are those of inheritance of property. Children expecting to inherit would be vexed at being denied their inheritance. A son who had taken over the family business would not welcome the return of his father who would demote him or oust him from management. The Internal Revenue Service would be faced with problems collecting taxes. The economic cost of large-scale freezing would be incalculable, considering the maintenance of freezatoriums, with all precautions against infection, periodic inspection by medical staff of the freezes, and so on. One must also wonder about the staggering problems of social adjustment in entering a futuristic era from a past age, as well as the environmental pressures of making space for an undying population.

Professor A. S. Parkes of Cambridge University declares: "Science fiction notwithstanding, the prospect of suspending animation for indefinite periods in man by freezing him is remote." But elsewhere he expresses another attitude: "All this of course sounds fantastic, but we have learned to use the word 'impossible' with caution. Ten years ago no normal mammalian cell had been frozen to temperatures compatible with long storage. Today this procedure is commonplace." Gordon Taylor, who delves into the subject in *The Biological Time Bomb*, says: "If anything in this line is achieved . . . it seems more likely that it will be by means of induced hibernation: a slowing of the bodily processes rather than a complete cessation. After all, we know this to be possible: nature does it regularly."

# PART III
# THE CULTURAL REVOLUTION

*For what is occurring now is, in all likelihood, bigger, deeper, and more important than the industrial revolution. . . . Change sweeps through the highly industrialized countries with waves of ever accelerating speed and unprecedented impact.*
                                        *Alvin Toffler,* Future Shock
                                                              *(1971)*

# THE CULTURAL REVOLUTION

All around us, people are shedding the old and predictable roles in society and opting for new and as yet undefined life-styles. In a very real sense, most of the material in this book is an elaboration of that phenomenon, but two developments seem particularly appropriate.

The first is women's liberation. By now, it should be undisputed that this movement is more than the petty frustrations of a few tired and shrill harpies. It is, at its best, an honest attempt to carve out a more meaningful place for women in this society. It did not grow out of anything but an underlying sense of uselessness and unfulfillment, and it will not be gone until those feelings are gone.

This is not a minority problem, obviously. And whenever women make adjustments, men will have to adjust accordingly. As in all the issues that run throughout this book, everybody is involved. More than one man has waved a disparaging hand toward the liberationists only to find soon after that the women in his life have changed because of it.

While women's liberation is essentially an effort to get more leverage in the establishment world, the communal movement is a rejection, in varying forms, of that establishment itself. "Going back to the roots" is the ultimate commitment to a new society, away from technology and "progress." The adherents are convinced that humanity has been lost somewhere in the shuffle and that the only way to find it again is to surround themselves with nature and rediscover those elemental human feelings.

This part, then, will focus on the motivations of those who seek to make a new way for themselves, for the purpose of achieving a greater understanding.

# WOMEN'S LIBERATION

### Historical Background

Will Durant, in *The Pleasures of Philosophy*, noting the progress of women toward equality in the twentieth century, says: "History has seldom seen so startling a transformation in so short a time." He goes on: "That woman should be anything but a household slave, a social ornament, or a sexual convenience, was a phenomenon known to other centuries than ours, but only as a phenomenon, as an immoral exception worthy of universal notice and surprise." The more usual view of woman was summarized by Aristotle, who classed woman as an arrested development, and explained her as nature's failure to make a man. She belonged with slaves as naturally servile, and quite unworthy of participation in public affairs.

This was also the opinion of the ancient Hebrews who grouped wives and mothers with cattle and real estate. The Jews, like most warring people, looked upon woman as a mishap, a necessary evil to be suffered as the only available source of troops for the time being. No candles were lit when a female was born among the ancient Jews. When a mother gave birth to a daughter she was commanded to undergo a double purification; and boys regularly prayed: "I thank thee, God, that thou hast not made me a Gentile nor a woman."

Other cultures eclipsed the Jews in the measure of disesteem and depreciation shown for women. Everywhere in the East women were scorned until they became mothers of sons, and were never fully honored until their sons died gloriously on some battlefield. Even Plato, who pleaded for equal opportunity without regard to sex, thanked God that he had been born a man.

In our own century women have been subject to almost as much maltreatment and malignment. Otto Weininger wrote a treatise purporting to show that women were soulless creatures. Schopenhauer, in his "Essay on Women," describes them as "that undersized, narrow-shouldered, broad-hipped, and short-legged race." Nietzsche counseled, "When thou goest to woman, remember thy whip." It is instructive to point out that all three of these truculent defamers of women were unrequited lovers.

Until 1900 or so a woman had hardly any right which a man was legally bound to respect. In the nineteenth century the women of Africa were still bought and sold as slaves. In Tahiti and New Britain they suckled the pigs. In England the husband could legally beat his wife nearly to death. Only if he succeeded in killing her, would the courts take notice. In Italy even until recently it was legal for a man to engage in adultery but illegal for his wife. Under common law if a wife earned money it belonged to her husband, and if she brought property into marriage it was his to spend. In France, after the Revolution which was fought for liberty and equality, a woman could still not vote nor own property.

Though in the past fifty years enormous strides have been made by the feminists, there is still a long way to go.

The American woman generally has a lower-paying job than a man does. In many jobs she does not earn equal pay for equal work. Her average earnings have actually declined relative to men's earnings. In time of recession she is, like blacks, the first to be fired. She represents only one percent of America's judges, one percent of its technicians, one percent of its engineers, one percent of its general surgeons, and one percent of the American Institute of Architects. Government is also virtually a no-woman's land. In 1971, out of a total of seven thousand legislators in the fifty states, only 340 were women. In religion, God is our Father and almost all preachers and priests are earthly sons. In education the percentage of women among college and university faculties has declined since 1920; in fact, the percentage of women going to college has also declined since that year. For most of Anglo-American legal history, when a woman married she became subordinate to her husband. A survey of the law shows that she is still subordinate. A 1972 Supreme Court decision denied a woman the right to retain her maiden name at marriage. Under California Civil code sections 1261 and 1263, a husband selects the homestead. He is the head of the family and may choose any reasonable place and mode of living, and the wife must conform thereto. The husband has management and control of the community property, and the absolute right of disposition over any community personal property. A married woman may become a sole trader, an independent businesswoman only by judgment of the Superior Court in which she resides. A married woman intending to become a sole trader must publish that fact in the newspaper along with her husband's name. Under California's labor code a woman cannot work on a job where she must carry objects weighing over fifty pounds, or ten pounds if it entails climbing stairs. Most states allow a husband to sue for loss of consortium if his wife is injured, but only a minority extend a parallel right to the wife when the husband is injured. North Carolina and Missouri even allow a woman to defend herself against a criminal charge by arguing that her husband ordered her to commit the crime. On the status of women, *Psychology Today* received twenty thousand replies to a questionnaire that sampled men, women not associated with a women's group, and women who were. Of the men, 51 percent agreed that "U.S. society exploits women as much as blacks." Nongroup women agreed by 63 percent, and group women by 78 percent.

### The Movement

The fundamental impact of the women's liberation movement cannot really be measured in terms of legal victories, employment coups, and sensational confrontations with the arch-forces of male chauvinism. What is more significant is the national soul-searching that it has generated, the collective reexamination of the male-female relationship in America. If law and morality are reflections of the predominant attitudes and feelings of the citizens to whom they apply, then they must flow from the consensus that emerges from the marketplace of ideas and philosophies. In the matter of women's liberation specifically, the legal consequences of the movement are the products of the frustration and impatience that pushed the entire subject of the woman's role in society into the forefront of our national consciousness.

It has never been easy to generalize about women's liberation, because of both the multifaced nature of its adherents and the differing degrees of equality they are demanding. On the one hand, there may be an organization entitled Women, Inc., of San Francisco, comprised of generally conservative women of conventional morality, seeking essentially employment equality only and supporting the war effort in Vietnam. On the other hand, there are those determined to annihilate, by whatever means necessary, every last vestige of male domination—e.g., WITCH (Women's International Terrorist Conspiracy from Hell). It is precisely this seemingly infinite variety of plans and goals that led Ti-Grace Atkinson, a prominent radical, to declare in 1968: "The whole thing is in a mess. We need a revolution in the revolution."

If it appeared at one time that the movement was doomed to an early death because of intra-sister clashes, the passage of time has brought a more durable image to women's liberation in general. What is most striking in 1972 is the degree to which it has been institutionalized by the American media. One need only take a fleeting glance at the local newsstand to discover an imposing array of new magazines devoted to the "new, aware woman." The bra-less phenomenon, far from being an incident of scandal, has been co-opted by respectable fashion; it was once the undeclared symbol of the defiant element in the movement. Various leaders of the feminists are now established as public personalities, their status secured either exclusively or primarily on the strength of their activity within the movement. Germaine Greer, Gloria Steinem, and others are household names. Already in the movies *The Diary of a Mad Housewife* has documented the trials of a bored, hemmed-in woman, and entertainers in general are not so quick to pattern their routines around dumb-blonde jokes.

Similarly, advertising agencies and the companies they represent are finding that they must pay a certain deference to the increased sensitivity of women or suffer the repercussions. When National Airlines instituted a campaign of attractive young stewardesses imploring potential customers to "fly me," incensed members of the National Organization for Women picketed both the National ticket agency and the offices of the advertising agency, many of them carrying signs imprinted, "Go fly yourself, National."

More seriously, the business world is consciously exhibiting an awareness of the vocational problems that beset women, and though the eagerness to hire sometimes smacks of tokenism, it is an important and observable change in attitude. So, too, with colleges and professional schools, in their admissions policies.

In short, women's liberation has secured a foothold on the American scene. It is no longer a novelty item, an aberration vulnerable to abrupt, impatient dismissals from those who disagree with it. An aura of permanence surrounds it now and, consequently, it receives better and more intense analysis. Almost every college and a good number of high schools have incorporated liberation-oriented courses in their curricula. Leading academicians in the fields of anthropology, history, and biology have turned their inquiring attention this way. So while there still remain the inevitable fringe groups and antagonistic extremists, and the movement still suffers from a lack of cohesiveness, the quest for a redefined role for womanhood is on for good.

A line tracing the evolution of women's liberation (at least in its current form) must begin in the area of the colleges and universities. Feminists are fond of embracing nineteenth-century predecessors such as Susan B. Anthony and rallying around their pronouncements—and, to be sure, there is some legitimate identification between today's militant and yesterday's suffragette. But it is equally true that the movement languished, if it existed at all, through the first half of the twentieth century and that the problems and motivations of the second feminist wave are unique enough to make their uprising a basically independent one. There were legal barriers in the early 1960s—and there still are—but for the most part it was an undercurrent of uselessness and lack of purpose and identity that surfaced in countless college discussions among women. The disenchanted found a ready and able heroine at this time in the person of Betty Friedan, author of *The Feminine Mystique* in 1963. Friedan's target in her book was not so much any institutional or personal oppressor such as marriage or men, but rather, as the title suggests, the entire vacuous syndrome of feminine passivity and do-nothingness:

> If I am right the problem that has no name stirring in the minds of so many American women today is not a matter of loss of femininity or too much education, or the demands of domesticity.... We can no longer ignore that voice within women that says: "I want something more than my husband and my children and my home."
>
> The only way for a woman, as for a man, to find herself as a person, is by creative work of her own. There is no other way ... Drastic steps must now be taken to re-

educate the women who were deluded or cheated by the feminine mystique. Many of the women I interviewed who felt trapped as housewives have, in the last few years, started to move out of the trap. But there are as many others who are sinking back again, because they did not find out in time what they wanted to do, or because they were not able to find a way to do it.

Asserting that marriage and a creative life were not incompatible, Ms. Friedan formulated "a woman's G.I. Bill" to sponsor the continuing education of married women. It is clear that the ideas embodied in *The Feminine Mystique*, working well within the established patriarchal system, were quite mild in the light of what was to come—however radical they might have been upon publication. Nevertheless, *The Feminine Mystique* supplied a strong, tangible starting point as a declaration of feminine discontent.

Three years after the publication of her book, Ms. Friedan organized NOW—the National Organization for Women. In the last six years, NOW has endured a host of factional disputes within its membership as regards proper methods and purposes, and stands today as the largest and most vital organizational force within the movement.

If the philosophical basis for NOW was originally the emptiness and creative ennui of the married housewife as depicted in *The Feminine Mystique*, it took only a short time for the members to expand their alienation. The immediate activity concentrated on legal strategems to safeguard employment rights. Among the first targets was the *New York Times* and its advertising procedures. For years, the *Times* had split its classified help-wanted headings into separate "male" and "female" columns. Claiming that such categorization violates Title VII of the Civil Rights Act of 1964, which prohibits sex discrimination in employment, NOW members picketed the *Times*. Finding little solace in talks with *Times* representatives, they sued the Equal Employment Opportunities Commission and eventually won their case.

A second sacred cow to be attacked was "protective legislation," most of which had been passed in the periods of heavy industrialization to limit the work-hours and stress of female blue-collar workers. NOW contended that many of these laws no longer served their purpose and often prevented women from making better money and reaching better jobs.

Other active fronts were (and are) the repeal of all abortion laws—part of the drive to allow women to control their own bodies; the creation of a nationwide network of day-care centers for children of working mothers; an alteration of the tax laws to allow a full deduction for housekeeping and child-care expenses of working parents; establishment of increased maternity benefits provided by employers, including paid leave and a guaranteed right to return after childbirth; the facilitation of divorces and new marriages by simplifying the laws; and, finally, a constitutional amendment which would deny federal funds to any agency, institution, or organization which would discriminate against women.

There was good reason for such a pragmatic schedule. The objective facts on the employment status of women were overwhelmingly clear. The Commission on the Status of Women called by President Kennedy found that women earned up to 40 percent less than men for the same work. As of 1968, 90 percent of the 28 million women in the job market earned less than $5,000 annually.

But as the members of NOW shared personal experiences and delved deeper and deeper into the causes of their frustration, a more subjective and inclusive indictment evolved. It became no longer possible for some feminists to isolate their legal struggles from the stifling and, in their minds, oppressive cultural roles of women or the masculine attitudes that shaped them. The charge of sexism was born and behind it was the growing feeling that genuine equality for women could come only as the product of a social revolution.

As the new feminist militants emerged, more and more traditional institutions came under their skeptical scrutiny, especially marriage. Ti-Grace Atkinson, who eventually left NOW in 1968, offered this view as to what was really plaguing women:

> The institution of marriage has the same effect the institution of slavery had. It separates people in the same category, disperses them, keeps them from identifying as a class. The masses of slaves didn't recognize their condition either. To say that a woman is really happy with her home and kids is as irrelevant as saying that the blacks were happy being taken care of by Ol' Massa. She is defined by her maintenance role. Her husband is defined by his productive role. We're saying that all human beings should have a productive role in society.
>
> We've always been so defensive. "Oh, no, we're not feminists, but can we just have a little more, huh?" I think

it's time for us to go on the offensive. I think we ought to say, "Listen, you, you dumb broad, you look funny. You stay home, you're kind of empty, you're bored, you take out your frustrations on your husband, you dominate your kids, and when you get older, you disintegrate. You fill the doctors' offices with headaches and backaches and depression, you tell the psychiatrist you don't feel fulfilled, you get menopausal breakdown. . . . What good are you? *Who are you? Get with it!*"

Clearly, the emphasis was switching from the legal and vocational condition of women to their entrenched life-styles and the blunted, confused self-perceptions that grow out of them. Marriage, childbearing and husband-keeping were now seen as incompatible with a meaningful, creative life.

With the castigation of marriage underway, there followed by logical necessity broadsides at the time-honored concept of the family. Feminists began to question the need for one-to-one parent-child relationships, asserting that the love that children need may be obtained equally well in communal settings where all children would love all adults. Some went further, claiming that the collective experience would benefit not only unburdened mothers but the children as well. Sociologist Suzanne Schad-Somers makes the case: "My own conclusion, based on the empirical evidence, is that children raised collectively are more independent, more cooperative, with fewer psycho-sexual problems than kids raised in the United States."

By 1968, what may be designated as the left wing of NOW found strong support in the ranks of numerous radical organizations that proliferated, mostly on college campuses and seemingly overnight. The new university groups fed on the experiences of its members in earlier reform movements in the early sixties, most notably the civil rights crusade. Women found it to be one short step from the effort to secure others' rights to that of fighting for their own. But while the liberation movement inherited a good dose of reformist zeal from the earlier activities, many of these women came to the sobering realization that they were definitely on their own—that there were unmistakable traces of sexism and chauvinism even within "the revolution." Few were content to trust the largely male leadership of radical campus action groups with the problems that were exclusively female. As one news-weekly put it, "Most radical organizations saw to it that the 'chicks' operated the mimeograph machines and scampered out for coffee while the men ran the show."

Steeped, then, in radical experience and philosophy yet disillusioned with male direction, college women started their own organizations. Most of them regarded the majority leadership of NOW as a bit behind the times since the makeup of the new university groups was decidedly militant. In their ranks today stand Redstockings, Media Women, Radical Mothers, and Bread and Roses—the implication of the last-named group being that women desire more than just flowers but money as well. And further left, on the fringes, a number of half-bitter, half-comical, quasi-guerilla groups poured out their disdain for the male world—not so much in pursuit of a precise program for change but rather in a calculated display of anarchic outrage. Probably the most virulent of these bizarre offshoots is SCUM, the Society for the Cutting Up of Men, whose Manifesto evidences the neurosis and misanthropy that marks the extremes of women's liberation:

> Life in this society being, at best, an utter bore and no aspect of society being at all relevant to women, there remains to civic-minded, responsible, thrill-seeking females only to overthrow the government, eliminate the money system, institute complete automation, and destroy the male sex.
>
> It is now technically possible to reproduce without the aid of males (or for that matter, females) and to produce only females. We must begin immediately to do so. The male is a biological accident. The Y (male) gene is an incomplete X (female) gene, that is, has an incomplete set of chromosomes. In other words, the male is an incomplete female, a walking abortion, aborted at the gene state. . . .
>
> The male, because of his obsession to compensate for not being female combined with his inability to relate and to feel compassion, has made of the world a shitpile. . . . SCUM is against the entire system, the very idea of law and government.

While the posture of SCUM seems infused with an intentional note of nihilistic absurdity, even less-alienated liberationists began, around 1968, to adopt more aggressive tactics. Karate classes for women became common. A Berkeley group petitioned the city council for the free issuance of guns so as to enable them to protect themselves from "male assaults." Some hysterical leaders dropped hints about the possibilities of armed conflict against men.

In essence, the late sixties witnessed the peak of feminist rhetoric. Much of it was rightly branded as hysteria and self-indulgent whining, and the more responsible leadership soon began to emphasize the need for cooperation with men and to clean up the appearance of the movement. Aware that opponents were only too happy to disparage the entire effort by pointing to its destructive elements, many of the groups underwent a thorough house-cleaning.

One of the thorniest problems to reconcile has been that of the lesbian. All allegations by disgruntled males aside, the presence of a healthy lesbian population among the feminists has provoked vigorous policy dissent. Those who emphasize the sexual and emotional dehumanization that issues from traditional male-female relationships are more welcoming; those with more immediate, objective goals, less interested in a cultural reorientation, tend to shun them as liabilities. Many lesbians have rejected the movement in anger, hurling charges of hypocrisy as they leave.

From the first awakening to the age of rhetoric and back to "respectability," women's lib has progressed to the seventies, winning over many supporters, male and female, along the way. A few unlikely enemies have emerged, however, and though liberationists are wont to describe them as mere victims of a sexist society, their presence is real enough.

The most nettlesome opponents are unsympathetic sisters. Since they are the individuals to whom the problems should be most apparent, non-comprehending demurrers such as that of Posey Carpenter, a Los Angeles real estate broker, are especially maddening: "I don't know what these women are thinking of. I love the idea of looking delectable and having men whistle at me." Others are not so puzzled—they are outright chauvinists. The Pussycat League, Inc., of New York swears that "the lamb chop is mightier than the karate chop" and issues instructional reading geared to help women serve, flatter, and generally overwhelm their men with feminine love.

In a more serious vein, scores of successful women in business, the arts, and the professions express agreement with the ends of liberationists, but deride their need or desire to resort to political group activity to achieve them. In their minds, the obstacles in the path of a successful career and a rewarding life, while greater than those that men might meet, are relatively insignificant in the face of a determined and talented woman's resolution.

For the black woman, if she is inclined to subscribe to the movement at all, liberation as a woman invariably remains subordinate to liberation as a black. Having done without the material comfort and attention that her white counterpart has become bored with, the black woman has trouble identifying with the cultural malaise that frustrates so many feminists. "They're just beginning to get the kind of good treatment as women that white women have always had," says Anne Osborne of the Southern Christian Leadership Conference. "They don't want to give it up too fast. Black men have just gotten enough money to take them to nice places and women like it." There are less selfish reasons too. Many black men and women pinpoint the failure of the black family as one of the prime reasons for the problems and disorganization that blacks face in America. If a black woman feels that her greatest contribution lies in complementary, self-sacrificing support of a black man and family, it is not likely that she will forego that to join other women, many of whose problems she does not share in the first place.

And, of course, there are the men. It would be impossible to catalogue all the masculine reactions to a phenomenon that affects such a fundamental part of their existence. Some have lost wives or had relationships quashed as their mates' viewpoints changed. Some denigrate out of ignorance, others out of a deep-seated cynicism rooted in a lifetime's observation of the differences they see between the sexes. And still others have lent their encouragement and active participation. But among the most interesting of male reactions is that of social anthropologist Lionel Tiger. Challenging the generally unwritten premise of the movement—that men and women are virtually identical and hence able to swap their roles if necessary—Tiger asserts that there are definite, inheritable bio-genetic traits that shape different lives for men and women. Casting the male-female relationship in terms of primitive animal behavior, Tiger speculates that male domination may very well be the result of an instinctual drive to maintain the species. As he says, "One of the problems here may be that primates physically have intercourse with females that they can dominate. It may just be that the phenomenon of sexual encounter depends on a sexual politic. And that without this politic, in the way it has been contrived for several million years, there may not be *any* sexual encounter." In any event, many men and women are querulous as to what female characteristics, if any, are inheritable and which have been produced and shaped by the system. The question goes to the heart of the problem.

Undoubtedly, the women are not about to be deterred from carrying on. But what direction women's liberation will take and what methods will prevail are still at issue. NOW has opted to continue the legal assault within the existing framework and, despite the passage by Congress of the Equal Rights Amendment, there is much yet to be done. Protective laws and antiabortion laws remain on the books in many states. Married women remain prey to restrictions on credit and property rights. And there is always the need to exert pressure for employment equality. With about 255 chapters in forty-eight states, a membership of 18,000 in 1972, and growing lobbying power, NOW is a force to be reckoned with.

Nevertheless sizable numbers of feminists view NOW's efforts as a futile attempt to exact token tribute from a system which is hopelessly corrupt and are taking a broader, revolutionary tack. Incorporating Marxist ideology and class-struggle theory into feminism, men become agents of oppression who force females into a lower caste in all existing social structures, and into a powerless economic class in capitalistic America.

Germaine Greer, the controversial author of *The Female Eunuch*, takes a cooler look, renouncing the efforts of NOW but describing men as equal victims of outmoded role-playing rather than oppressors. Speaking of Betty Friedan, she opines, "What she wants for (women) is equality of opportunity within the status quo, free admission to the world of the ulcer and the coronary." In a recent interview in *Playboy* magazine, a rather ironic forum (yet logical in reaching the other side), she expounded on the notion that men and women are in this struggle together. "We must be part of the general pressure for revolution in a capitalist society. We can't just be yet another privileged group applying pressure for our personal interests . . . neither of the sexes is truly liberated at this time. . . . You see, it's impossible for superiors and inferiors to love, since the superior can only condescend and the inferior can only admire. Whereas what you really want is recognition between two equals, which means that they don't need to exploit each other. They simply rejoice in each other's presence, because what they see is a reflection of themselves in each other."

In recognizing that our present sexual and psycho-sexual conditions are so irretrievably mired in long-standing economic and historical realities as to make unqualified and indiscriminate attacks on men meaningless, Ms. Greer and her adherents have taken a giant step—up from the shrill vituperation that marked earlier feminist rhetoric. But her thoughts too smack of the utopian, of academic exercise, for the American experience has shown that change comes slowly. The revolution seems hardly imminent. Perhaps more accurate are the words of Kate Millet, whose massive piece of scholarship, *Sexual Politics* awakened many to the cause: "We really don't have any fatuous hopes of taking over. We would, very much, like a fair shake."

Whatever transpires, women's liberation has succeeded in prodding this nation into reconsidering a matter in which every citizen has something at stake. The collective morality of the country can't help but be affected by the reordering of intersexual relationships. Even those who remain steadfastly resistant must defend and reinforce their traditional morality.

America's legal system and moral sense are being challenged to show their flexibility and adaptability. How well they respond to the currents raised by the women's liberation movement will be a significant measure of their continuing vitality.

# COMMUNES

Somewhere in the course of the moral and social upheaval that has come to be called "the revolution," it must have occurred to the participants that a new living structure would be necessary to maintain the force of the new movement. Or perhaps the changes were simply spontaneous adjustments to new philosophies, a natural expression of the proper way to live. Whatever the origin, a significant number of Americans are demonstrating their preference for the communal way of life, and leaving traditional family habits behind.

## The New Collectivism

The trend toward collectivism in America has already spawned a variety of kinds and sizes in communes. Some offer an alternative to urban boredom and a chance to get back to nature and a subsistence existence. Some grow out of political motives and are designed to foster solidarity in promoting given ideologies. Others seek to supplant the biological family, extinguishing all parent-child relationships and discouraging the ownership of private property. And still others are simply efforts to escape the dehumanization its members feel in a highly technological society and to rediscover a sense of brotherhood.

Undoubtedly, some communes are flaunting an irreverence for the style of Middle America and exist only as a convenient vehicle for easy sex and drugs. But these are definitely a minority. For the most part, the commune movement has flourished as an honest reaction to the stultification inherent in an increasingly mechanized and urbanized society. The formation and running of a commune can be a difficult and serious business. Whatever the mores of a rural commune, sex and drugs do not occupy more than a fraction of its time; eking out a living from the earth, often without tools or know-how, does not leave much time for sport.

Defining a commune defies simple generalizations, but common to all of them is a gathering of like-minded people in an undivided unit, with each member contributing to and sharing in the fruits of the community. Communes are both a product of the moral revolution and a source of moral revolution, as members grope for the life-style and mores that yield the peace and harmony they seek. For communalists, this kind of life is the bridge from empty rhetoric to the living of one's faith—a personal contribution to the revolution. If the silent majority inclines to disparage these early radical alternatives, it must at least concede the actual commitments that have been made.

Actually, the modern collectivist phenomenon is not without its roots. There is a rich if largely unknown heritage of utopian settlements dotting the path of American history. The original colonization of America, especially the Pilgrim settlements, supplied a model of the basic organic community centered on religious principle. Two groups with contrasting marital philosophies flourished in upstate New York late in the nineteenth century. Unorthodox Quakers called Shakers preached celibacy in their rural commune while the Oneida Community endorsed community marriages, a position so novel and shocking for its time that it eventually hastened its dissolution. Rural Massachusetts was the site of Brook Farm, a short-lived (1841-1847) but well-known experiment instituted by New England intellectuals. Running their own school and following the precepts of French socialist Charles Fourier, they "strove for a harmonious life that would combine the activities of 'thinker' and 'worker.' " In addition to these formal innovations, the neo-communalists have drawn inspiration from just the ordinary life patterns of preindustrialized America.

Sheer numbers (the *New York Times* has estimated that there are now over two thousand communes) preclude any listing of absolutes pertaining to the new collectivism, but there are some characteristics shared by many of them. The first is a strong, almost religious conviction about the primacy and beauty of nature. There is a rapport between many communes and the land, dedicated as they are to reaffirming the simplicity and joy of being alive. As one long-time observer of the movement, Herbert A. Otto, expresses it: "Commune members generally believe that a very small but politically influential minority with no respect for the ecological system or the beauty of nature exploits all of the land for its own gain. Surpassing the credo of conservationist organizations, most commune members stress the rehabilitation of all lands and the conservation of all natural resources for the benefit of all the people." Tilling the soil and growing their own food, the new agriculturists withdraw from modern, material society. In many ways it is a recapturing of the natural gratitude the Pilgrims must have felt at the first Thanksgiving.

Equally pervasive in the communes is a strain of spiritualism and religious philosophy which, like the life-style, is usually uncomplicated and nature-oriented. The trend is away from the customary, structured religions and toward a more intensely personal commitment. Mysticism, Eastern religions, and various forms of meditation are in widespread practice.

Not all communes represent a political position in the strict sense of the term, but those that do lean decidedly leftward, almost by definition. One would not expect those enamored with the status quo or anything right of it to embrace an alien life-style. Almost universally, members speak of the need for an overhaul of the existing social and political institutions, to halt depersonalization and the blunting of human potential. While many are working political revolutionaries, more are cultural radicals, in the sense that their communal lives are their examples and weapons for conversion.

Other settlements center around more particularized purposes. Homosexual groups or "gay communes" provide an opportunity for homosexuals to live in a community free from the legal and psychological harassment of the straight world. One such arrangement in Hollywood operates out of a large apartment building renting only to gays and offering a regular schedule of social and entertainment services, as well as an informational pool designed to assist gays in their necessary maneuvers through heterosexual society. On the other hand, there are those with a more aggressive approach, heavily engaged in the gay liberation movement. Presumably, if they are successful, the need for communes exclusively gay will diminish.

Another specific communal type, identified by Otto, is the gypsy commune. Living and traveling in assorted (and often outrageously decorated) trucks and buses, these mobile bands of artists, musicians, and generally funky vaudevillians roam up and down the country, nickel and diming their way through impromptu college appearances and street shows. It is not by any means a comfortable life, but it is a free one and the participants are living symbols of the restless, shifting moral currents of our time.

Of a different character are neighborhood service communes, whose members are busy in the formulation of neighborhood action agencies, rehabilitating and upgrading the local quality of life. Similar to these are teaching communes, usually created to spread a single philosophy through the establishment of a school; some teaching, others learning.

In essence, communes proliferate much the way political interest groups do, a new type blossoming to suit whatever interests people might bring to it. Some special groups evolve the way they do simply because a good number of their element share a particular vocation or interest; others, such as artists' or crafts' communes, enhance talents existing prior to the formation. In any event, they are strong enough by now in number and purpose to dispel any outside notion that they exist only for promiscuity and irresponsible idleness.

## Problems of Communal Living

Not all communal life is rapture, though. A number of problems have surfaced, some imposed from without, others growing from within. The urban type particularly is frequently subject to legal restrictions which often have the thinly disguised ulterior purpose of ridding an area of unfamiliar practices. Renting often proves unsatisfactory, for even a sympathetic landlord can become hostile when he, in turn, feels the thrust of community pressure. Consequently, large and, if possible, inexpensive houses have become valuable commodities, but finding one of these is not the end of the problem. As Albert Solnit, Chief of Advanced Planning for Marin County in California, explains it: ". . . many residents are becoming notably eager to force cooperative living groups out of their single-family districts. Where local politicians have responded, the favorite anti-commune ploy has been that all-around tool of exclusivity, the zoning ordinance." These laws typically limit the number of people unrelated by blood or marriage to

around four or five per housing unit—on the theory that traffic congestion, overcrowding, and excessive noise will result
otherwise.

Naturally, communes bear the full brunt of these policies, and it
is not surprising that they have entered the struggle against them.
The thrust of the attack on these laws is that they are naked
attempts to enforce social preferences through a method, the
zoning law, which is not proper for that purpose. Additionally,
authorities are not applying the laws straight across the board. If,
as the American Civil Liberties Union has hypothesized, six airline
stewardesses were to take up residence in a single house, it is
doubtful that there would be prosecution. For all intents and
purposes, the laws are being used to register disapproval of the
unconventional morals and living practices of communalists and,
hopefully, to eliminate them.

The struggle promises to be a long and arduous one. The first
test case, *Palo Alto Tenants Union* v. *George Morgan et al.*, in the
District Court for Northern California, came down against the
collectivists. The text of the decision exhibited little patience with
or understanding of the new communal spirit.

> There is a long-recognized value in the traditional family
> relationship which does not attach to the "voluntary
> family." The traditional family is an institution reinforced
> by biological and legal ties which are difficult or impos-
> sible to sunder. It plays a role in educating and nourishing
> the young which far from being voluntary is often
> compulsory.
>
> The communal living groups represented by the plain-
> tiffs share few of the above characteristics. They are
> voluntary, with fluctuating memberships who have no legal
> obligations of support or co-habitation. They are in no
> way subject to the state's vast body of domestic relations
> law. They do not have the biological links which charac-
> terize most families.

The judge's text is flawed for a number of reasons. It suggests a
durability and efficiency about the traditional nuclear family
which is not borne out by the divorce rates and generation gaps. It
reflects little awareness that many communalists have chosen their
method sincerely to live and raise children. Sooner or later the
laws concerning domestic relations will have to adjust to this
reality. But even more striking is the fact that the decision says

nothing about whether or not the law is being applied for the reasons it was drawn up. Clearly, the court is more concerned with promoting a certain set of mores than in preventing supposed disruptions such as excessive noise or congestion. So far, it seems, the law is reflecting many of the misconceptions about communes that circulate through the general public.

The Department of Agriculture in the Nixon administration has supplemented this kind of legal harassment with a bar against the issuance of food stamps to households composed of nonrelatives. As Solnit reports, "Agriculture Department officials concede that the new amendment is intended to deny food stamps to 'unrelated youths following the hippie family life-style.' " Eventually, the courts and the government will be forced to make a better distinction between genuine communalists and the restless transients that mar the movement.

## Reasons for Joining Communes

The real watchword of the collectivists is freedom—freedom to determine which of society's institutions deserve ongoing observance and which are the waste products of an arid culture. By withdrawing from mindless consumerism, prescribed sexual and marital relationships, and the confines of private ownership, commune members search for the fundamental feelings and emotions that our computer culture often tramples. In many ways, they are the new pioneers, making the transition from individualism and all its connotations to group living and loving.

Because so many of the new collectivists were brought up in the family system, the forging of a new life means that old habits must give way to new demands. The following interview with a Los Angeles couple, who declined to identify themselves or give the name of their commune for fear of adverse public action, lends insight to this kind of adjustment.

Q: Why did you join the commune?

A: (M) Neither of us were especially happy with the normal family setup, and now after living like this for a while, we're glad that we made the switch. I couldn't imagine living any other way.

Q: What do you see as the advantages of communal life?

A: (F) Well, I can only speak for our own commune but there are a lot of good things about it. From a practical standpoint, it makes sense economically. We have eleven adults in our group and they all contribute financially. We don't ask everybody to pay any required amount—there's just a sense of giving according to your means. Nothing rigid. It would be a tension-producing situation though if some contributed nothing at all.

Q: Is yours the kind of group in which biological family ties are obliterated—where all the children belong to all the adults and vice versa?

A: (F) No, not really. I suppose it's something of a compromise. The children don't live with their parents in the apartments we have. But they do look more to their natural parents than to the others for things.

(M) The important thing is that the kids don't grow up with the kind of perverted dependence on their parents so many children seem to have today. They learn not only to relate to different kinds of people but also to depend more on themselves as well. I definitely think it's a healthier environment for kids to grow up in.

(F) One of the hard things about erasing all family ties is the energy you have to expend making decisions about the kids. For example, choosing a school. In our commune there are differences of opinion about what kind of schooling is best, and it would be almost impossible to hammer out which schools which kids would attend. But under our setup, natural parents can still make that kind of decision individually.

Q: Do the children perceive that they are growing up in a different way?

A: (F) Most of them are still too young to understand any difference—or at least to show that they understand any. We have two ourselves and sometimes the older one, who is six, wants me to be around him more. For the most part, though, they really enjoy it. I know that the kids who come to visit like it. It's like a big playground for them.

Q: What kind of governing structure do you have? Are there difficulties in making group decisions?

A: (M) We have weekly meetings, kind of a town-hall democracy. Nobody really has any self-interest to push so it's rare that there are any extended disagreements.

Q: Are there any clashes over sexual relationships?

A: (F) People in the commune relate to each other as people and relationships grow just as they would in any situation, some lasting longer than others. There certainly isn't the kind of promiscuous mate-swapping that most people suppose goes on in a commune. The atmosphere may be looser and people might be more independent as far as their sex lives go, but sex is by no means an end in itself.

Q: Do you see communes as one facet of a larger cultural revolution? Are they related to or designed to facilitate a certain philosophy or movement?

A: (M) Ours is probably more an expression of women's liberation than anything else. We don't have any role-playing by sex and the men and women share all the work around the apartments, including caring for the children. The careers of the women are as important as those of the men, and they aren't hung up in the mother-husband syndrome which is probably the most debilitating condition a person can be in.

   (F) That's true but it's also part of the whole change in attitude about how people should interact with each other. We're out of the rut in which everybody confines all their feelings and thoughts to one other person. And we're finding out that sharing ourselves with more people and, in turn, sharing in the lives of more people makes for a happier life.

Q: Have there been any significant problems that you would care to discuss?

A: (M) There have been some couples that were together for a long time but just recently broke up. As a matter of fact there were two breakups almost simultaneously. Some of the partners have left but others have stayed, which is kind of an indication that the commune doesn't depend on those kind of personal relationships. Other than that there haven't been any real problems. It's been a pretty static thing, not a lot of coming and going.

Q: Do you have any observations or predictions about the future of communes in general? Do you see them replacing the family as we know it?

A: (F) That's pretty hard to say, really. We're not that eager to sell our life-style as the best for everybody though we do think this would be a better country if most of the people lived collectively. People would have more consideration for each other's welfare and problems. And, in turn, our political institutions would be more responsive to the people. I mean you couldn't have communes as the main way of living and still have the same politics, the same educational institutions, and the same morality. This is both a way of changing things and a way of showing the changes that have already taken place.

This couple's experience grew out of an urban commune. A good example of the rural-type settlement is Twin Oaks in Virginia. Consciously designed around the concepts expounded in *Walden Two*, the utopia created by behavioral psychologist B. F. Skinner, Twin Oaks, claims twenty-four members living on a former tobacco farm of 120 acres. Income revolves around the making and selling of hammocks, industrial piecework, and, when necessary, whatever menial jobs members can find in surrounding towns.

Like many of the country settlers who have found living off the land a bit more onerous than expected, the Twin Oaks population purchases some of its food and grows the rest. The members' days are divided into work details named with a childlike simplicity: cleanup, food, cows et al. These are called managerships. In the governing hierarchy, three "planners" who serve terms lasting one and one-half years, never running consecutively, appoint each of the other members to two or three managerships. Labor credits are awarded for work done and upon accumulation to a certain point, vacations are earned. Everyone enthusiastically follows a behavior code under which drugs and personal property are forbidden.

Richard Todd, editor of *Atlantic Monthly*, talked to a number of members upon visiting Twin Oaks and elicited a number of reasons for being there. One graduate of the civil rights and peace efforts offered this overview: "I realized that it's not a matter of reforms. It's an overall problem. What we have here is a post-revolutionary society, a model so that society can look at it and know: 'There's a better way.' We're building a sane society from the ground up." Others traced a more personal motivation: "I've tried everything. Man has no reason for being on earth. He's just born. Might as well make it so people can be happy." And a third voice pinpointed exactly how real the feeling and desire for change has become. "We're sort of pretending that there's been a revolution and we're going on from there. I think the United States is a crummy place but I don't go there very often and I don't pay much attention to it."

The attention that the media pay to the communal movement is proportional to its novelty; a romantic aura hovers over the very idea of forsaking organized society and all its electronic conveniences and electing to rough it in the wilderness. And when you get to the core of it, the truly dedicated communalists would probably prefer as little attention as possible from the outside world. Nevertheless, the acid test of collectivism as a growing trend in America is occurring right now.

There is a question of durability in many people's minds. Is the entire phenomenon, as some have suggested, just a new way of running away from home? Will it collapse as the newness wears off and as establishment life-styles are liberalized? Or, if the American government responds to the discontent of its citizenry, will the movement be robbed of a prime motivating force? And, finally, can this radical alternative sustain its spirt of denial and sacrifice when comfort is so close at hand? It is a question that the original pioneers did not have to answer.

Surely, there will be some disassociations in the future and some new efforts may be aborted. But for the most part the indications point to the continued, healthy existence of group living in the United States. There may have been other upheavals and agitations that produced a hospitable climate for the emergence of collectivism, but regardless of how the movement started, thousands of Americans are now convinced that communal living is a saner way of life. If many groups began as a means of facilitating "the revolution," they now have become ends in themselves, logical extensions of the personality makeup of the revolutionaries. Furthermore, the nonpolitical communes, each with their own affiliations and commitments, are so numerous today that it would be foolhardy to contend that communalism is inextricably tied to any single outside phenomenon.

In their own minds, the new pioneers view their work not as an escape from society but as the only way to save it. "The cities teach violence and destruction," says one Vermont communalist. "The country teaches time and space and life and creation. . . . Our technology functions as an end unto itself with nothing whatever to do with the rhythms, harmonies, and cycles of life." It is a subtle conversion that they preach, though, for when all is said and done, their happiness is their best argument. The communalists are revolutionaries that cannot be accused of rhetoric or mindless idealism. No one who expects to last can afford naiveté, because the life is not always one of idyllic pleasures, sitting back and taking in the majesty of nature.

When Middle America points to the lack of morality in the communes, it misses the point. Communalism is a new morality, a new way of relating to people and the world. It is a brand new start, and perhaps the most reassuring thing about it is that however the participants turn out, the result will be their own experience, free of any preconditioned, tired ideas. And that actually is what the movement is all about—to find out what life, stripped of all the accessories, really is.

# PART IV
# FRONTIERS
# OF THE
# CRIMINAL LAW

*"There is a revolution coming . . . It is now spreading with amazing rapidity, and already our laws, institutions, and social structure are changing in consequence. At the heart of everything is what we shall call a change of consciousness. This means a new head—a new way of living—a new man."*
*Charles A. Reich*, The Greening Of America
*1971*

# THE RIGHT
# TO MARIJUANA

Despite the tremendous amount of material available to the public on the subject of marijuana, large segments of the population remain ignorant of the physiological, psychological, social and/or political aspects of the drug. Although the current world literature on cannabis (the name for the plant from which marijuana and hashish are derived) numbers some two thousand publications, few of these papers meet modern standards of scientific investigation. They are often ill-documented ambiguous, emotion-laden, or just plain biased. This is in part due to the fact that some people have a vested interest in maintaining general ignorance of the facts in order to retain the illegal status of the herb. Others have simply been unable to depart from their preconceived notions concerning marijuana despite evidence of its relative harmlessness.

The public image of marijuana is mainly the result of the diligent efforts of the Federal Bureau of Narcotics. Allen Ginsberg, in his *First Manifesto to End the Bring Down* writes:

Following Parkinson's Law that a bureaucracy will attempt to find work for itself, or following a simpler line of thought, that the agents of this Bureau have a business interest in perpetuating the idea of a marijuana "menace" lest they lose their employment, it is not unreasonable to suppose that a great deal of violence, hysteria and energy of the antimarijuana language propaganda emanating from this source has as its motive a rather obnoxious self-interest, all the more objectional for its tone of moralist evangelism.

In the 1930s Harry Anslinger, who was at that time head of the Federal Bureau of Narcotics, spearheaded a scare campaign and this was largely responsible for the grossly distorted picture conveyed to the public. In his book, *The Murderers: The Story of the Narcotic Gangs*, Anslinger depicts marijuana users as wild, irresponsible, sadistic people. The book is filled with scenes of brutal rapes and entire families murdered.

But, that equally unreliable information has been foisted on the public from other sources can easily be seen in this excerpt from a pamphlet entitled *Marijuana or Indian Hemp and Its Preparations*. issued by the International Narcotic Education Association:

Prolonged use of marijuana frequently develops a delirious rage which sometimes leads to high crimes, such as assault and murder. Hence marijuana has been called the "killer drug." The habitual use of this narcotic poison always causes a very marked mental deterioration and sometimes produces insanity. . . . While the marijuana habit leads to physical wreckage and mental decay, its effects upon character and morality are even more devastating. The victim frequently undergoes such degeneracy that he will lie and steal without scruple; he becomes utterly untrustworthy and often drifts into the underworld where, with his degenerate companions, he commits high crimes and misdemeanors. Marijuana sometimes gives man the lust to kill unreasonably and without motive. Many cases of assault, rape, robbery, and murder are traced to the use of marijuana.

Contrary to the beliefs of the author of the above piece, it has been demonstrated that marijuana tends to pacify the smoker. The marijuana experience is by nature private, introspective, and spiritual. On the other hand, we have an enormous literature concluding that alcohol has a strongly criminogenic effect under a wide range of conditions, and there is almost universal agreement on the subject. According to Professor Kaplan the lowering of inhibitions caused by alcohol is not accompanied by a lowering of aggression and an increase in passivity as in the case of marijuana.

In fact, if one is concerned about violence such as that described in the excerpt above, one should seriously consider the fact that marijuana (as discussed later in this chapter) is conspicuously absent from crimes of violence and sexual aggression; and one should also consider the effects of the excessive use of alcohol. According to the study of the President's Commission on Law Enforcement and Administration of Justice entitled *1967 Task Force Report: Drunkenness*, homicide is an alcohol-related crime. An Ohio study found 43 percent of homicide offenders had been drinking previous to commission of the murders. And in a study conducted by Professor Marvin E. Wolfgang from 1948 to 1952—probably the most comprehensive of its kind—among 588 Philadelphia homicide cases, alcohol was absent from both victim and offender in only 36 percent of the murders. Another interesting fact is that in homicides involving alcohol, stabbing is the most common method of inflicting the death wound. On the basis of a study of all criminal homicides in Philadelphia from 1948 to 1952—some 588 cases—Wolfgang states that of 228 stabbings, 72 percent involved the presence of alcohol. Beating by fist, feet, or blunt instrument ranked second, for of 128 cases, 69 percent revealed alcohol in the situation. Another interesting statistic is that in a survey of over two thousand new inmates of California State Penitentiaries, over 60 percent of those involved in crimes of great risk (aggravated assault, sex crimes, etc.) had been drinking prior to commission of the crime. Different interpretations may be given to these statistics. Although they do not constitute any irrefutable indictment of alcohol, they may certainly suggest possible effects of the habit that so many of the older generation seem so desirous of convincing the young to take up in favor of marijuana.

## Marijuana as a Symbol

What seems quite obvious is that the subject of marijuana is capable of eliciting highly emotional responses. Cigarettes cause lung cancer, alcohol is responsible for all sorts of physical and mental deterioration, and tranquilizers and amphetamines are not only physically addicting but are unquestionably harmful in large doses. Yet parents seem to fear marijuana more than any of these other substances.

Years ago the public was fed horror stories handed the press by the Federal Bureau of Narcotics. It was insisted that the herb drove normal individuals to madness and depravity and that it was a satanic destroyer of the will. In the light of such publicity, panic was an understandable reaction to the subject of marijuana. But today the story is somewhat different. There is still plenty of misinformation passed on to the public, yet the more liberal press has certainly printed enough refutations of the marijuana myth to cause anyone who has seriously considered the subject to doubt the veracity of some of the wilder claims concerning the destructive effects of the drug.

It has been widely suggested that many of today's exceedingly negative responses to the subject of the drug may be the result of the association in the adult mind between marijuana and antisocial youth. Marijuana has come to symbolize all the negative aspects of the younger generation. To people so disposed, the word marijuana provokes images of dirty long-haired youths, who are capable of little more than objecting to the way their parents live. To both sides of the generation gap, marijuana has come to symbolize youth's rebellion, and the more that parents exaggerate the ill effects of the drug and the more they seem to react hysterically to any mention of it, the more youths are tempted to flaunt their use of what seems to them, to be an innocuous herb. The greater one's abhorrence of the change of values and life-styles that seems to have been visited upon us by the young, the greater the possiblity that one will react negatively to the subject of cannabis. There are a surprisingly large number of people who are capable of putting marijuana, hippies, long hair, homosexuality, political radicalism, sexual excesses, communism, defiance of authority, lack of patriotism, laziness, and rock music into one category in which distinctions between the various things blur, and each is capable of producing an equally ominous feeling in the pit of the conservative stomach. Many youths feel that adults merely begrudge them the free time, the freedom, the financial security, and the opportunities to have a good time that were unavailable when their parents were young. The marijuana laws are felt by many to be an expression of the resentment that one side of the generation gap feels for the other. Youth cannot help but feel that it is somehow unjust that their parent's drug (alcohol) is legal whereas their drug is not. (And to anyone who is in doubt, alcohol is pharmacologically as much a drug as marijuana.) Millions of dollars are spent each day in advertising alcohol, tobacco, pills to help you wake up, and pills to help you calm down, pills to help you sleep and pills to do just about anything else. The adult example of frequent use of alcohol, tobacco, barbiturates, diet pills, etc., renders the outlawing of marijuana singularly unfair.

## The Law

The drive by the Federal Bureau of Narcotics to inflame public opinion against the use of marijuana was a huge success, and the congressional legislation enacted in 1937 is a monument to the incredibly talented public relations work done by the bureau. Congress, however, showed itself to be considerably lacking in critical judgment in accepting unquestionably the claims of the Federal Bureau of Narcotics. It equipped the Marijuana Tax with what was hoped would prove a quite potent power to deter—five years of imprisonment, a $2,000 fine, or both. This applied to possession of even the tiniest quantity of marijuana.

In 1930, the year that the Federal Bureau of Narcotics was established, only sixteen states had laws prohibiting the use of marijuana, and those statutes were as a rule mild and infrequently enforced. By 1937, largely as a result of almost eight years of determined efforts on the part of the Federal Narcotics Bureau, nearly every state has been obliged to adopt some statutes prohibiting the use of the controversial substance.

In all states both the possession and use of marijuana constitute a crime with penalties which vary drastically, depending on the state. For example, the law in the state of Alaska reads: "To possess or to control marijuana or any depressant, stimulant, or hallucinogenic drug is a misdemeanor if the possession or control is for one's use; the penalty is imprisonment for no more than one year or a fine of up to $1,000 or both." There do not appear to be any restrictions on suspension, probation, or parole regarding sentence imposed. However, in the state of Alabama the law reads: "It is a felony to possess, sell, deliver, transport, or give away marijuana. A first offense is punishable by imprisonment for not less than five nor more than twenty years and a fine of up to $20,000." Suspension and probation are not permitted.

In many instances both the federal and state laws controlling marijuana are essentially the same as those covering heroin and other such "hard drugs." Reference is often made to penalties applicable to "marijuana and any narcotic drug" with little, if any, distinction made between the so-called dangerous drugs, such as heroin, and the clearly less harmful marijuana.

There are a number of constitutional arguments that have been raised against the illegality of marijuana; however, thus far, none of them have been successful in convincing the courts. These arguments can be grouped into two general categories: the first is comprised of challenges to the right of the government to regulate the use of marijuana at all. The constitutional bases for such a challenge are the rights of privacy, fundamental peripheral rights, and substantive due process. In addition, the free exercise of religion guarantee of the First Amendment could provide a constitutional protection for those who use marijuana as part of their religious rituals. The second general category includes arguments against the manner in which marijuana is presently controlled and the severity of the penalties associated with these laws. Under this category equal protection and due process arguments can be raised in regard to the classification of marijuana with "harder" drugs and the distinction made in the legal treatments of marijuana and other intoxicants such as alcohol and tobacco. Also in this category can be included arguments arising out of the Eighth Amendment's prohibition of cruel and unusual punishment with regard to the excessive punishment for the use of marijuana. A final challenge to the marijuana laws might arise out of the federal laws which provide that anyone dealing in marijuana has to register with the government and file a special tax return. These federal laws might be seen as violation of the Fifth Amendment in that they are in effect requiring one to incriminate oneself.

## Negative Aspects of Present Marijuana Laws

In order to accurately assess our present marijuana laws, it is necessary to consider their disadvantages. A growing number of people are finding the costs of the laws out of all proportion to the benefits they accrue.

Margaret Mead believes that "we are damaging our country, our laws, and the relation between young and old by marijuana prohibition. This is far more dangerous than overuse." Dr. Stanley F. Yolles, former director of the National Institute of Mental Health, has stated, "I know of no clearer instance in which the punishment for an infraction of the law is more harmful than the crime." Professor John Kaplan, author of *Marijuana: The New Prohibition*, says, "all laws have costs and the costs of the marijuana laws far outweigh their benefits." He claims that "a drastic change in our whole approach to the problem is necessary to avoid national tragedy."

One of the most obvious disadvantages of the present marijuana laws is the cost in dollars and cents of enforcing those laws. In California in 1968, approximately one-fourth of all felony complaints were for violation of marijuana laws. More than 34,000 adults and 17,000 juveniles were arrested. California state and local governmental agencies spent $72 million enforcing the marijuana laws in that year.

But the real cost of these arrests is the toll taken on the lives of such "offenders." In California approximately 80 percent of the adult marijuana law violators had either no previous difficulty or only minor difficulty with the law. Of the juveniles arrested, this was the first major difficulty with the law for over 98 percent of them. Putting these people into jail with other criminal offenders will more likely prove detrimental to both them and society at large. The marijuana law violator, in prison for use of a relatively harmless drug, may well feel persecuted and harbor bitter feelings toward society. In contact with other criminals, such a person may well feel motivated to learn from his prison acquaintances efficient means for taking out his frustrations.

But imprisonment is not the only way marijuana convictions or arrests may hurt cannabis users. There are any number of firms, schools, and even governmental agencies that make it a general practice to turn down applicants who have been arrested (even if the charges were subsequently dismissed). A conviction for any offense is sure to curtail one's chances for ever getting a decent job, and considering the job market in the early 1970s, a person with a marijuana conviction would probably have difficulty in getting hired for any job at all.

The inequity of the laws, subjecting users of small quantities of the drug to the possibility of arrest, job loss, reputational harm, and years in prison while allowing alcoholics to misuse their drug with legal impunity seems clearly hypocritical. The hostility engendered in youth for what appears to be blatant discrimination is perhaps a high price to pay for laws that have proved to be largely unsuccessful. The problem of the alienation of many of today's youngsters is not one to be taken lightly. Turning a sizable portion of our youth into felons will do little to narrow the generation gap.

Another disadvantage of the laws is that many of them have put marijuana into the same category as that of much more dangerous drugs. To many people this seems to be a statement as to the equally deleterious effects of marijuana and, for example, LSD. Someone having used marijuana and having found it to be quite harmless, might therefore assume that LSD is similarly innocuous, because of the similar legal treatment of the two substances and also because of the equally negative picture of the drugs that has been presented to the American public. Likewise, children taught in drug education classes that marijuana is harmful, and having tried it and found this not to be the case, might well assume that if their teachers can lie about marijuana they might certainly lie about heroin. In other words, the smear campaign of which marijuana has been the victim is calling into question the credibility of claims as to the horrors of other drugs.

As Allen Ginsberg has said, it is not a healthy activity for the state to be annoying so many of its citizens in this manner; it creates a climate of topsy-turvy law and begets disrespect for the law and the society that tolerates execution of such excesses. It also creates a climate of fear and hatred for legal administrators. Such a law is a threat to the existence of the state itself, for it sickens and debilitates some of its most sensitive citizens.

The law itself is responsible for much of the paranoia or fear frequently claimed to be the effect of marijuana itself. It is little wonder that marijuana smokers in this country may be subject to paranoia while smoking. With the increased sensitivity visited upon the smoker, he is likewise confronted with the fact that he is doing something illegal and that thousands of investigators all over the country are out there, trained and paid to discover users and put them in jail. It is certainly frightening to think while you are attempting to get high that police may break into your home and unceremoniously arrest you, interrogate and take you through the entire hassle of being booked, fingerprinted, and then thrown into a cell with great numbers of delightful characters; and, finally, given plenty of opportunity to contemplate your forthcoming trial with its endless red tape; expensive legal fees; cold, severe courtrooms; and unsympathetic judges. In short, the illegality of the drug clearly makes enjoyment of marijuana more difficult, although this fact may be a source of comfort to those of an antimarijuana position.

The illegality of the drug also makes it impossible to control the purity and strength of the marijuana that one is purchasing, smoking, or ingesting. There are many gradations of potency, and the exact strength cannot be known until a person tries it. There are also dealers who "cut" marijuana with other substances to make it look like more. These substances are generally harmless, but they cause many people to pay for more marijuana than they are getting. If marijuana were made legal the government could control its purity and potency. It might outlaw only the stronger forms of the weed such as hashish, or it might outlaw sale to minors. With the government in control of the weed, it might be taxed very heavily. Since marijuana is so cheap and easy to grow, most of the price could simply be the tax. The government could make a great deal of money and perhaps use the funds to deal with real crime instead of victimless crimes such as smoking grass.

## Extent of Marijuana Use

With the possible exception of speeding on the freeways, pot smoking is almost certainly the most widely committed crime in the United States. Dr. Stanley F. Yolles, former director of the National Institute of Mental Health, has estimated that the number of Americans who have tried grass at least once may be as high as twenty million. James L. Goddard, former commissioner of the United States Food and Drug Administration, estimates that about twenty million Americans have used marijuana at one time or another, while as many as three million smoke it regularly. Other estimates put the total of occasional users at about three to five million, with regular users ranging around one million. In 1951 the United Nations estimated that there were 200 million marijuana users in the world and quite clearly, the figure has increased considerably since then. In other words, the number of people in the world who use marijuana is greater than the entire population of the United States.

Having established as accurately as possible (considering the illegal status of the drug) the number of marijuana users, the next question is, "Who smokes pot?" Although there have been numerous studies disproving the notion that the marijuana smoker is a specific personality type, some professionals in the field of narcotics still perpetuate the myth of the marijuana smoker. For example, Dr. Robert Baird, chairman and organizer of the Harlem Haven Clinic, a rehabilitation center for narcotic addicts, has claimed in lectures on college campuses that people who use pot generally have severe mental problems. He has said that you can always spot a pot user—he's the boy on campus with the set of shoulders as broad as a toothpick. He has the typical caveman head, the long hair and the beard, but from the neck down he has that swishy look. Such gross distortion and generalization is enough to turn off an entire campus audience. The fact is that the largest category of students who have smoked grass is comprised mainly of the "average" students, the women or men who maintain acceptable grades, and meet general standards of dress and behavior. These students have only indulged in anywhere from a few nervous puffs of grass to about ten marijuana cigarettes.

The next largest category of student marijuana users is comprised of students who indulge in the weed regularly but generally limiting their smoking to weekends. Students in this group maintain average grades but tend to be more socially active than the students in the category mentioned in the previous paragraph. These students often smoke socially to maintain membership in a group where smoking grass is almost a social necessity, membership in the subculture being more important than the drug itself. Therefore, in such a group, drug obsession is rare.

The smallest segment of marijuana users on the college campus are the "heads," or those who are high a great deal of the time. This group consists of only about 5 percent of the students experimenting with marijuana. Heads turn on by themselves or in small groups, and frequently such people become suppliers. They usually consider marijuana to be one of the most important things in their lives and tend to have psychological difficulties. They often end up dropping out of school, but some continue to reside within the college community. Heads are most apt to become involved with harder drugs.

Of course, college students aren't the only ones who smoke grass, although many people estimate that up to 50 percent of these students have tried the drug. There are also large numbers of high school students who smoke grass and growing numbers of professional people. Other frequent users of marijuana are those who were smoking it back in the thirties—minorities (blacks and Mexican-Americans) and artists, especially musicians.

## Why People Use It

The hardest question to answer is why people smoke grass. Dr. Howard Becker, a sociologist at Northwestern University, claims that in a study he conducted of fifty regular marijuana users, the only possible conclusion he could come to as to why these people smoked was because they had tried marijuana and found it to be pleasurable. Of course, different people have claimed all sorts of psychological reasons why people smoke, and while these reasons are probably accurate when applied to some smokers, they are clearly inapplicable to the vast body of marijuana users as a whole.

Marijuana probably meets different needs for different people. It enables some to relax, it facilitates social interaction for others, it is a means of rebellion for some, it enhances sensual enjoyment for others. The list is endless, and it could probably be said that there are about as many reasons for smoking grass as for drinking alcohol. Many claim that instead of dropping out of life marijuana smokers are merely probing it more deeply. According to many, marijuana shifts attention from stereotyped images; that is, it alters one's normal patterns of thoughts so that things which one has experienced many times before appear in a different light. This often leads one to question things one has always taken for granted. William Burroughs, a former addict of fifteen years, claims that "sedative drugs (and this includes alcohol) act to decrease awareness, and increased dosage is generally required to achieve or maintain this state of decreased awareness. The consciousness-expanding drugs (such as marijuana) act to increase awareness, and this state of increased awareness can be a permanent acquisition." Burroughs also claims that marijuana is unquestionably a very useful drug to the artist, "activating trains of association that would otherwise be inaccessible." He also claims marijuana can provide a key to the creative process.

## Scientific Research

Quite a bit of research has been done on the subject of marijuana, but unfortunately much of the public is not aware of the findings. In 1938, in the midst of the marijuana hysteria promoted by the Federal Bureau of Narcotics, Mayor LaGuardia of New York had a many-faceted study undertaken to explore the various aspects of marijuana. The findings of the researchers comprise many pages. The report clearly stated that the drug was not found to be addicting, that it does not cause individuals to commit crimes, but instead is conspicuously absent from crimes of violence and sexual aggression (as compared with the very high correlation between crimes of violence and use of alcohol). Another finding of the researchers was that use of marijuana did not lead to the use of harder drugs. This finding is also corroborated by a 1967 report of the United States Task Force.

The most recent report issued by the National Institute of Mental Health claims that for most people the drug "does not seem harmful," although this report is qualified by a statement as to the possibility of future findings to the contrary.

Studies have been done to determine the frequency of

marijuana-induced psychosis. In one of these conducted by Barbara Durham, assistant district attorney of Seattle, she reports:

> An attempt has been made to contact the doctors and clinics most likely to have encountered examples of abnormal behavior caused by marijuana. The institutions involved were the Student Health Centers at Stanford University and the University of California at Berkeley, the University of California Medical Center and Clinic in the Haight-Ashbury district, the San Francisco General Hospital, and the Stanford-Palo Alto Hospital. At the risk of making the rest of this section anti-climactic, it is impressive to find not a single case of marijuana-induced psychosis reported from any of these facilities.

This may seem somewhat surprising especially in regard to the finding from the clinic in Haight-Ashbury. Of the thirty thousand admissions to the clinic since its opening, not one case of marijuana psychosis was seen.

A study conducted at the USC Medical Center yielded similar results. There were three admissions for marijuana-induced difficulties in one year. All were teenagers, two with "acute intoxication" and one with headache after marijuana ingestion. All were released within three days. Professor Kaplan compares these figures from the USC Medical Center with others representing the number of admissions over the same period for other drug-induced difficulties: 35 admissions traceable to Doriden, 16 to Sleepeze, and similar numbers for other easily available psychoactive agents. In addition, in one month there were 140 hospital admissions and 11 fatalities traceable in whole or in part to barbiturate use. Clearly, marijuana is less apt to produce psychological difficulties than a good many other products to which the public has access, and which, despite the possibility that they may produce negative results, we do not consider putting under public sanction. We still do not know the long-term effect of birth control pills and many patent medicines. Even aspirin, in the case of many people who are sensitive to it, can be especially dangerous. In statistics reporting hospital admissions classified as resulting from drug-induced disturbances, aspirin is often the most frequent cause. There were 5,700 poison cases in Florida in 1966, of which 418 were reported by the four hospitals in Pinellas County. Of these 418, there were 199 cases of poisoning resulting from internal medicine, and 92 were aspirin.

What must be realized is that even if marijuana is known to produce negative effects upon its users, this is not necessarily sufficient reason to make it illegal. For the most part the state allows us to worry about ourselves and to use or abuse ourselves as we see fit. If, in the case of substances which are known to definitely be responsible for illness (cigarettes), the government chooses to do little or nothing, it seems that in the case of marijuana the decision to retain the illegality of the drug must be motivated by reasons other than just protection of public health.

Government should step in and regulate marijuana in situations where marijuana use reasonably appears to be a threat to society— as, for example, when someone drives an automobile while under its influence. Such use should be considered a criminal act, and those who peddle marijuana should be subject to stringent penalties. But the government should not make criminals out of those who merely indulge in moderate social use in the privacy of their own homes; to continue to do so is the most deplorable kind of hypocrisy and inequity.

# PENAL
# REFORM

"We must renounce the philosophy of punishment, the obsolete vengeful penal attitude if we are to have a society safe from crime. In its place, we would seek a comprehensive, constructive social attitude—therapeutic in some instances, restraining in some instances, but preventive in its social impact." This declaration by Dr. Karl Menninger in his book *The Crime of Punishment* (1966) represents the view of a growing number of modern social engineers. The traditional Judeo-Christian model of human nature is being challenged. Under the traditional model, if an individual committed an antisocial act he did so by free will, which made him a wicked person, and therefore punishment was warranted. Today, crime is being viewed with less moral absolutism. Antisocial acts are being interpreted from scores of perspectives now. Psychiatrists emphasize pathology, maladjustment, or environmental factors; anthropologists underline cultural influences; radicals and militant political groups talk of rebellion against repression and poverty.

Menninger calls for a greater role for the social sciences in dealing with crime and offenders.

> Scientists are not illusion proof. We are not always or altogether objective. We are not oracles. But we have been trained in a way of observing and interpreting things that has produced rich harvest for the civilized world. This is the systematic collection of certain facts, the orderly arrangement of those facts, and the drawing of tentative conclusions from them to be submitted to further investigation for proof or disproof. . . . Crime problems have been dealt with too long with only the aid of common sense. Catch criminals and lock them up; if they hit you, hit them back. This is common sense but it does not work . . . social scientists all share a faith in the scientific method as contrasted to obsolete methods based on tradition, precedent, and common sense.

## The Death Penalty Is Dying

The death penalty has been abolished in almost all of western Europe, and is on its way out in the United States. Over the past three decades there has been a steady nationwide decrease in the number of executions. In 1935 there were 199 executions; in 1967, only two, despite population growth and despite the fact that capital punishment is sanctioned in forty-one states. Since 1968 no one has been executed. This moratorium could continue indefinitely, either through U.S. Supreme Court action, or if that fails, by the actions of individual state legislatures. On February 18, 1972, the California Supreme Court rendered an historic decision when it ruled that the death penalty was unconstitutional. In a 6-1 decision, written by California Chief Justice Wright, the court said: "It degrades and dehumanizes all who participate in its processes. It is unnecessary of any legitimate goal of the state and is incompatible with the dignity of man and the judicial process." This landmark case interprets a section of the California constitution which prohibits "cruel or unusual punishment." The question, said the court, was whether the death penalty when judged by contemporary standards "is either cruel or has become an unusual punishment." The court found it to be both.

Not only is actual execution cruel, declared the court, but the lengthy imprisonment prior to the execution constitutes a psychological torture with a dehumanizing effect. That punishment carrying such a psychological impact could be cruel was recognized by the U.S. Supreme Court in 1958 when it held that denationalization was barred as a punishment under the Eighth Amendment.

As to unusual punishment, the California court adopted the criterion set forth by the U.S. Supreme Court for measuring acceptable punishment under the Eighth Amendment—"the evolving standards of decency that mark the progress of a maturing society." The court recognized that many condemned prisoners have committed crimes of the utmost cruelty and depravity and are not entitled to the slightest sympathy from society, but the court found it incompatible with the dignity of an enlightened society to attempt to justify the taking of life for purpose of vengeance.

The California court pointedly refrained from considering the Eighth Amendment to the U.S. Constitution which prohibits "cruel and unusual" punishment. The U.S. Supreme Court is itself reviewing that question at this writing. If the U.S. Supreme Court concludes, as the California high court did, that capital punishment is "cruel and unusual," it will bring down the final curtain on the death penalty in the United States. A ruling by the U.S. Supreme Court will be binding on all states.

One can only speculate on how the presently constituted Court will decide. Given the recent number of Nixon conservative appointments, the Court may retain the death penalty. This would not, however, permanently arrest the movement from the eventual abolition of the penalty; it would only delay it. From the perspective of history, the use of the death penalty in western civilization is fading into oblivion. The death of the death penalty appears inevitable; it seems only a matter of time.

## Clashing Voices

There is a certain style and fervor with which men have debated the question of capital punishment. The Romans, from a motive of pride, would not execute free men, but rather saw banishment from the state as the ultimate punishment. Slaves, however, were apparently executed with impunity. Montesquieu condoned the death penalty only for those who had threatened to take lives, but discouraged it in cases where the dispute had been over property. Throughout American history, the death penalty—in the form of hanging—was quite common, sometimes without the encumbrances of litigation. But with the advent of "advanced" civilization, it has become *de rigueur* to question the need— indeed, the morality—of revenge by the organized state in the form of capital punishment.

If a person were to look without any preconceived notions at literature on the subject of the death penalty, he would be left swimming in a sea of contradictions, casuistry, emotional pleas, and *somebody* v. *somebody*. The Bible can be used to support both sides of the argument on capital punishment. The pro group quotes scriptures such as: "Whoever strikes a man so that he dies shall be put to death" (Exod. 21:12). "He who kills a man shall be put to death" (Lev. 24:17). "If anyone kills a person, the murderer shall be put to death of the evidence of witnesses" (Num. 35:30). Finally, they point out the "eye for an eye, tooth for tooth, life for life" revealed in Deut. 19:21.

Those who wish to abolish capital punishment also quote scripture: "Render to no man evil for evil" (Rom. 12:17). "Judge not, that ye be not judged" (Matt. 7:1). "Thou shall not kill" (Exod. 20:13). "Vengeance is mine; I will repay, saith the Lord" (Rom. 12:19).

In modern literature, the works of Camus, Dostoevski, Tolstoi, Henry Fielding, Arthur Koestler, William M. Thackeray, Justice Bok, and court cases which alternatively support both sides are quoted. In *The Idiot*, Feodor Dostoevski presents his viewpoint:

> . . . Isn't that a mockery? Just think how cruel it is, and yet, on the other hand, these innocent people do it out of pure kindness of heart and are convinced that it's an act of humanity . . .

From one side of the chasm we are told the sad and poignant story of a little five-year-old girl who was raped in a pool of blood by a convicted murderer who had been released on parole from state prison. From the other side we hear of the unbearable mental torture which has led several convicted criminals to attempt to commit suicide on the eve of their impending execution. We are told that one reason why the death penalty should not be revoked is that we elect presidents in our country who have the power to kill people in possible wars. We are told so many different things that those who have not yet made up their minds will have great difficulty doing so, and those who have decided where they stand on the issue of capital punishment should reevaluate their decisions and make sure they are the result of logical thought rather than internalized prejudices.

## Historical Origins and Background of Capital Punishment

The taking of life was the primitive and supreme satisfaction of personal vengeance. The most expert fighter, the one who killed the most often, was the one ultimately most feared, the one who took the leadership in the early communities. In the beginning such a man slew his enemies through his personal prowess or cunning. Leadership would bring him the power, and the ultimate ability, to delegate the act of slaying to others.

Historically, the death penalty has existed for different reasons. In ancient times the death penalty rested primarily on man's effort to placate the gods, lest the gods become angry over some transgression by a member of society. In the earliest records of China, Egypt, and Assyria there is mention of capital punishment. The oldest death sentence on record can be found in the Amherst papyri, which contains the accounts of trials of state criminals in Egypt some fifteen hundred years before Christ.

In ancient Rome there is evidence of the infliction of capital punishment. Curiously enough, it was only the slaves who were so punished.

It was not until comparatively recent times that the punishment of death was specifically reserved for murder and other major offenses, although as far back as the time of Moses the right of the state over the individual in cases of capital offenses was recognized. With the approach of the Middle Ages, the number of capital crimes increased. By the late eighteenth century, 222 crimes were punishable by death in Britain.

Much of the American criminal law is patterned after both the form of the British legal system, and its substantive laws. By the time of the War of Independence, English law had recognized eight major capital crimes. These included: treason, petty treason (killing of a husband by his wife), murder, larceny, robbery, burglary, rape, and arson. The new American republic adopted much of the British policy toward the death penalty. The major capital crimes were retained and supplemented by piracy, sodomy, and from time to time, counterfeiting, horse-theft, and slave rebellion.

In some states a more severe code persevered to as late as 1837 when North Carolina required the death penalty for such crimes against the state as statutory rape, castration, burglary, highway robbery, stealing bank notes, slave stealing, "crimes against nature" (sodomy, bestiality, etc.), burning a public building, assault with intent to kill, breaking out of jail if under a capital indictment, concealing a slave with intent to free him, taking a free Negro out of the state with intent to sell him into slavery, the second offense of forgery, mayhem, inciting slaves to insurrection, being an accessory to murder, robbery, arson, and bigamy.

In addition to the wide variety of crimes that were subject to the death penalty, history shows a great number of ways of putting a person to death. In less enlightened times, criminals were boiled in oil, crucified, hung, thrown from a rock, burned alive, sawed in half and starved in dungeons. Present-day forms of execution include electrocution, hanging, asphyxiation, shooting, and beheading.

While the popular forms of execution have been limited to the electric chair or asphyxiation in a gas chamber, the current list of capital crimes in the United States has not been similarly limited. In the fifty states the possible capital crimes are as follows:

1. murder
2. treason
3. kidnapping
4. rape
5. carnal knowledge
6. robbery
7. bombing (includes bomb throwing and dynamiting)
8. assault with a deadly weapon by a life-term prisoner
9. train wrecking
10. burglary
11. arson
12. perjury in a capital case
13. espionage
14. machine-gunning
15. insurrection (Georgia)
16. forcing a woman to marry (Arkansas)
17. second conviction for selling narcotics to a minor
18. desecration of a grave
19. castration
20. piracy of interstate or foreign commercial aircraft

In addition to this list of civilian capital crimes, there are also about a dozen military capital crimes. Many apply only during wartime. They include desertion, spying, misconduct in the face of the enemy, compelling a subordinate to surrender, aiding the enemy, assault or willful disobedience of a superior officer, and misbehavior while on duty as a sentinel.

## History and Background of the Abolitionist Movement

Dr. Benjamin Rush is usually recognized as the father of the movement to abolish capital punishment in the United States. In 1788, his essay entitled, "Inquiry into the Justice and Policy of Punishing Murder by Death" put forth the following points: "(1) scriptural support for the death penalty was spurious; (2) the threat of hanging does not deter but increases crime; (3) when a government puts one of its citizens to death, it exceeds the powers entrusted to it."

Several prominent citizens of Philadelphia, notably Benjamin Franklin and the attorney general, William Bradford, helped achieve the repeal of the death penalty in 1794 for all crimes in Pennsylvania except for the crime of first-degree murder. These reforms of predominently Quaker Pennsylvania, however, had no immediate influence in other states. It was not until several decades later that any other major movement toward abolition was made.

In the early nineteenth century, the distinguished American attorney Edward Livingston prepared a revolutionary penal code for Louisiana. At the heart of his proposals was the total abolition of capital punishment. The legislature rejected his proposals, but for the next few decades Livingston's writings were the leading ones among abolitionists.

The efforts of Rush and Livingston finally began to bear fruit in the 1830's. Petitions on behalf of abolition were sent to legislatures, and anti-capital punishment organizations were formed. In 1845, an American Society for the Abolition of Capital Punishment was organized. The movement for abolition reached its highwater mark in the late 1840's when Horace Greeley, the editor and founder of the *New York Tribune*, became one of the nation's leading critics of the death penalty. In 1847, Michigan and Maine abolished the death penalty. In 1852, Rhode Island abolished the gallows for all crimes; the next year Wisconsin followed.

In several states, capital punishment for lesser crimes was replaced by life imprisonment, and other reforms affecting the administration of the death penalty were adopted. During the 1920s, eight states had abolished the death penalty for murder and for most other crimes. However, this situation did not last since shortly thereafter five of the eight states had reinstated the death penalty.

By the late 1950s abolitionist groups were again quite active, and anti-capital punishment bills were again being discussed in various state legislatures. Although intensive efforts in California and Massachusetts failed to obtain repeal of the death penalty, they did achieve legislative committee reports recommending abolition. Both Hawaii and Alaska, while still territories, eliminated the death penalty in 1957.

## Current Status

> Joseph Edward Smith eats two meals a day off a metal tray with a spoon—the only utensil he is trusted with. Three times a week, he is allowed to walk for two hours around a barren, 20-foot-square "recreation" room. The rest of the time he spends reading books or playing chess by sprawling on the floor of his cell and reaching through the bars to an adjoining cell. It is hardly enough activity for Joe Smith, a stocky twenty-nine-year-old Negro who has followed the same routine for the past nine years. "When I was put in the street," says Smith, "I played all types of sports. Now I do push-ups and I have a rubber ball I squeeze and I try to run in place. Sometimes I get to thinking I'm Gale Sayers or something and I forget my cell is only five feet by nine. But there ain't nothing like bars to bring you back to reality." ("Death Row: A New Kind of Suspense," *Newsweek*, January 11, 1971.)

For thirty-four other men as well as Joe Smith at Texas State Penitentiary, "reality" is death row. In 1971 there were approximately 675 condemned men and women on the death rows of this nation. The lives of these people have taken on a quality of surrealism. At the time of this writing, the executions have stopped. A moratorium has been declared pending a decision of the legality of capital punishment by the U.S. Supreme Court.

Capital punishment in the United States is today at its most critical crossroads. Never before in history has there been a greater movement for change. The first year in American history in which no executions took place was 1968. There have been none since that year, and this trend could continue indefinitely. Abolition of the death penalty, either through U.S. Supreme Court action or, if that fails, by the actions of individual state legislatures, is regarded as inevitable by some Americans. Many have worked diligently to accomplish this abolition; thus, it is no accident that from 1968 to the time of this writing, there were no executions. Hard work by concerned groups and a growing uneasiness on the part of society about the death sentence indicate the signs of change. As previously mentioned, there were 199 executions as opposed to two in 1967, and only one in 1966. However, it should be noted that in this recent moratorium period, despite the decline in executions, there has been a steady increase in prisoners awaiting execution. Only the deaths, not the death sentences, have thus far stopped.

The reason for the current moratorium is that lawsuits were filed in 1967, in the courts of Florida and California (the two states with the largest death-row populations), seeking stays of execution on behalf of all condemned persons. The argument was that the death penalty was unconstitutional. The courts upheld the stays of execution, and the same issues were later offered and upheld at lower and appellate levels in other states. Since then, different appeals concerning the death penalty have been consolidated and have reached the U.S. Supreme Court. At the time of this writing, arguments have been heard, and a decision is awaited.

Aside from the judicial channels, there is also considerable activity on the legislative front. In many parts of the nation, state assemblies and senates are considering bills to abolish the death penalty, regardless of what the decision of the court may be. On the national level, Congressman Emanuel Celler and Senator Philip Hart have bills before their respective chambers of Congress which would impose an official, legislative moratorium on all executions for a two-year period.

Finally, what is the trend of current thinking on the issue of capital punishment? In the public eye, the efficiency of the death penalty, specifically for the crime of murder, evokes sharply divided opinions. Based on Hanes and Gallup polls of the 1960s, there is an indication of a slight trend against support for the death penalty. At present, opinion seems to be fairly evenly divided. In February 1965 the poll on the question "Do you favor the death penalty?" showed a positive response of 45 percent; a negative response of 43 percent, and 12 percent with no opinion.

With the question of the continuance of capital punishment still quite open, and public opinion seemingly evenly divided, let us proceed to the pros and cons of the death penalty itself.

## Arguments in Favor of Capital Punishment

The three theoretical objectives of punishment are retribution, deterrence, and rehabilitation. The death penalty represents the ultimate implementation of the first two. Of rehabilitation (an objective which some argue is the only legitimate one), capital punishment is the total antithesis.

Since the goals of deterrence and retribution are achieved so simply and directly by the death penalty, much of the argument for the death penalty has been carried out in terms of a defense against the arguments of the abolitionists. Jacob Villenga, who serves on the National Board of Administration of the United States Presbyterian Church, states that we hear the following abolitionist statements made: "Capital punishment brutalizes society by cheapening life." "Capital punishment is morally indefensible." "Capital punishment is no deterrent to murder." "Capital punishment makes it impossible to rehabilitate the criminal."

> Villenga rejects these arguments in favor of the "eye for an eye" approach: No one can deny that the execution of a murderer is a horrible spectacle. But we must not forget that murder is more horrible. The supreme penalty should be exacted only after guilt is established beyond the shadow of a doubt and only for wanton, willful, premeditated murder, but the law of capital punishment must stand, no matter how often a jury recommends mercy. The "law of capital punishment" must stand as a silent but powerful witness to the sacredness of God-given life. Words are not enough to show that life is sacred. Active justice must be administered when the sacredness of life is violated.

The late J. Edgar Hoover, director of the Federal Bureau of Investigation from 1924 to 1972, has made very strong comments favoring the death penalty:

> Experience has clearly demonstrated, however, that the time-proven deterrents to crime are sure detection, swift apprehension, and proper punishment. Each is a necessary ingredient. Law-abiding citizens have a right to expect that the efforts of law enforcement officers in detecting and apprehending criminals will be followed by realistic punishment.

A judge once said, "The death penalty is a warning, just like a lighthouse throwing its beams out to sea. We hear about ship-wrecks, but we do not hear about the ships the lighthouse guides safely on their way. We do not have proof of the number of ships it saves, but we do not tear the lighthouse down."

One of the major arguments for abolishing the death penalty is that these convicted "killers" can be rehabilitated. J. Edgar Hoover rejects this argument by stating:

> There can be no doubt of the sincerity of many of those who deplore capital punishment. A realistic approach to the problem, however, demands that they weigh the right of innocent persons to live their lives free from fear of bestial killers against statistical arguments which boast of how few murderers kill again after rehabilitation and release. No one, unless he can probe the mind of every potential killer, can say with any authority whatsoever that capital punishment is not a deterrent. As one police officer has asked, how can these "authorities" possibly know how many people are not on death row because of the deterrent effect of executions?

Historian Jacques Barzun in an article entitled "In Favor of Capital Punishment" also takes a defensive approach in his arguments. Barzun allows that there are four arguments against the death penalty. These are, briefly, that (1) it is rooted in revenge; (2) it does not deter; (3) judicial error being possible, taking a human life is an appalling risk; and (4) a civilized state must uphold the sanctity of life. Barzun takes issue with the third and fourth:

> ... a man's inability to control his violent impulses or to imagine the fatal consequences of his acts should be a presumptive reason for his elimination from society. This generality covers drunken driving and teen-age racing on public highways as well as incurable obsessive violence; it might be extended ... to other acts that destroy, precisely, the moral basis of civilization.

Among the salient points which Barzun makes are that the abolitionist is inconsistent, narrow, and blind. They quibble over the value of human life when they talk of capital punishment, but they live in nations which arm themselves to the teeth against other nations and against internal disturbances. Therefore, the sanctity of human life is only a "slogan" to the abolitionist. Barzun believes that it follows that since the abolitionists are hypocritical, capital punishment should not be abolished.

Barzun continues asking how the abolitionists can attack capital punishment when animals are killed in laboratories. He claims that the problem is not so great because there are only about fifty people who could/should be executed per year; that psychiatrists overlook the innocent victims because they would rather study the pathological criminals; and, finally, that rehabilitative cures are always quite uncertain.

Barzun finally brings us to his conclusion:

> As in all great questions, the moralist must choose, and choosing has a price. I happen to think that if a person of an adult body has not been endowed with adequate controls against irrationally taking the life of another, that person must be judicially, painlessly, regretfully killed before that mindless body's horrible automation repeats.

Finally, retentionists point out that imprisonment is more expensive. It has been estimated that to keep a person in prison for life runs about $1,200 to $1,800 per year. Even though most prisoners work in prison industries, and this helps to defray the cost of their upkeep (death-row prisoners do not work), such upkeep is still very costly for the state. If a capital offender were to be put to death, a large expenditure of time and money could be avoided.

## Arguments in Opposition to Capital Punishment

That the concept and practice of capital punishment greatly offend the sense of morality of many in this society is beyond any doubt. However, arguments based solely on the immorality of the death sentence have not met with great success. Thus, the modern-day abolitionist takes a pragmatic view of capital punishment in demonstrating the areas in which he thinks it has failed. The major arguments which are being voiced today are that capital punishment is unconstitutional, and that it is totally ineffective as a deterrent to future crime. Moreover, modern-day abolitionists argue that the death penalty has been inconsistently and prejudicially applied; that it is too uncertain; that it even serves to promote violence; and that juries are often incapable of fair and rational decisions when it comes to their power to impose the death sentence.

*Constitutional Argument:* The constitutionality of capital punishment rests upon the Eighth Amendment which states ". . . nor cruel and unusual punishment be inflicted." The cruel and unusual punishment clause is taken to be highly elastic in meaning. In the case of *Trop* v. *Dulles,* the U.S. Supreme Court stated that "the amendment must draw its meaning from the evolving standards of decency that mark the progress of a maturing society." Thus, in theory, the death penalty can be struck down if it conflicts with moral precepts universally held. An example of this type of reasoning was seen in the U.S. Supreme Court case of *Robinson* v. *California* where it was decided that a criminal penalty for narcotics addiction was cruel, since the current opinion was that addiction is a disease.

There are three tests of a cruel and unusual punishment. The first is its analogy to torture. In *Trop* v. *Dulles,* it was decided that expatriation constitutes cruel punishment. The Court reasoned that the expatriate is potentially subject to untold physical abuse and/or psychological hurt.

The second test is the penalty's unusualness. Even before the present moratorium, fewer and fewer executions were taking place. Since the penalty has been applied so seldom, it is therefore unusual.

The final test is the penalty's severity. It was argued in *Rudolph* v. *Alabama* that the death penalty should be held in violation of the Constitution because it produces hardship disproportionately greater than the harm it seeks to prevent, and since a less severe penalty could as effectively achieve the permissible ends of punishment.

Capital punishment may also violate the Eighth Amendment in the manner it is administered. The lack of criteria to guide judges and juries in imposing a death penalty may render it cruel and unusual. Cruel because it is extreme and wanton, unusual because it is rare and arbitrarily removes the individual from the ordinary penological regime.

An additional constitutional argument rests not on the Eighth Amendment, but on the due process clause. The due process of law which the Constitution requires is violated by vagueness. It can be argued that such vagueness exists because jurors in capital cases are not required to observe the purposes of punishment, or the pertinent aspects of the defendant's conduct. There is no criteria to assure that there will be a connection between the sentences they give and a reasonable justification for giving them.

*Capital Punishment Ineffective as a Deterrent:* There are several sub-arguments for the proposition that the death penalty has failed as a deterrent. One is that individuals who are the type to commit murder or other capital crimes are not the type who can be deterred by threatening to kill them, or by killing others so as to frighten them. Murderers are incapable of understanding the consequences of their acts; therefore they cannot be deterred by the death penalty. Murderers can be divided into three groups: (1) those who suffer from physical, mental, or cultural deficiencies which make it possible for them to contemplate murder as a natural form of conduct; (2) those who are subjected to intensely difficult or inciting emotional situations, which prompt them to commit murder; and (3) professional gunmen. It can be seen that the members of the first two groups would not be deterred by the thought of death, while those in the third group would have great faith that they would not be captured and punished.

If capital punishment were truly a deterrent, it is argued that the following four propositions would be true:

1. Murders should be less frequent in states that have capital punishment than in those that have abolished it (other factors being equal).

2. Murders should increase when the death penalty is abolished and should decline when it is restored.

3. The deterrent effect should be greatest and should therefore affect murder rates most powerfully in those communities where the crime occurred and its consequences are most strongly brought home to the population.

4. Law enforcement officers would be safer from murderous attacks in states that have the death penalty than in those without it.

Abolitionists argue that none of the above statements are true. Statistical studies show there are no differences (other than normal fluctuations) in the number of "capital" crimes committed in states with and without the death penalty. Murders have not declined in places where the death penalty has been restored; murder rates have remained relatively stable in the communities in which they are committed; law enforcement officers seem to be subject to an ever increasing number of attacks, regardless of the death penalty.

*Capital Punishment is Inconsistently and Prejudicially Applied:* Abolitionists argue that frequently such factors as wealth, education, and position, rather than those that make a person a threat to society, may determine whether criminals are executed. Records show that it is very seldom, or never, that a rich or powerful person sees the inside of an execution chamber.

Accurate death penalty statistics for the United States have been available for the last forty years. An analysis shows that in this period, there have been close to four thousand executions. Of those executed, 2,066 were blacks and 1,751 were white persons, although blacks make up only one-eighth of the United States population. And of the 455 of those men executed for rape, 405 were blacks. In his *The Death Penalty in America*, Hugo Adam Bedau points out:

> Analysis of the . . . cases in which the death penalty was exacted, discloses that more than half were Negroes, that a very significant proportion were defended by court-appointed lawyers, and that few of them were professional killers. Whether a man died for his offense depends not on the gravity of his crime, not on the number of such crimes or the number of his victims, not on his present or prospective danger to society, but on such adventitious factors as the jurisdiction in which the crime was committed, the color of his skin, his financial position, whether he was a male or female, and indeed oftentimes what were the character and characteristics of his victim. (p. 188)

*Uncertainty Argument:* Abolitionists point out that the death penalty is one of the most uncertain punishments in our legal system. It is suggested that a relatively mild punishment that is certain to follow a crime has a much more deterrent effect than a severe penalty which is rarely enforced, or which can be predictably evaded. Thus, life imprisonment would be a more effective deterrent because of its greater certainty.

In 1963, for example, there were twenty-one persons executed in the United States while there were 8,404 cases of murder and non-negligent manslaughter. In that same year in California there were 656 willful homicides reported by the police; 208 convictions for murder; twenty-four death sentences; and one execution. (Statistics from Trevor Thomas, *This Life We Take*, The Friends Committee on Legislation, San Francisco, Calif., February 1970, p. 14.) Thus, there is no certainty as to who are these few who get executed, and why. Abolitionists therefore argue that if certainty cannot be found in the application of the death penalty, its use should be discontinued on this ground alone.

*Argument on Fallibility of Jury System:* Murder always produces a violent emotional public reaction, and a demand for vengeance. Jurymen cannot help but share this feeling. According to Thorsten Sellin, *(Capital Punishment*, 1967):

> The idea that a jury weighs the evidence in a criminal case to decide whether the accused is guilty beyond a reasonable doubt conveys a wrong picture of the process. In many cases it is merely a question of what evidence the jury chooses to believe. Where there is conflict of testimony, people tend to believe that which they would like to believe.

There is also often public hostility against the accused, and the jury may listen to the defendant's evidence with ears that are stone-deaf. In the case of Sacco and Vanzetti, the jury, after thirty-five days of trial, received the case in the afternoon and returned a verdict of guilty in the evening. It is also often true that some prosecutors, because of political ambition or simple vanity, are not above deliberately seeking the headlines by inflaming the jurors against the accused, and by playing upon every prejudice and ghastly detail.

*The Death Penalty Promotes Violence:* Finally, there is even an argument to be made that the death penalty actually promotes violence. The effect of executions on other inmates in a prison where the condemned wait to die is devastating. The penitentiaries where executions take place house thousands of serious criminal offenders, most of whom will some day return to the streets. Inmates are constantly aware of the men on death row. Seeing the condemned wait month after month on death row, the other inmates wonder what kind of a society surrounds them. Since it appears to be a violent one inside, there is no reason for it not to be the same on the outside.

*Alternatives:* Abolitionists are usually quick to point out that stopping the executions will not mean that these convicts should go free. Life imprisonment without possibility of parole is often cited as an alternative to the death penalty. However, while the idea of no possible parole satisfies to some extent the need for retribution, many argue that this also is an archaic concept. However, this raises issues of the efficacy of the penal system in this country and its ability (or lack of ability) to serve a rehabilitative role.

It should be noted though that a 1967 study on the behavior of parolees after imprisonment for willful homicide showed that only 0.2 of 1 percent were convicted again of willful homicide during the year after parole. Ninety-one percent were found to have favorable parole performance. The study concluded that persons convicted of capital crimes are generally the most reliable prisoners and parolees. ("Case for the Abolition of Capital Punishment," *Louisiana Law Reviews*, Vol. 29, February 1969, p. 399.)

## Conclusion

It has been seen that the death penalty cannot be approached as an exercise in logic or proof. It is contingent upon the merciful or vengeful aspects of mankind, upon the likelihood of emotional sway, and upon religious and ethical questions which remain nebulous. It is also contingent upon legal and political questions, and upon the disciplines of sociology and psychology. The few points which could be successfully debated must rely upon statistical data which is inaccessible because of the variables involved. There is no conclusively pragmatic or objectively right or wrong answer. It is ultimately a moral and philosophical decision for the individual to decide how our evolving society should deal with its hateful and crazed offenders. In my personal view, executing a man, however heinous his offense, is incompatible with mature civilization. We can give sufficient protection to society by rewriting our legislative codes to ascertain that dangerous murderers are confined for life without opportunity for parole. Society does not have to retain the barbaric vestige of human sacrifice in the name of self-defense.

# THE RIGHT
# TO DIE

Not long ago when the point of death was reached, there was usually nothing that could be done about it. Now, due to incredible advances in medical science, patients are kept alive long after what used to be the final crisis. The pacemaker, a cardiac machine can restore a heart that has stopped beating; the artificial respirator continues to breathe for a patient who can no longer breathe for himself; the kidney machine can sustain the vital functions of the human kidneys in a patient who has lost his own. Modern drugs, a defibrillator, and a pacemaker helped Dwight D. Eisenhower survive seven heart seizures, an acute intestinal blockage, and pneumonia before he died at the age of seventy-eight. To many it was an example of medicine's technical virtuosity at its best, but to Dr. Kenneth Vickery, a British health official, it was "the most dreadful example of medicated survival." The miraculous techniques of modern medicine can sometimes restore an elderly critically ill patient to a full life, but in a growing number of cases death is held off for a kind of half-life or vegetable existence that may be full of pain, misery, and tragedy for all concerned.

The late Philip Wylie, author of *A Generation of Vipers*, regarded most of the lingering terminal cases in our hospitals as a gross waste and misallocation of society's resources. He cited the case of Mrs. Wrigley of Chicago who was sustained in a coma for seven years by chemical transfusions and intravenous feeding. The huge sums of money that were expended for her costly care could have been better spent on a ghetto child's education. The half facetious solution proposed by Wylie was to go into the hospital wards with machine guns and wipe out all these old people; he noted that history abounds with examples of societies which have killed their old when they have become parasitical and useless.

Not many Americans would take Wylie's proposal for genocide seriously, but a wave of feeling for voluntary euthanasia is growing in this nation. More and more people who have gone through long, agonizing vigils with dying relatives are embracing the view that death may not always be worth fighting at any cost; that it may not be merciful to prolong a failing life. Using the techniques of modern medicine to keep a dying man alive for extended days or months can be needlessly cruel. Usually it creates an onerous emotional and financial burden on his family and merely prolongs his own suffering.

## Differing Viewpoints

A classic science fiction short story illustrates the time when society has "euthanasia parlours"—luxurious places resembling our high-priced beauty salons or cocktail lounges—where the individual can go, by appointment or off the street, for one last, sensational, totally artificial experience, which will end with a death pill. In this futuristic society there is no longer any question of morality. Voluntary euthanasia has become an assumed and unquestioned right.

Does a person have a right to death, or a right from life, as well as a right to life? In 1972 a circuit court judge in Miami ruled that a 72-year-old woman who had been receiving painful medical treatment "has the right to die in peace." Judge David Pepper said that Mrs. Carmen Martinez can refuse surgery that might prolong her life. Her physician, Dr. Rolando Lopez, told the judge that further surgery would be painful and could kill her but might prolong her life. The judge said, "A person has the right not to suffer pain."

It is becoming increasingly more common for people to express in writing the desire that they not be kept alive at any cost. The Euthanasia Educational Fund, founded in 1967, has answered demands for over forty thousand copies of what it calls a "living will," which recites in part: "If there is no reasonable expectation of my recovery from physical or mental disability I request that I be allowed to die and not be kept alive by artificial or heroic measures."

Arval A. Morris a scholar in this area, discusses this basic "freedom," guaranteed, he believes, by the Bill of Rights. He argues, ". . . the appropriate question should be, 'Why should our criminal law restrain the liberty of the doctor and the patient, denying them from what they want?' In a free society it is the restraint on liberty that must be justified, not the possession of liberty." He also believes:

> The time has come for man to rethink his traditional attitudes toward death. We cannot continue to view death in every circumstance as necessarily bad, something to be avoided, or something for which punishment must necessarily follow when it is inflicted upon another. Nor can we persist in believing that any kind of life is so sanctified as to be preferred absolutely over death—rather, we must replace our neurotic attitudes toward death with a more realistic view of death as a biological function.

Jurist Glanville Williams touches on the right to die when he says, "Many people still fail to comprehend that the question of whether conduct is wrong or foolish or undesirable is not the same as the question whether it ought to be punished by law. There is a sphere of conduct in which men are, or ought to be, free to act according to their consciences."

However, in a highly moralistic probe, Russell Kirk, in the *National Review* (March 23, 1971) states that once we subscribe to the politics of death, then why should we bother with the politics of order and justice and freedom? Mr. Kirk states that the criteria by which we measure the vigor and health of any society is by the strength of the love of life prevalent in that society. He queries, what test must we apply to any social order if we wish to evaluate its goodness? He answers that we must ask whether that society adequately protects the innocent and the weak, the young and the old. "If a social order fails to defend those who cannot defend themselves, then that order is impotent, heartless, or both." Viewing the movement for euthanasia, he rails: "Indeed, this really is a brave new world—the one so loathingly described by Aldous Huxley."

## Historical Overview of Euthanasia

*Euthanasia* is a word of Greek origin, which literally translated means happy death (*eu*-happy, *thanatos*-death). In Western civilization it has become associated with the social policy of killing those suffering from incurable disease, old age, or serious physical malformation.

Compulsory euthanasia on eugenic or utilitarian grounds was widely accepted in the ancient world. In primitive societies it was a common practice to abandon the aged. In Greece and Rome, while they did not abandon the aged, they did dispose of defective children. Aristotle said: "As to exposing or rearing the children born let there be a law that no deformed child shall be reared but on the ground of the number of the children, if the regular customs hinder any of those being exposed, there must be a limit fixed to the procreation of offspring." A more limited form of euthanasia was advocated by Seneca: "If one death is accompanied by torture, and the other is simple and easy, why not snatch the latter? Just as I shall select my ship, when I am about to go on a voyage, or my house when I propose to take a residence, so shall I choose my death when I am about to depart from life. Moreover, just as a long drawn-out life does not necessarily mean a better one, so a long drawn-out death necessarily means a worse one." India long had a practice of stuffing the mouths and noses of the aged with mud of the Ganges, then throwing them in the river.

Before World War II, compulsory euthanasia for the aged or incurably ill was gaining support in England, but the horrendous experience of Nazi Germany dealt a severe blow to the movement. In 1939 Hitler inaugurated a program of compulsory euthanasia. Initially confined to Germans, it was later extended to foreigners. Estimates range up to 275,000 people exterminated in German euthanasia centers. Allegedly by the Nazi version these were foreign slave laborers suffering from incurable tuberculosis. Euthanasia of foreign citizens has since been held to be a crime against international law.

The Reverend Charles Potter in 1938 formed the Voluntary Euthanasia Legalization Society with an aim toward changing the law in the United States. The Society framed a model bill which was introduced into the Nebraska Assembly but failed to secure acceptance. The New York Assembly rejected a similar bill. Initially the Society sought to also legalize compulsory euthanasia for monstrosities and imbeciles, but in consequence of unfavorable criticism from physicians, decided to limit its campaign to voluntary euthanasia.

In 1946, a total of 1,776 physicians joined a committee in New York State to crusade for legalizing voluntary euthanasia. The majority signed a petition to the legislature to amend the law, but their efforts were unsuccessful. Six years later a joint petition of English and American clergymen, doctors, and scientists requested the United Nations to amend the declaration of human rights to include the right of incurable sufferers to voluntary euthanasia. The general public, however, does not appear too responsive to euthanasia proposals. A poll in 1937 by the Institute of Public Opinion indicated that 54 percent of the American people were in favor of mercy-killing, but a Gallup poll of two years later gave a figure of only 46 percent in favor. A poll of American doctors in 1947 revealed that only 37 percent favored euthanasia.

In England, legislation to legalize voluntary euthanasia was debated in the House of Lords in 1969 and was defeated by a 61 to 40 vote. On April 7, 1970, a proposal was made in the House of Commons "to make lawful, administration of euthanasia at the request of the patient." This bill, the fourth of its kind, was defeated. The Royal Commission on Capital Punishment ruled that it would be "impossible to define a category of mercy-killing which would not be seriously abused."

Euthanasia as practiced in Switzerland is the most liberal in the Western world. Under Swiss laws it is legal to ease into death a patient suffering a painful and grave illness and for whom death is only a matter of time. No penalty is visited upon a doctor who administers a lethal pill out of compassion. The Swiss reason that if animals have a legal and moral right to a merciful death, so do humans.

### The Law on the Books

Voluntary euthanasia under American law is almost invariably regarded as suicide in the patient who consents and murder in the doctor who administers. The fact that the physician might act from the highest of motives in carrying out mercy killing on a willing patient would not change the characterization of the offense as murder. The most lenient interpretation by the law would hold that it could not be less than manslaughter for the doctor, the punishment being anything up to imprisonment for life, depending on the jurisdiction.

*First-Degree Murder:* If the doctor gives the patient a lethal injection with the intent of killing him the doctor is a common murderer under the law. The fact that the patient consents is not a defense, nor is the fact that the patient was in great suffering and his death imminent. When the doctor administers the fatal dose himself, it is first-degree murder. Legal writer M. Hale states the relevant rule: "If a man is sick of some disease, which, by the course of nature might possibly end his life in half a year, and another gives him a wound or hurt which hastens his death, by irritating or provoking the disease to operate more violently or speedily, this is murder . . ." The "malice aforethought" requirement of murder does not require any evil motive, anger, hatred, or revenge to be in the mind of the actor, but only an intent, plain and simple, to take the life of another.

*Second-Degree Murder:* If the doctor furnishes poison or an overdose of sleeping tablets for the purpose of enabling the patient to commit suicide, and the patient, with full knowledge of the consequences, takes either accordingly and dies, this is suicide, and a kind of self-murder in the patient at common law. The doctor, as an abettor, becomes again guilty of murder in the second degree, at least in strict legal theory.

*Doctrine of Legal Necessity:* In both the above situations, it is conceivable that a humane judge would instruct the jury that voluntary euthanasia may in extreme circumstances be justified under the doctrine of legal necessity. In the case of *Rex* v. *Bourne* this doctrine was invoked when the court instructed the jury that the unborn child may be destroyed for the purpose of preserving the yet more precious life of the mother. In the situation of voluntary euthanasia, it is possible to imagine the jury being directed that the sanctity of life may be submerged by the overwhelming necessity of relieving intolerable suffering in the last stages, where the patient consents to what is done and where in any event no measure of useful life is left to him. While this argument appears persuasive, there has been no hint of it being accepted by the courts in an actual case.

## The Law in Practice

The administration of the law in euthanasia cases is more humane and liberal than as it reads on the books. In England it has been customary for a long time to reprieve those guilty of murder for mercy killing. A typical English case was the trial of Mrs. Brownhill in 1934. She had undergone a serious operation and was worried about the future of her thirty-one-year-old imbecile son; so she killed him by gassing. Sentenced to death, she was reprieved two days later, and after three months received a pardon.

The harshness of the law is also mitigated by juries who bring in verdicts of acquittal or conviction for a lesser offense than that charged in the indictment. For example, in 1947, an American named Repouille killed his imbecile, blind child, and was indicted for manslaughter in the first degree. The jury returned a verdict of manslaughter in the second degree and strongly recommended clemency. The judge imposed a sentence of five to ten years imprisonment, and placed him on probation. In 1960 an army officer killed his three-month-old mongoloid son. He was acquitted of murder but found guilty of manslaughter and sentenced to twelve months imprisonment. Juries will sometimes return verdicts of temporary insanity or totally disregard the facts presented and acquit. In the case of *State* v. *Sander*, a physician admitted causing the death of a cancer patient by injecting air into the veins. The jury refused to recognize this as the cause of death. Very often mercy killers in the United States are not indicted at all. It is extremely difficult to prove a charge against a doctor.

## Explaining the Difference Between Law and Practice

*Death Taboo:* A number of theories have been advanced to explain the difference between the law as written on euthanasia and the actual effect of the law in practice. It may be harder for Americans to reach the acceptance of death than for any other people. Death is the primal taboo in our civilization. It is preceded by old age, is inevitable, and hence is frightening to our youth-oriented population. Americans vigorously deny their own finiteness. "We never talk about death, or if we do we resort to euphemisms. We have deep-freeze societies where bodies are frozen at the moment of death to be unfrozen sometime later when scientific advances will supposedly make regeneration possible. We have drive-in funeral homes where mourners do not have to face the bereaved; you can just drive in and sign the guest book. We have 'slumber rooms' in funeral parlors.

"Children should be taught to accept death as a natural part of life, like birth. We make preparations for birth. . . . We anticipate birth. We share it. But we do little like that for death. . . . As a result we grow up fearing death in our unconscious as a catastrophic destructive force that we can do nothing about. . . . Before parents can teach their children to accept death, however, they must come to grips with their own fears of dying. It's not the words you use but the attitude you convey. . . . We do not look at the subject of euthanasia squarely, come to any practical conclusion, or form any realistic attitude towards it. We prefer to say that euthanasia is homicide and treat each case with a 'there but for the grace of God' attitude when we are faced with a situation as a juror or judge."

*Wedge Theory:* Many legal authorities are fearful that the introduction of limited legal sanctions would open the door to mass voluntary euthanasia, i.e., genocide. This is the so-called "wedge" thesis. Advocates of this position argue that once the principle of the sanctity of every individual life is abandoned, it is an easy step to get rid of the diseased because they are a burden to society, and to rationalize eliminating those whose racial and religious beliefs may appear to pose a threat. Yale Kamisar, a proponent of this theory says:

> At present the problem has certainly not reached the degree of seriousness that would warrant an effort being made to change traditional attitudes towards the sanctity of life of the aged. Only the grimmest necessity could bring about a change that, however cautious in its approach, would probably cause apprehension and deep distress to many people, and inflict a traumatic injury upon the accepted code of behavior built up by two thousand years of the Christian religion. It may be, however, that as the problem becomes more acute it will itself cause a reversal of generally accepted values.

Postulating a theory contrary to this "wedge" thesis, Luis Kutner says: "The present state of the law, as it is evolving from judicial practice, may in effect be permitting mercy killing without adequate protection for the victim whose death may be unwarranted and uncanted. Clearly, the lack of definiteness in the present state of the law does not comport with notions of due process of law. From another perspective, the current state of the law does not recognize the right of the victim to die if he so desires." Implicit in Kutner's statement is an important question: Should the law be more specific as regards a very special instance of suicide or homicide?

Public confidence in the administration of criminal justice is hardly strengthened when, rather than coming to grips with the moral issues involved, we relegate these questions to a jury. Our system of justice might give more serious consideration to permitting "motive" to enter the substantive law, instead of restricting its use to evidentiary matters. For example, if the motive of a killer is the altruistic desire to comply with the victim's express wish to be killed, should not the law perhaps extend the mercy killer more lenient treatment under statutory law? Instead the law resorts to various devious devices to achieve the same result.

## Religious Attitudes

The Semitic religions, Judaism and Mohammedanism, have traditionally been opposed to taking one's own life. Neither the Bible nor Koran explicitly condones or condemns suicide; however, the absence of clear approval has been taken to mean disapproval. The overwhelming weight of Christian doctrine and history condemns euthanasia. In his encyclical *Mystici Corporis*, Pius XII denounced compulsory euthanasia: ". . . when to our profound grief we see the bodily deformed, the insane and those suffering from hereditary disease, at times deprived of their lives, as though they were a useless burden to society . . . hailed by some as a new discovery of human progress . . . what sane man does not recognize that this not only violates the natural and Divine law written in the heart of every man, but flies in the face of every sensibility of civilized humanity?" Voluntary euthanasia has also been rejected by the Pope as contrary to Christian teachings. The cornerstone of the Christian position is the belief that man has no absolute control over life, but holds it in trust. The disposal of life is in God's hands. Man has the use of life, and therefore may prolong it, but he may not by his own decision end it. Another point emphasized by Christians is that no man has the right to take an innocent life. "The innocent and just man thou shalt not put to death," says Exodus (23:7): "The innocent and just thou shalt not kill," admonishes Daniel (13:53). Only in self-defense against an unjust agressor may a Christian take another life.

As illustrated by the story of Job, suffering for Christians is not an absolute evil. The individual in physical travail may grow in spirit and wisdom. Suffering is also a means of expiating for sins; it can make one feel spiritually clean.

Within Christianity, voluntary euthanasia also finds articulate supporters. Episcopalian theologian Reverend Joseph Fletcher values life by its quality, not its quantity. "The mere fact of being alive and breathing is not so important to the man of moral integrity and spiritual purpose as are the terms of quality of that living. Euthanasia does not raise the issue of life and death, but rather the kind of death—peaceful or agonized—which the person is to meet. He feels that God has given man the power over life to some extent and has provided him with the tools and the knowledge for bringing the cause of dying to a merciful end when the individual has prepared himself for death and requested it of his physician."

A petition by Protestant and Jewish ministers in New York echoed the same principle: "We believe in the sacredness of the human personality, but not in the worth of mere existence or 'length of days.' We no longer believe that God wills the prolongation of physical torture for the benefit of the soul of the sufferer. For one enduring continual and severe pain from an incurable disease, who is a burden to himself and his family, surely has no value. We believe that such a sufferer has the right to die, and that society should grant this right showing the same mercy to human beings as to the sub-human animal kingdom. 'Blessed are the merciful.' " The New Testament has been quoted as favoring a death of dignity. "Lord, now thou lettest thy servant depart in peace." (Luke 2:29.)

## Medical Profession on Horns of Dilemma

The dilemma facing a doctor in euthanasia is, on the one hand, his duty to relieve suffering and, on the other, his commitment under the Hippocratic oath to preserve life. A section of the oath reads: "I will use treatments to help the sick according to my ability and judgment, but never with a view to injury or wrongdoing. I will not give anyone a lethal dose if asked to do so, nor will I suggest such a course." But Francis Bacon in *New Atlantis* says, "the office of a physician is not only to restore the health, but to mitigate pain and dolours; and not only when such mitigation may conduce to recovery, but when it may serve to make a fair and easy passage."

# SUICIDE—
# NO LONGER A CRIME

### England's New Suicide Law

"It seems a monstrous procedure to inflict further suffering on even a single individual who has already found life so unbearable, his chances of happiness so slender, that he has been willing to face pain and death in order to cease living. That those for whom life is altogether bitter, should be subjected to further bitterness and degradation seems perverse legislation."

The above quotation represents the new humanistic view of the Anglican Church which, in 1961, discontinued certain burial dishonors for suicide that had been retained by the Church for centuries. In the same year the English government, influenced by a committee set up by the Archbishop of Canterbury, abrogated the law whereby it was a felony to commit suicide. The English government also repealed the crime of attempted suicide and lifted its forfeiture of property laws for suicide, which dated from 1554.

Shortly after the passing of the Suicide Act of 1961, which contains these changes, the Ministry of Health in London issued a memorandum advising all doctors and authorities concerned that attempted suicide was to be regarded as a medical and social problem and that every such case ought to be seen by a psychiatrist. This attitude to suicide is in keeping with the scientific, humanistic emphasis of modern society in contrast to the punitive, superstitious thinking of the past.

Like many laws which are out of keeping with public sentiment, the English law of suicide was not implemented consistently. In many cases the coroners gave a verdict that the person who took his own life was of unsound mind, which avoided the pronouncement of a felony. However, the number of prosecutions for attempted suicide was substantial. During the period 1946-55 over five thousand suicidal attempts were brought to trial, and the overwhelming majority were found guilty. As late as 1955 a sentence of two years in prison was imposed on a man for attempting suicide. Thus, the English repeal of its criminal laws against suicide represents a significant action, not merely a formality.

In the United States attempted suicide is a crime in only a few states, and in those states prosecution is becoming nonexistent. Suicide per se is only a crime in Massachusetts and South Carolina, but the suicide suffers no penalties. The trend is to treat a suicide as a mental health problem rather than an act of evil, or a crime to be punished. Los Angeles County has established a Suicide Prevention Center where individuals with suicidal impulses are encouraged to get help at psychiatric clinics. This attitude of seeing a need for help and relying on treatment represents a major facet of the moral revolution. Under the old morality society more frequently resorted to the formula of sin and punishment.

## Frequency of Occurrence

Suicide is the intentional taking of one's own life. Somewhere in the United States during the last twenty-four minutes a man has committed suicide. In an average day sixty Americans commit suicide; over the course of a year more than 22,000 Americans end their own lives. The statistics of the World Health Organization for the year 1965, list the American suicide rate as 11.1 per 100,000. The rate for some European countries such as Austria and Hungary is more than twice that of the United States, while some countries such as Italy and Ireland have a suicide rate which is less than half of ours.

It has long been recognized that the official suicide statistics are not completely reliable. These statistics tend to underrate the frequency of occurrence. It has been estimated that the number of suicides in the United States is probably from one-fourth to one-third higher than is recorded. This means that in the United States there are probably more than 27,000 suicides a year. The reason that suicide tends to be understated is, since it is morally condemned in most of Western civilization, families of suicide victims try to hide the fact that a suicide has been committed, and they are frequently successful at doing this. Another reason for actual suicides being higher than reported suicides is that it is often difficult for a coroner to determine that the cause of death was actually suicide. A man who has killed himself and left no suicide note, may appear to have met an accidental death. Since in our society accidental death is a less shameful way to die than suicide, many coroners may report the former as the cause of death in doubtful cases.

## Who Commits Suicide

Sociologists and others who have studied the problem of suicide have recognized for a long time that people belonging to certain social groups are more likely to commit suicide than others. The suicide statistics tell us that the older you are, the more likely it is that you will kill yourself. The average age of suicides is in the late fifties. Older people are more likely to end their lives probably because they are more prone to serious illnesses which they regard as intolerable, and because they are more likely to live alone than younger people with families. It has been shown that the larger your immediate family (the family you live with), the less likely it is that you will commit suicide.

One exception to the fact that older people are more likely to kill themselves is the high incidence of suicide among college students. It would seem that the pressures of academic competitiveness are the crucial factors in giving college students much higher suicide rates than others of the same age who are not attending college. But it has also been suggested that those who go to college are more likely to come from the social groups which are most prone to suicide.

Race is also a significant factor in determining the likelihood of taking one's own life. Both in the United States and in South Africa, where blacks and whites live side by side, the suicide rate of blacks is much lower than the corresponding rate for the white population. In the United States a white person is three times more likely to kill himself than a black. This does not really prove that blacks are happier or more well adjusted than whites since, when homicide rates are examined, it is observed that blacks are more likely to kill other people than whites are. It seems that blacks are more likely to turn their frustration and hostilities outward toward others, while whites are more likely to take out their frustrations and hostilities on themselves. Obviously the physical color of one's skin does not determine one's propensity toward suicide or toward homicide. Rather, blacks would appear to have a lower suicide rate because of cultural differences and because in the United States and in South Africa they tend to be members of different socio-economic classes.

Social class and occupation are also significant factors in who commits suicide. The suicide rate is highest among people engaged in professional and managerial occupations, followed by businessmen and executives. Skilled workers and semi-skilled workers tend to have the lowest suicide rates, while unskilled workers tend to have higher suicide rates than the skilled and partly skilled. Doctors and dentists have the highest suicide rate of all professions. This can be ascribed to both the pressures of their work and to their easy access to poisons and other means of ending their lives.

Although females attempt suicide four times as often as males, many more men than women actually kill themselves. The fact that more women attempt suicide than men has been attributed to their more hysterical and emotional nature. One theory as to why women's suicide attempts are less successful is that women who attempt suicide do not really want to end their lives, but are acting for other reasons. A half-hearted suicide attempt is a cry for help, or, in some cases, an unconscious wish to punish someone close to the person who is making the attempt. Also, many who attempt suicide probably really wish to kill themselves but lack the courage. The discrepancy between male and female suicide rates is rapidly narrowing. This would seem to be the result of a breakdown in the sex roles. More women are working than ever before and are thus living more like men. The male suicide rate has not changed that much during the twentieth century in contrast to the rate for females.

The closer family ties one has, the less likely he is to end his life intentionally. People who are married have a much lower suicide rate than people who are single, divorced, or widowed. Divorced males have an exceedingly high suicide rate of 70 per 100,000, while 18 divorced females out of each 100,000 take their own lives. Again, we must use caution in regard to these statistics. It is probably true that living in a married state makes one less apt to take one's own life, but it may also be true that those who are single by choice or divorced are those of a particular personality type that is simply more suicide-prone. It is not whether or not they are married but their personality that determines their likelihood of committing suicide.

Religion is also a factor influencing suicide rates. Roman Catholics, Jews, and Moslems all have lower suicide rates than Protestants. This is especially true in countries which have a majority of Protestant citizens. Some Roman Catholic countries such as Ireland, Italy, and Spain, have a very low incidence of suicide, but Austria and Hungary, two predominantly Roman Catholic countries, have the world's highest suicide rate. Religion may be a factor, but in some cases it may be outweighed by cultural differences. One reason that Catholics in predominantly Protestant countries, and also Jews, have low suicide rates is that they are minorities. As we have seen with the blacks in the United States, the minority ethnic and socio-economic groups in any given country are less suicide-prone than the ruling class.

A member of a minority group may blame his station in life on the ruling majority, and he may spend his life trying to rise in social position. On the other hand, a member of the ruling class may have no one to blame but himself, and he has nowhere to go insofar as bettering his social and economic position. One who has made it in life may find himself with no more goals to attain, and being dissatisfied with his life, may choose to end it.

*Where Suicide Occurs:* Where one lives may also determine the likelihood of suicide. The nations with the highest suicide rate are Hungary, Austria, Germany, Finland, and Sweden. A number of factors enter into the high suicide rates such as greater cultural acceptance of suicide, more accurate reporting of suicide statistics, and the degree with which the people are able to express themselves emotionally. The Swedes are known for not being an emotionally demonstrative people. They are more likely to keep their feelings inside themselves, and so are less able to rid themselves of frustration by verbal or physical means. Suicide may be for them one of the few means for dealing with despair and unhappiness. The Italians, on the other hand, are known to be a very emotional people who readily express what they feel. Perhaps their frustrations are let out frequently enough to prevent any significant buildup of hostilities that may result in severe frustration and finally suicide over a period of time. Another possible explanation is the stabilizing influence of the Roman Catholic

Church. The suicide rate in Italy is only one-fourth that of Sweden.

In the United States the West Coast has the highest regional suicide rate. Nevada is the state where people are most suicide-prone. There, 22.5 per 100,000 end their lives. This must be attributed to gambling, drinking, and the high divorce rate, which create a high crisis quotient. California also has a very high suicide rate, while states on the East Coast tend to have lower rates. This is attributable to the fact that more people who live in the East have roots and family ties where they live. The West Coast in this country seems to be the epicenter of the moral revolution. When people come west they tend to leave some of their moral and cultural ties behind, along with their families.

*When Suicide Occurs:* The incidence of suicide fluctuates with the seasons. The months when the most suicides are committed are April and May, while the fewest suicides occur in December and January. One would think the opposite would be true as December and January usually bring the most depressing weather. One explanation for this phenomenon of a higher suicide rate in spring is that the increasing temperature of this season leads to greater excitability with a greater tendency toward suicide. Emile Durkheim thought that with the increasing length of the day, social life becomes more intense and this factor causes the greater number of suicides. Another answer in that someone who is already depressed feels lonelier and more alienated when the rest of the world is elated by spring.

### History of English and American Law on Suicide

Early English law on suicide was, of course, derived from canon law and the teachings of the Roman Catholic Church. The Bible itself does not condemn suicide. In fact, the suicides of Saul and Razis are actually praised, while Abimelech, Samson, and Ahithophel who also committed suicide in the Bible are not condemned for taking their own lives.

The idea that suicide was a sin was developed by St. Augustine in *The City of God.* Augustine argued that suicide is a violation of the sixth commandment. A suicide deprived himself of the opportunity for a healing penitence. Augustine also argued that a truly great man will bear the ills of life, or, to put it another way, suicide was seen as an act of cowardice. These arguments probably served as rationalizations for Augustine who had other reasons for condemning suicide. Glanville Williams suggests that the reason Augustine had to condemn suicide was that suicide followed as a natural corollary to the Church's teaching. The Christian belief was that life on earth was important only as a preparation for the hereafter. The supreme duty was to avoid sin. Since everyone had desire to commit sin, many Christians, therefore, committed suicide to avoid the temptation of sin and so to enter the hereafter in a pure state. Augustine was probably seeking to prevent suicide on a massive scale by making it appear as an act of cowardice rather than an acceptable alternative to struggling with the temptations of life on this earth.

Augustine's teachings on suicide gradually crept into canon law. The Fifteenth Canon of the Council of Braga in A.D. 563 denied to suicides the usual funeral rites with Eucharist and the singing of psalms. This was affirmed in England by a canon of King Edgar in the year 967. The synod of Nimes in 1284 refused suicides the right of burial in holy ground. To this ecclesiastical penalty, popular custom added a further punishment of dishonoring the corpse which eventually became incorporated as part of the law. Jurist William Blackstone reported that suicides were buried at the highway or crossroads and a stake was driven through their bodies. Also, a stone was placed over the face of the suicide. Stake and stone were intended to prevent the body from rising as a ghost or vampire.

These practices were not abated until the nineteenth century. In 1824 a statute was passed abolishing the crossroads burial for suicides. In its place burial took place privately in a churchyard at night, and without religious rites. In 1882 for the first time, suicides were allowed to be buried at normal hours. To this day, the burial rites of the Church of England are denied to suicides who are adjudged to have been of sound mind. If, however, the coroner holds that the suicide's mind was unbalanced at the time of the act, the prohibition does not apply.

Suicides were also subject to civil penalties which took the form of forfeiture of land and personal property. This rule gradually worked its way into the law from the time of Edgar's canon in 967, which provided that a suicide's goods were to be forfeited to his lord. As the forfeiture of property was a penalty for commission of a felony under English law, suicide gradually became recognized as a felony in England, provided that the person who intentionally took his own life was of sound mind. In 1563, in an investigation into the alleged suicide of Sir James Hale, Judge Brown stated the reasons for treating suicide as a crime. He thought suicide was against nature as it was contrary to the rules of self-preservation, it was an offense against God, and it was also an offense because it caused the king to lose one of his subjects. In 1870 the forfeiture of goods of felons was ended by statute, and in 1961 suicide and attempted suicide were repealed as crimes by Parliament.

In the United States there was no general adoption of the English law on suicide. Massachusetts followed the English practice, and in 1660 passed a statute forbidding a Christian burial for suicides and directing that they should be buried in the highway with a cartload of stones laid on the grave. This statute was not copied in other states and was finally repealed by Massachusetts in 1823. Other states declared suicide a crime, but since forfeiture of goods was never a punishment for crime in this country, a suicide suffered no penalty as there was little else the law could do to a man once he had ended his life. The definition of the offense was the same in this country as in England—there must be the intentional taking of one's life by one of sound mind and of the age of discretion.

## The Present Law

Suicide is still a crime today in the states of Massachusetts and South Carolina, but the person committing the act suffers no penalties. The states of New York and Oregon hold that suicide is not a crime. In a minority of the states where suicide is a crime, one can be punished for attempting to take one's life. This would seem to logically follow from holding that suicide is a crime, since to attempt any crime is always considered a legal offense. However, the justification for prosecuting people attempting to end their lives is doubtful. It does not seem possible that laws punishing attempted suicide could deter anyone wishing to take his own life. People who want and intend to commit suicide usually do not consider the possibility of their not being successful. A man who is going to jump off a bridge does not consider the possibility that he may not succeed in killing himself and thus be liable for prosecution. On the other hand, there are those who attempt suicide but do not really wish to end their lives. Rather, they are merely expressing a need for help. In this case they do not really intend to take their lives and should not therefore be guilty of attempted suicide at all. One must intend to commit a completed crime in order to be guilty of an attempted crime.

California is typical of a majority of states. Suicide is not a crime, nor is attempted suicide. But under penal code section 401, one who aids, abets, or encourages a suicide is guilty of a felony. This position may appear illogical. How can it be a crime to encourage an activity that is not a crime? It is obvious that where suicide is no longer considered a crime, it is nevertheless considered an immoral act. It is not a crime because it really cannot be punished. In some states aiding a suicide is treated as murder, on the ground that the consent of the victim in no way alters the quality of the act. In other states it is treated as a lesser offense.

One who commits suicide today may still suffer some consequences (if the dead can be said to be capable of suffering) because our society still strongly disapproves of suicide. Along with the stigma associated with taking one's own life in some states, the beneficiary under a life insurance policy is not allowed to recover the value of the policy when the insured meets his death by his own hand. This would seem, however, to be more of a punishment of survivors of a suicide than of the suicide himself. In fact, any attempt to punish a successful suicide falls into this category of punishing only the survivors. It is almost as if society, frustrated at its inability to take out its hostility on the deceased, tries instead to get back at the people who were closest to the suicide as a substitute for the actual object of their frustration who is now immune from further attack.

## The Causes of Suicide

There are countless reasons why people commit suicide, and in any one particular case there are usually a number of factors involved. Why two people may react differently to the same stimulus, one with suicide and one with only frustration, has been the subject of considerable research although there have been no clear-cut answers. The difficulty in obtaining data from suicide victims is obvious. Various types of studies have been conducted— psychological, sociological, anthropological, etc.—and even within any one such category there exists disagreement. Freud and Jung had quite different approaches to the problem of suicide. A psychological and a sociological approach may result in overlapping hypotheses in some areas, but generally in contradictory results. When dealing with a subject such as suicide one always encounters numerous obstacles. Unconscious factors operating on men's minds when dealing with the specter of death make objectivity into an almost unapproachable ideal. Any writer dealing with the subject of suicide cannot help but be influenced by unconscious forces within him: his own fear of death, his attitudes toward suicide acquired as a result of religious upbringing and parental and class attitudes, the occurrence of suicide in his family, and his own intimate relation to the possibility of his own suicide.

Emile Durkheim, in his study of suicide, treats it as a phenomenon caused by social conditions. He makes a distinction between three types of suicide. Egoistic suicide results from an individual's lack of integration into society, the chance of one's taking one's own life increasing with the degree to which one is alienated from the rest of the community. Altruistic suicide may result when society has too strict a hold over people and they thus lack individualism; these people may be driven to suicide by excessive altruism and a sense of duty. This kind of suicide was more common in primitive than in highly developed societies. Altruistic suicide occurred among the old and the sick who wanted to relieve society of the burden of having to take care of them; among women who followed their husbands to the grave; and among servants or among followers of chiefs who killed themselves upon the death of their leader. The self-sacrifice of martyrs as well as the hara-kiri of Japanese officers were suicides fitting into this category. The third category of suicide explained by Durkheim is called anomic suicide. If society loses its hold over the behavior of individuals, if there is some sort of social relaxation of sexual codes, there develops a state of anomie. The individual, unable to find strength in the collective organization, becomes more apt to commit suicide. Anomic and egoistic factors may both enter into an individual case of suicide. That these factors are, in fact, significant can be seen in the statistics which show that suicide was less frequent in strict and rigid societies than in those of a comparatively more liberal and flexible nature. In a more rigid society, the individual is not confronted with the question of what to do with his life or how he should live. If a society perpetuates a system which determines one's role 'in life and almost prescribes what one's relations will be with other people, there is much less chance that the individual will commit suicide.

Erwin Stengel in *Suicide and Attempted Suicide* discusses a study done in East and Central Africa where the discovered motives were, in order of frequency, among men—physical disease, quarrel with spouse or lover, impotence, mental illness, shame, and bereavement; and among women—physical disease, quarrel with spouse or lover, and infertility. Fifteen percent of the suicides followed homicidal acts. A frequently recurring theme was also that of a suicide as revenge upon a person with whom the victim had had a quarrel and who, it was hoped, would feel responsible for the death. Motives for suicide in Africa and Western countries appeared to be similar except that impotence and infertility were less often precipitating factors in Western nations.

The study of conscious motives alone, however, cannot fully elucidate the causes of suicide. Freud was the first to probe the psychological origins of suicide. He postulated that from birth there existed side by side in each individual the sexual drive (or the life force) and a death instinct (or a tendency toward disintegration and destruction). Any action in an individual's life could be seen as the result of one or a combination of both of these drives. In this way, any behavior such as reckless driving or excessive use of alcohol or, finally, suicide could be seen as a reflection of the death instinct. Freud's theory has not received much acceptance among members of the psychiatric profession; however, his postulation of a primary aggressive tendency provided stimulus for further research and a starting point for dealing with the root of destructive behavior directed against oneself or others.

Karl A. Menninger, an American psychiatrist and author of *Man Against Himself*, followed in Freud's footsteps in his explanation of suicide. Menninger sees any behavior which is inimical to health or life, e.g., antisocial behavior, asceticism, martyrdom, and some types of mental illness, as chronic or partial suicides.

Some psychoanalysts have rejected the idea of a death instinct and interpreted suicide as a desire for new life, a desire to be reborn and start over. Suicide is seen as an act in which the individual denies the barrier separating life and death. Taking one's own life may also be an assertion of omnipotence; by so doing one is evading natural death and endowing oneself with the power of God to take away life.

Suicide is seen as a means by which one may force others to feel sympathy and love. It may also be a means of making others feel guilty for not having shown sufficient affection during one's life. It may be used as a means of revenge, making a disappointing parent, friend, or lover feel responsibility for not acting in such a way as to prevent one's suicide. The social stigma that may descend upon the family in which there has been a suicide can also be part of the revenge.

A particularly frequent factor in the background of suicide victims is a broken home. The prolonged or permanent absence of one or both parents may cause personality problems that in later life may lead to suicide. Dr. Joost Meerloo of the New York School of Psychiatry claims that the early death of a parent often brings about an urge to join the lost parent. He claims that men have a tremendous need to dramatize old parental tragedy such as the case of a twenty-year-old student reenacting in his suicide attempt the death of his mother after divorcing his father when the student was five.

Suicide and unconscious (that is accidental) suicide sometimes occur as the result of the death of a person that one has either consciously or unconsciously wished dead. Such suicides are the result of guilt feelings stemming from a feeling of responsibility for the death of the person one has hoped would die.

Meerloo discusses the case of many children with over-conscientious parents who have instilled in their offspring feelings of inordinate guilt, thus stifling their children's initiative and creativity. Suicide in such cases is interpreted as a furious anger against those who have caused them excessive frustration and self-reproach.

Examples of psychological backgrounds or situations that might predispose one toward suicide, or of sociological factors that might play a major role in suicide occurrence are almost endless. It seems reasonable. to suppose that both psychological and sociological factors usually interact to bring about a suicide.

## The Morality of Suicide

Western civilization's abhorrence of suicide is in part a legacy of centuries of Christian teaching. Suicide is condemned as immoral and cowardly by the clergy. Even if the suicide is done in protest of war out of conscience, it is condemned by the Church unless there is a last breath left to repent. In 1965, a twenty-two-year-old Roman Catholic student, La Porte, doused himself with gasoline and set himself on fire outside the United Nations building in protest of the war in Vietnam. His friend, also a Roman Catholic, did likewise and died. He was buried, without ritual, as a sinner. La Porte, however, lived thirty-three hours and in that time was reported to have said to a friend, "I want to live." A priest thought that was sufficient for contrition and allowed the boy to be buried normally.

Not all cultures have looked upon suicide as immoral. Among the ancient Greeks and for the Roman stoics it was an ethical ideal. Seneca reflected that no one need be wretched by choice. "Against all the injuries of life, I have the refuge of death." Pliny maintained that the power of dying when one pleased was God's best gift to man. In Asia certain types of suicide have been admired such as hara-kiri, the death of World War II kamikaze pilots, and the self-immolation of monks in Vietnam. Even within Christianity not all suicide has been condemned. Bishops who took their own lives were often considered to be divinely inspired and were thus canonized as saints. Sir Thomas More, Voltaire, and Montesquieu have all maintained the morality of suicide. David Hume wrote, "By retiring from the arena man did no positive harm, but merely ceased to do good." This view was challenged by Madame de Staël who condemned suicide as inconsistent with the moral dignity of man and stressed that suffering is essential for spiritual growth. The controversy continued into the nineteenth century with Schopenhauer becoming the apostle of suicide. He depicted life as an unpleasant dream, the sooner ended the better. In modern times Albert Camus has observed that there is only one truly serious philosophical problem, and that is suicide. Camus sees man's mission as the revolt against the meaninglessness of life, and to take one's life is merely cowardly submission.

Part of our abhorrence of suicide seems to be due to the fact that society is threatened by individuals taking their own lives. What if large segments of the population started committing suicide? When a man takes his own life he is saying that life in his society is not worth living, and he is expressing his feeling in the most powerful terms. He creates uneasiness for others because, when confronted with a suicide, people are almost forced to consider suicide in relation to themselves and to question the worth of their own lives—something they would perhaps rather just take for granted and avoid dealing with. No one really wants to consider whether his life is sufficiently meaningful to warrant his continued existence. An added problem that confronts us when dealing with suicide is the problem that we always face when dealing with the subject of death. In the presence of death, Western culture has tended to run, hide, and seek refuge in group norms and statistics. There is nothing quite so fearful as death, and anyone throwing himself into the abyss in preference to life must really have some strong objections to living. We do not like to think that anyone could treat so contemptuously the life we assume to be so precious. The uneasiness we experience over an act of suicide, and perhaps the partial responsibility we cannot help but feel because we have not helped to make the world a more worthwhile place to live in (and perhaps thus have helped to prevent a suicide) may sometimes be too difficult to deal with. As individuals and societies often do in such cases, the guilt and anxiety we experience may often be repressed, reemerging as hostility, which is in this case directed either toward the individual who has taken his own life (and thus caused our anxiety) or toward the family of the suicide victim whom we may hold responsible. '

Maintaining a moral taboo on suicide is one way in which society tries to protect itself against the possibility of large numbers of the population taking their own lives. By exerting pressure of this sort, by assuring that the family of a suicide victim and the memory of the victim itself shall be invested with some sort of stigma, society not only hopes to make people consider suicide a less attractive possibility in their own case, but also something to try to prevent at all cost from occurring in their immediate circles.

Perhaps society has a legitimate interest in attempting to prevent the occurrence of suicides at any price. If a society wishes to perpetuate itself without major changes, perhaps it is in its best interest to maintain moral and legal sanctions against taking one's own life. Significant numbers of suicides could certainly pose a serious threat to the continuance of life as it is in this society. But the question is perhaps whether or not, if large enough numbers of people are unhappy with their existence in this society, they should be forced to go on living in it against their will; and whether they should bend their will for the sake of the perpetuation of the status quo. If many people want to commit suicide, should they not be allowed to and should not society thus be forced to deal with its inability to satisfy its members? If the individual has such great responsibility to his society that he should remain alive against his will as his duty to that society, then one must consider that any society that deserves such allegiance from its members must likewise have a responsibility to its members, and this should perhaps include providing the individual with a life worthwhile enough for him to wish to go on living. The responsibility cannot all be on the side of the individual. No society can be considered worthwhile if its citizens owe more to it than it owes to them. If one is forced to take responsibility for one's society, one should likewise be able to have complete responsibility for one's own life. A necessary and logical extension of one's taking full responsibility for oneself includes the right to determine the time, place, and the manner of termination of one's life. Perhaps we should say that the responsibilities of man and his society should be reciprocal, and if the society cannot live up to its responsibilities to the man, then the man has the right to terminate his life if he so chooses.

A frequent argument as to the immorality of suicide is that it is unfair to the people who are left behind. It is true that it may be immoral to kill oneself and leave a family with no one to support it, but the immorality in this case should not be attributed to the act of suicide itself. Suicide is basically a neutral act in terms of morality. It may assume moral or immoral overtones as a result of the circumstances in which it occurs, but this should not be confused with the morality of the act of suicide per se. If a father gives his only water to his children when they are lost in the middle of a desert, and he thus preserves his children's life at the expense of his own, one can hardly say he is acting immorally. But if a father takes his own life and, as a result of this impairs the lives of others, he may be said to be acting immorally. However, immorality is not an absolute. In some cases one is forced to choose between two acts, both of which may be regarded as immoral. The fact that someone may be unhappy as the result of one's suicide is not necessarily sufficient reason for one to go on living. As in the case of all other actions, one must weigh all the factors and determine as best one can what one should do. Perhaps the pain a person will have to endure if he is forced to go on living is much greater than the pain it might cause those around him if he were to die, especially in the case of those upon whom no one is significantly economically or emotionally dependent. As in the case of all other actions, a person must have the right to consider the factors and to make his own decision as to whether he feels he can morally take his own life. If we believe in man's right and freedom to choose how to live his life, we must allow him to end that life in the manner he sees fit. The moral decision must be up to him. In a time when changes in morality and philosophy have provided us with an existential ethic as to man's responsibility to himself and the world, it seems only fitting that we should allow each man the responsibility for his own death.

# PART V
# THE ABORTION CONTROVERSY

*A new morality is emerging. This morality demands liberation and freedom for the individual to realize his own potentialities and satisfy his own needs, desires, and tastes as he sees fit, with a minimum of intolerant social rules and regulations.*

*Paul Kurtz*, The New Sexual Revolution
*(1971)*

# ABORTION— PAST AND PRESENT

### Illegal Abortion Tragedies

In the July 1969 issue of *Dissent*, Alice S. Rossi commented cogently:

> Free association with the word "abortion" would probably yield a fantastic array of emotional responses: pain, relief, murder, crime, fear, freedom, genocide, guilt, sin. Which of these associations people have no doubt reflects their age, marital status, religion, or nationality. To a forty-four-year-old Japanese or Hungarian woman, the primary response might be "freedom" and "relief"; to an unmarried American college girl, "fear" and "pain"; to a Catholic priest, "murder" and "sin"; to some black militants, "genocide."

Abortion, with all its religious, medical, legal, and philosophical dilenmas, is undertaken by an estimated 1.5 million women annually in the United States. Kinsey's figures show that married women account for 85 percent of the total number of induced abortions. In half the cases where a girl has become pregnant before marriage, she is under twenty years old. About 89 percent of these teenage girls will have an abortion.

Dr. Robert Hall, president of the Association for the Study of Abortion, says there are now about a million criminal abortions each year in the United States. Botched illegal abortions are the largest single cause of maternal death in the United States. Dr. Christopher Tietze claims that those who die from abortion do so as a result of infection or hemorrhage. Estimates range from one thousand to five thousand on the number of women who die each year from illegal abortion.

The world of illegal abortion is a dirty, degrading world. In it women die from trying to burn themselves out with Lysol, from having their uteri torn with coat hangers, from being turned out of an abortionist's kitchen to bleed to death in the street. Women have been raped under anesthesia, and have been treated like sides of beef in abortion mills by assembly-line operators who carry their instruments wrapped in rags in their pockets. One case has been reported where a woman's insides were used to smuggle heroin from Tijuana to Los Angeles. It has been said that a considerable portion of our knowledge of poisonous drugs is derived from the human experiments performed by women upon themselves to induce abortion. The victims of illegal abortions are invariably members of the poor who cannot afford to travel to a state where abortion is legal or pay the price of a competent, sanitary illegal abortionist in their own state. Where abortions have been legalized, maternal deaths resulting from the operation have become almost nonexistent. Bulgaria reported 67,000 legal abortions for a recent two-year period without a single maternal death from that cause. Awareness of the danger of illegal abortion, and the safety of the legal one, has been a significant factor in the current abortion reform movement.

The President's Commission on Crime reports that criminal abortion is the third largest racket in the United States. A group of abortion mills operating in the city of Miami were raking in $20 million yearly. The enforcement of these nonenforceable laws cost the American taxpayers $120 million yearly for police and court time.

Violation of abortion laws is a felony in seventeen states and carries sentences ranging up to twenty-one years. In almost every case it is the doctor or abortionist who is charged, never the woman. Some have criticized this practice. They ask why the doctor and not the woman should be prosecuted since she is an accomplice. Lincoln once said: "Law is no stronger than the sentiment in the community." The typical jury will not convict a woman. They do not consider her action criminal. She is not in the business of abortion for profit. Her motive for seeking an abortion is usually to avoid hardship. There is also the problem of making enough room in prison for two million women.

## Abortion Reform Movement

On March 5, 1970, the Wisconsin Eastern District Federal Court in *Babbitz* v. *McCann* ruled that a woman "has the right to determine whether to carry or reject an embryo that has not quickened." In March of 1972, a federal court sitting in New Jersey held "that a woman has a constitutional right of privacy under the Ninth and Fourteenth Amendments to determine for herself whether to bear a child." In the early stages of gestation, the court declared, "a mother's right transcends that of the embryo." Though these decisions have limited reach, they reflect a growing movement across the nation. Since 1967 seventeen states have liberalized their abortion laws. A Gallup poll of 1971 indicates that nearly five hundred college newspapers accept advertisements for birth control devices, and more than six hundred accept advertising for abortion agencies. At the University of Maine each student is assessed seventy-three cents for an abortion loan fund called the Population Control Fund. A national clergy group in large cities has been sending 25,000 women a year to physicians for therapeutic abortions. The *Nation* now carries advertisements listing abortion prices at various hospitals. Similarly, radio broadcasts give information to pregnant women on whom to contact should they seek an abortion. When one considers that only two decades ago the mere word "abortion" was unmentionable in many quarters of the press (newspaper editors substituted "illegal operation"), it is clear that a social change of revolutionary dimension is taking place.

While the right to abortion has gathered momentum in recent years, the traditional Christian antiabortion view still remains the predominant position of society. Thirty-three states have strict laws against abortion. Even in states where the law has been liberalized, a woman seeking an abortion can find obstacles. Many doctors are reluctant to perform abortions. The number of hospitals willing to handle a substantial number of abortion patients is still limited. In Los Angeles, of the more than two hundred hospitals in the city, only six are willing to handle more than a token number of abortions.

Notwithstanding the obstacles, however, the opportunity for abortion has been made much easier for pregnant women in seventeen states as compared with the situation ten years ago. This trend may be abhorrent to antiabortionists, but to girls who are in trouble and who would otherwise be driven into the hands of an illegal abortionist, it is welcome. The fact remains that despite the traditional morality's disapproval of abortion, innumerable women will go to dangerous extremes to rid themselves of an unwanted pregnancy. Many people have realized that to maintain the prohibition of abortion is simply to condemn thousands of women to risky and sometimes fatal operations. Numerous countries have all but removed abortion restrictions, and in this country we seem to be headed in that direction. People see that liberalized abortion in other countries has caused no tremendous difficulties. It has not prompted greater promiscuity nor has it otherwise threatened the family. In the age of the moral revolution, people are more prone to question religious dogma that has been handed down for centuries and to decide for themselves what is morally permissible.

The general attitude of the women's liberation movement is that the question of abortion should be left entirely to the discretion of the individual woman. The issue for them is not whether a woman should be allowed to have an abortion but rather whether a woman should be compelled to be pregnant against her will. They see no reason why laws made by men should impose upon women the necessity to unwillingly give birth to a child. As Dr. Natalie Shainess of the Women's Liberation Movement puts it, "Men have borne up well while forcing women to bear down in unwelcome labor and to bow down in lifetime subservience to the unwanted fruits of sex. . . . In all consideration of abortion there has been almost no consideration of the woman. She is regarded as nothing more than an encapsulating amniotic sac."

In 1962 the American Law Institute drafted a Model Penal Code which takes a less radical yet still progressive stand. It proposed that licensed physicians be able to legally terminate pregnancy (1) if there is a risk that continuation of pregnancy would threaten the life or gravely impair the physical or mental health of the mother; (2) if the child would be born with a severe mental or physical defect; or (3) if the pregnancy resulted from rape or incest. The American Medical Association which had for sixty years opposed legalized abortion adopted this proposal with minor changes and now proclaims that abortion is a private matter to be decided by a woman and her physician. Various nonprofessional groups have also been instrumental in the abortion reform movement. The Association for the Study of Abortion in New York and the Society for Humane Abortion in San Francisco for years have been mobilizing public opinion for new legislation.

## New Abortion Legislation

Starting in 1967 liberal changes were brought about in the laws of Colorado, Mississippi, California, Georgia, North Carolina, and Maryland. All these states legalized abortion if performed in order to save the life of a pregnant woman, to preserve her physical or mental health, or to terminate a pregnancy resulting from rape. More recently Hawaii has enacted extensive reform in this area. Its new statute provides for abortion on request for a nonviable fetus, which means a fetus unable to survive outside the mother's body or in practical terms no more than twenty-four weeks old. Alaska passed a similar statute.

In 1970 New York passed the most liberal abortion law in the nation. It provides that abortions can be performed by licensed physicians within twenty-four weeks of the commencement of pregnancy. There is no residency requirement, and the law does not specify that the abortion must take place in a hospital. In New York City, however, regulations requiring abortions to be given in a hospital or equivalently equipped clinic were enacted after passage of the reform law.

First-year experience with the new and more liberal laws in Colorado and California indicates that hospital abortions will increase six to eightfold. If the laws were similarly modified in all fifty states there would probably still be more than 900,000 illegal abortions performed each year. The Association for the Study of Abortion suggests that one reason for this is the fear of doctors that they may be persecuted for incorrect interpretation of the new and ambiguous liberalized statutes. Doctors also do not want to risk ruining their reputations by performing operations that a large segment of the public and many conservative hospital boards consider morally wrong. To protect their reputations, several doctors privately admit to performing illegal abortions covertly outside the hospital.

Dr. Robert Hall, a distinguished physician active in abortion reform, points out that the changes proposed by the American Law Institute would merely legitimatize many abortions now being done in non-Catholic hospitals. He further points out that although the new liberal abortion laws enable abortions to be done in cases where they could not have been performed otherwise, at the same time they are so riddled with restrictions that there are cases where they make abortion impossible even when they might have been performed previous to the restrictions. One example is the frequent requirement that the abortion must be approved by a board of doctors. Dr. Hall claims that when such a board was formed at his hospital, the abortion rate fell two-thirds. Some states require that for a woman to qualify for abortion on grounds of rape, she must report the incident to the police within one week of the time it occurs. Most rape victims never report such incidents to the authorities. Police subject the victim to embarrassing questions and cross-examination, sometimes attempting to establish guilt on the part of the woman for enticement by means of seductive clothing or conduct. Reporting a rape to police may also entail publicity and, in the few cases where the criminal is actually apprehended, a public trial can be a tremendous ordeal for the rape victim. Most women would not report a rape to the police just in case they should get pregnant and decide that they want an abortion. In fact the law regarding abortion would probably not be one of the first things to occur to someone who has just been raped.

Change in abortion law is not only being brought about by legislators. The courts also have had their effect in helping to liberalize the law. For example, in 1969 California's State Supreme Court declared a state abortion law unconstitutional on the grounds that allowing the operation to be performed only when it is "necessary to preserve the life" of the mother is unconstitutionally vague and in conflict with the right to due process of the law. Justice Raymond Peters in his opinion said:

> The rights involved in the instant case are the woman's right to life and to choose whether to bear children. . . . The fundamental right of the woman to choose whether to bear children follows from the Supreme Court's and this court's repeated acknowledgement of a "right to privacy" or "liberty" in matters related to marriage, family and sex.

Actually this opinion which was handed down in the case of *People* v. *Belous* was not terribly significant since California had just passed a new and more liberal abortion law, and so the judgement in this case merely overturned a law that had already been replaced by a new one. However, as mentioned earlier, although California had in 1968 amended its century-old law and replaced it with a therapeutic abortion law, it did not make provision for mothers with deformed fetuses. Originally, such a provision was written into the law but had to be deleted; otherwise Governor Reagan would not have signed it.

The courts also found fault with California's 1968 law. In a 1970 decision written by Judge T. L. Foley for a municipal court in Alameda County, the judge claimed:

> We cannot permit a legislative theory which decrees that life begins at conception. To do so would be to blandly adopt the philosophy of one of the country's major religions, an act which clearly would be in violation of the First Amendment to the United States Constitution. Thus the court can find no compelling interest of the state, and concludes that the right to choose to bear children is a fundamental right of the individual woman to be exercised in any manner she chooses and which may not in any way be abridged by law.

In Texas and Wisconsin, federal district courts in 1970 overturned abortion laws in their respective states. The courts ruled that laws limiting the availability of abortion to instances where the life of a woman is in danger are an unconstitutional infringement of the right to privacy. The Texas court further found the state's statute unconstitutionally vague.

In 1967 a New Jersey court refused to grant damages to a woman suing her doctor for failing to advise her of the certainty that she would bear a deformed child as a result of contracting German measles early in pregnancy. However, as a result of this case, New Jersey state prosecutors agreed to refrain from prosecuting cases in which doctors had performed abortions for reasons approved by the medical community.

In 1968 a New York court dealt with a case much like the one just discussed. A deformed child and its parents sued their hospital for failing to allow the performance of an abortion and failing to advise the woman to seek such an operation elsewhere. The court awarded $10,000 to the mother.

Although the courts may certainly help in the struggle for liberalized abortion, their influence is only indirect. They can deal only with individual cases and are no help to a woman until she has already given birth to an undesired infant. With the tremendous backlog of cases from which our courts suffer, it would be unlikely that a woman who is refused an abortion could get a favorable court decision in time to have the operation performed before the birth of her child.

## History of Abortion Laws

The earliest abortifacient recipe is more than 4,600 years old, and primitive people all over the world have been found to practice abortion as well as infanticide in order to prevent an increase in their numbers. Among primitive people, the more extreme methods were gruesome. One tribe encouraged large ants to bite the woman's body. In the royal archives of China records of abortion techniques date back three thousand years. Abortion was widely practiced in both Greece and Rome for economic, eugenic, and even cosmetic reasons; for example, to preserve a woman's breasts. Plato recommended that abortion be obligatory for every woman over forty and Aristotle, being concerned with population control, urged abortion for women after an allotted number of children. During the later Roman Empire attempts were made to suppress abortion, but the motivation was not our present-day one of protection of the unborn child but rather protection of the husband who might be deprived of offspring.

In the early days of the Roman Catholic church and continuing for centuries thereafter, controversy raged over the exact time during pregnancy when a fetus came to possess a soul. Deciding on the exact day this occurred was of great importance because after this time abortion was held to be murder. The controversy stemmed from the classical argument over the exact moment when life actually commences. Aristotle claimed that life commences about forty days after conception in male embryos and ninety days after conception in female embryos. Of course this speculation was of little help to a woman desirous of an abortion because she would have no way of determining the sex of the child until after it was aborted. The Stoics believed that life only began at birth. Hippocrates thought life in the male began at thirty days after conception and in the female at forty days after conception. Roman law settled finally upon forty and eighty days respectively.

In theology the question of when life commenced was linked to theories of the origin of the soul. According to Tertullian the soul was transmitted to the child by his parents, and hence was ensouled at the moment of impregnation. Another view held that the soul did not enter the embryo until later. In determining the time it arrived, theologians relied upon the views of classical writers on the commencement of life. Thus St. Augustine drew a distinction between embryo informatus and embryo formatus, the former being the entrance of the soul into the fetus, with abortion at the informatus stage in pregnancy considered as merely prevention of life and as such punishable only by a fine. But abortion of an embryo formatus was considered ending of a life already begun and thus a form of murder punishable by death. Exactly when an embryo reached the stage of formatus was not agreed upon until the fourteenth century. It was then resolved that ensoulment occurred on the fortieth day after impregnation for the male and eighty days after impregnation for the female. A well-known feminist writes: "To listen to judges and legislators play with the ghostly arithmetic of months and weeks is to hear the music by which angels used to dance on the head of a pin."

The Roman Catholic position on abortion has been a strong influence on Western law. In 1588 Pope Sixtus V made abortion an excommunicatory sin. Three years later Pope Gregory XIV qualified the earlier order and held abortion to be a sin worthy of excommunication only if it were performed over forty days after conception to a male fetus or eighty days after conception to a female fetus. This remained the position of the Church and the law in Western countries until the 1800s. During the nineteenth century, under the leadership of two Napoleons, France engaged in 100 years of war intent on building a world empire. Both the Catholic Church and the emperors had a vested interest in maintaining the numerical strength of France. Men were needed to fight wars, sustain the home economy, and serve as colonizers in new territory. French peasants were encouraged to have as many children as they could. Peasant fathers received tax incentives, social security benefits, and even medals if they sired a large family.

French women were given in marriage at the earliest possible age. They were to be kept pregnant and at home for their own fulfillment, but particularly for the fulfillment of French destiny. Attending church was their sole social function. A French peasant woman properly impregnated could be expected to produce up to fourteen children. French daughters under the Code Napoleon could not inherit property and had the status of brood mares.

In that age of frantic overbreeding for war and imperialism, scientists discovered the dynamics of impregnation and finally developed methods of contraception. These were immediately utilized by the French and in ten years the French birthrate dropped 50 percent. Napoleon Bonaparte was furious at this threat to the glory of France for the mere convenience of the peasants. He found it both necessary and moral to use any possible means to stop this growing use of contraception and to render abortion an impossibility.

Pope Sixtus IX in 1869 returned to the old bill of Pope Sixtus V and decreed that all abortion from the moment of conception on was murder. Pope Pius IX also stated that "all abortion is against the precept of God" and the "laws of Nature." Each sexual episode was to "be open to procreation" and a wife was to be sexually accessible at all times to her husband except during menstrual periods. Contraception was denied her, and once pregnant, no matter how unwillingly, she was to bring forth the infant for the church and state, regardless of the chaos in her own family or the threat to her life or health.

Under such regulation, abortion was still practiced, albeit illegally. Alarmed at the infanticides, the Catholic Church briefly reopened the infamous Tours. A compartment was placed outside the church into which a woman might put her unwanted newborn child. The infants were inspected by the church priests and nuns; healthy infants were placed in church orphanages, and substandard infants were allegedly consigned to the sewers for disposal.

Like the French civil law, English common law was heavily influenced by theologians, particularly St. Thomas Aquinas, in its attitude on abortion. St. Thomas claimed that the soul entered the body at the moment life began, and that the beginning of life could be determined by movement. Thus the fetus was considered to be alive as soon as the mother felt it move or "quicken" within her. English common law adopted this view. Life was held to begin at the moment of "quickening" and not at any particular day of pregnancy, although quickening usually takes place about four and a half months after conception. Before quickening, abortion was not held to be a crime. Even after quickening, abortion was prosecuted only rarely in early England. In 1803 British law was altered. Abortions before and after quickening were both felonies, although the former was less severely punished. The law had considerable impact since most abortions take place during the early months of pregnancy, and this had suddenly become criminal. Until a few years ago English abortion restriction rested on the Offences Against the Person Act of 1861 which established a maximum punishment of imprisonment for life whether an abortion was attempted before or after quickening. This statute outlawing all abortion has been attributed to some degree to the manpower needs of a nineteenth-century England engaged in global wars, colonization, and industrial growth.

Charles Dickens wrote his searing books about the travesties of human dignity resulting from the theory of the "sanctity of life in the womb." After a sanctified nine months inside the mother, the child was fair game for the sweatshops, coal mines and slums. Huge numbers of children died from malnutrition, consumption, fevers, and plague before reaching age twelve. The "sanctity" of these lives evidently did not extend to that portion of their lives beyond the womb.

## Early American Law

The Puritans regarded sex as one of the basest of human activities, and found the prohibitions against contraception and abortion useful in guarding their women against promiscuity and in encouraging population growth in a new continent. Forcing women to bear illegitimate pregnancies was seen as a desirable means of punishment for sexual sin. More often, however, such misfortune was the fate of poor women; the rich generally had ready access to an abortion.

American abortion laws have their origins in early British law. However, abortion before quickening was not held to be a crime in this country until the time of the Civil War (about sixty years after it became illegal in England). Dr. Horatio Stoner, who in 1866 wrote the earliest treatise on abortion, observed that abortion was a common practice during the Civil War. The first abortion law in the United States was passed by Connecticut, but until 1860 abortion before quickening remained lawful. By the late 1800s, with the increasing role that government began to play in the lives of its citizens, common law practices were replaced by statutes giving doctors control over abortion. This was the beginning of the legal medical abortion.

Clearly influential on the status of abortion here has been our Puritanical religious heritage. Sexual matters including birth control were not matters for open discussion. When Dr. Charles Knowlton published a book on methods of contraception in 1830, he was arrested for offending public morality. Birth control information had the legal status of obscentiy. Publications in that day would not even print the word "abortion" lest it offend the community's moral sensibilities.

## The Onset of American Reform

Birth control became a public issue after World War II through the efforts of such people as Dr. Mary Calderone and such organizations as Planned Parenthood. The concern about overpopulation and increasing talk of women's rights gave impetus to the birth control movement.

Abortion reform itself did not come into its own until the 1960s. Two outstanding incidents sparked public controversy on the subject. In 1962 Mrs. Sherrie Finkbine of Phoenix took thalidomide (a tranquilizer) while pregnant. She later discovered that this drug meant certain deformity of the fetus. With her physician's urging, a Phoenix hospital approved the abortion until publicity focused upon the case. The hospital then withdrew permission, claiming the Arizona law only allowed abortion to save the life of the mother and not to prevent the birth of a deformed child. Mrs. Finkbine was forced to fly to Sweden where liberalized abortion laws enabled her to have the operation performed, and it was found that her child would in fact have been deformed. The case of Mrs. Finkbine, as well as the large number of deformed thalidomide babies actually born, brought the need for change in abortion laws to the eyes of the public.

Also bringing out the need for more liberal abortion provisions was the 1964-65 rubella or German measles epidemic in this country. Contracted during the first three months of pregnancy, there is a fifty-fifty chance that rubella will cause cataracts, deaf mutism, cardiac anomalies, or mental retardation in the baby. It is estimated that due to the rubella epidemic fifteen thousand to twenty thousand infants were born defective or malformed. United States legal resources were strained in attempting to cope with the legal consequences of the epidemic. In California, doctors were indicted for having performed abortions on women who had contracted German measles during pregnancy, while in New Jersey doctors were prosecuted for not having performed such operations.

# ABORTION—
# PRO AND CON

### Is a Fetus a Human Being?

Perhaps the most crucial question in the abortion controversy is whether the young fetus is "tissue," as those favoring abortion argue, or "human life," as abortion foes contend. Professor Charles Rice of Notre Dame says the contention of "human life" can be supported by the data of embryology. "When the child is eighteen days old he has every single internal organ he will ever have as an adult. Not long after he has a mouth with lips and a tongue and buds for twenty milk teeth. At eighteen weeks he can suck his thumb, scratch himself, and even cry (although he makes no sound because there is no air in the womb). He can feel pain." Princeton ethicist Paul Ramsey, a Methodist, contends that science is now detecting "discernible brain waves at eight weeks in a fetus." The findings of genetics, says Ramsey, suggest a much earlier date. Since the individual's unique genetic code, or genotype, is established at the moment of fertilization, the zygote itself—the fertilized egg—should be considered "human."

Professor Garrett Hardin, noted biologist at the University of California, Santa Barbara campus, disagrees: "Whether the fetus is or is not a human being is a matter of definition, not fact; and we

can define any way we wish. In terms of the human problem involved, it would be unwise to define the fetus as human. . . .
Abortion-prohibitionists generally insist that abortion is murder, and that an embryo is a person; but no state or nation, as far as I know, requires that the dead fetus be treated like a dead person. Although all of the states in the United States severely limit what can be done with a dead human body, no cognizance is taken of dead fetuses up to about five months' prenatal life. The early fetus may, with impunity, be flushed down the toilet or thrown out with the garbage—which shows that we never have regarded it as a human being."

Under California law, whether a fetus is viewed as a human being depends on the facts. If injured during pregnancy by a negligent act, the child when born has a cause of action against the wrongdoer. However, if the fetus is accidentally killed by negligence, the parents are not allowed to bring a wrongful death action in behalf of the dead fetus. The courts will not allow a wrongful death action, refusing to recognize a fetus as a human being. What happens when the death is brought about not by negligence but by malicious intent? In the case of *Keeler* v. *Superior Court of Amador County* a jealous ex-husband seized his wife, pregnant by another man and said, "I'm going to stomp it out of you." He pushed her against a car, and shoved his knee into her abdomen, and struck her several blows. A Caesarian section was performed, and the fetus was examined *in utero*. Its head was found to be severely fractured, and it was delivered stillborn. The pathologist gave his opinion that the cause of death was skull fracture with consequent cerebral hemorrhaging, that death was the result of force applied to the mother's abdomen. Upon delivery the seven-month-old fetus weighed five pounds and was eighteen inches long. The defendant Keeler was charged with murder. The court found him not guilty because under the common law, a child in its mother's womb is not a "human being" within the meaning of the term *murder*. In reaction to the case, the California legislature enacted a new law making it manslaughter to intentionally destroy a fetus without the mother's consent.

## Psychiatric Opinion

Psychiatric opinion on abortion varies almost as much as public opinion. However, most psychiatrists claim that in the case of an emotionally disturbed woman who does not wish to have a child, forcing her to give birth may have a severely damaging effect upon both the woman and the offspring. Nine months of pregnancy entails a tremendous drain on the resources of any woman, and in the case of a disturbed woman who despises the fetus growing within her, suicide or severe difficulty may be the result of a refusal to perform an abortion.

Dr. Harold Marcus, Associate Professor of Psychiatry at Mt. Sinai School of Medicine in New York, stated that "if a woman is going to err in either direction, it is better that her error be in abortion. If she regrets the abortion, she can usually have another child at another time. But her regret after the child is born can be dangerous to the mother and the child."

The Committee on Psychiatry and the Law for the Advancement of Psychology stated, "There can be nothing more destructive to a child's spirit than being unwanted. And there are few things more disruptive to a woman's spirit than being forced into motherhood."

Psychiatric recommendations for therapeutic abortions are on the increase. Some women who must see a psychiatrist for evaluation turn out to be emotionally ill. The psychiatrist will recommend abortion for these women as a preventive measure to suicide or severe depression or an illegal abortion.

Ninety percent of the abortions performed in California in 1970 were for reasons of mental health. This percentage certainly indicates a rise in abortion for psychiatric reasons.

But psychiatrists also say that there are some neurotic women who may be treated during pregnancy, taught to accept the child and become good mothers. Some psychiatric opinion also maintains that abortion may bring about feelings of guilt and depression and should therefore not be performed. But in studies of large numbers of women who had undergone abortion, the percentage of women who expressed regrets that their pregnancy had been terminated was very small. If having an abortion may in fact cause feelings of guilt in some women (and perhaps if abortion were not illegal people would be less apt to feel guilty as they would not feel like criminals), there is some question whether the law or even psychiatrists should be put in a position to decide whether a woman should or should not be able to have the operation performed on the basis of whether they feel she may later experience guilt. In a free and democratic society one would like to think that mature adults are capable of making their own moral choices and taking responsibility for their own actions even if these actions should cause them to feel guilty. Although psychiatrists may be capable of foreseeing the result of a particular woman having an abortion, the thought of putting the power of deciding who can or cannot have her pregnancy terminated in the hands of such specialists is almost frightening. By taking the right to decide whether a woman must bear a child away from the woman, one is putting her into a position of childlike dependency upon psychiatrists. No one thinks that psychiatrists should be given power to make other moral choices for us even if they are capable of determining what would make us most happy.

## The Feminist View

"Don't Labor Under Misconception" and "If Men Got Pregnant, Abortion Would be a Sacrament." These were the slogans on the homemade signs and posters carried by the two-thousand women and men who marched through the downtown streets of San Francisco on November 30, 1971, at a rally sponsored by the Women's National Abortion Action Coalition.

Susan Dunn, who teaches a class on Women's Liberation at UCLA, says: "An unwanted child destroys a woman's mastery of her life and creates stress and anxiety, damaging to her and all those around her. When the more conservative are confronted with the idea of legalized abortion, they are quick to cry murder yet remain silent in the face of war, capital punishment, and the tremendous amount of violence passed off on us by the mass media. If our society accepts the murder of thousands of innocents in the pursuance of war, it seems almost perverse that so many should cry out in horror at the removal of an unfeeling cluster of cells from a woman who positively does not want to bear a child."

Many of the women in the women's movement see partial liberalization of abortion law as a threat in and of itself. They feel that once there has been some liberalization and the more obvious grotesqueries of illegal abortion are eliminated, it will be much harder to ever get the less stringent requirements thrown out and that it will lull the public into a false sense of accomplishment. Many women view the "reforms" of the old rape-incest-fetal-deformity variety as not being in the interest of women at all, but rather as an insult to a supposedly self-determining individual. Although some of the new abortion legislation may look good (especially to middle-class women who can afford the costs and can deal with endless red tape involved in obtaining a legal abortion) it fails to deal with what feminists consider the heart of the matter, and that is the right of any woman to decide whether to have an abortion.

Another gripe of some feminists is that newspapers often report change in abortion laws as "repeal." However, it is obvious that when you repeal an abortion law you do just that; you do not put something back in its place or make special restrictions on abortion and not on other medical operations. There has yet to be a state in this country that has eliminated its abortion law without substituting for it another law. Most feminists have objections to all the new restrictions. One such restriction is that abortions must be performed in licensed hospitals. Abortion is a relatively simple procedure that can be carried out in a clinic or a doctor's office. Most women need to lie down for a while after the operation but there is no reason to occupy expensive hospital beds and go through the present rigamarole of obtaining a hospital abortion. Most hospitals today are directed by conservative boards that are reluctant to grant abortions. In Hawaii where a new and more liberal law is in effect, hospital boards have established their own guidelines. Although the law appears to make it relatively simple to obtain an abortion, the hospital boards now insure that any woman desiring such an operation will have to ask a lot of strangers for permission to spend a considerable amount of their money on a hospital abortion.

Actress Romy Schneider expressed what is probably the view of the majority of women when she said: "Look, there's never going to be anything easy about an abortion. It isn't easy. No girl will ever make the decision simply. No matter what anyone says, it can't just be five minutes. The law, the church, stupid morals have nothing to do with the way a woman feels when she makes a decision like this. She herself knows how painful, difficult, complicated it all is, and no law needs to tell her how she should feel."

## Philosopher's View

One of the main philosophical arguments against abortion is that it violates natural law. Natural law represents the primitive, spontaneous urges of all living things. It is the state of existence as created by God. The tropism of plants is an example of an organism obeying natural laws for survival. To eat when hungry is another example. It is contended that when a woman is pregnant, natural law behooves her to have her child. To intervene and interrupt her pregnancy by artificial means violates natural law. Should we look to nature for moral norms? Upon simple reflection the answer is clearly in the negative. We cannot look to the rabbit for lessons in the morality of sex, or answers to the population problem. Nor can our wives take lessons in maternal duty from the behavior of the queen bee who destroys her mate as soon as he performs his conjugal duty. Nature is prolific when we do not want her to be, and so we have to control her. Nature is barren when we need fertility so we have irrigation. Frustration of nature, far from being immoral, is man's vocation. Since he invented the first tool, man has always frustrated nature and will continue to do so until his last day on earth. Every canal and dam that man has erected are monumental frustrations of nature's even flow. When nature is deficient in doing what it should for human welfare, human reason makes up for that deficiency. When it comes to population control, frustration of nature may be necessary for man's survival.

# ABORTION
# IN OTHER CULTURES

## Widening Our Perspectives

Moral norms in other cultures may not provide a model for our own society, but knowledge of them can help to enlarge our perspectives on moral issues. For a long time it was popularly believed that males were inherently aggressive and females inherently submissive, but then along came Margaret Mead who reported that in some far-off lands these traits were reversed in the sexes. In some cultures the male is not only submissive, but he wears jewelry, makeup, screams hysterically, gossips, and tends household chores. In several primitive tribes men engage in the practice of couvade, which is a ritual where a husband pretends to go through labor when his wife is about to give birth. Everyone crowds around the husband to fortify him as he sweats and groans. Meanwhile his wife is in a corner going through the real motions, practically ignored. After she had the baby she goes back to the fields to work. The baby is then placed at the side of the father who proudly displays it to visiting relatives.

The importance of Margaret Mead's work is that it shows that many of our perceptions of truth and reality are merely prejudices and inventions of our own culture. In the United States abortion is a profoundly emotional issue, but there are other cultures where it is as casually accepted as brushing teeth. We can seek to discredit these cultures by labeling them "primitive" or "uncivilized," but we should realize that such labels are also products of our own acculturation. All peoples are equal in the eyes of the universe. We have fabricated the criteria and created the game which says industrialized societies are superior to primitive societies. If mental health were the ultimate standard of merit many of the so-called uncivilized peoples would rank above our own society.

The following brief outline of abortion practices in other societies will show how universal the quest for abortion is, and the range of moral attitudes and motives surrounding it.

## Motives for Abortion in Other Cultures

Mataco: Mataco women abort the first fetus in order to make subsequent births easier.

Dahomeyan: If a pregnant woman is ill, the fetus is formally tried and if it is found guilty of having caused her illness, it is aborted in order to cure the mother.

Jivaro: The Jivaro believe demons can father monsters and there-fore abort what they anticipate will be an evil child. They believe "like father, like son." If the father has caused the tribe problems, they seek to end his hereditary line through abortion.

Purari: The women of this tribe abort simply because they are afraid of childbirth.

Chagga: Chagga women must not bear children after their daughters are married.

Uganda: In order to safeguard the senior male branch of the royal house of Uganda from competition, princesses are not permitted to marry. They lead promiscuous lives, and their pregnancies are terminated by abortion.

Samoa: Samoan girls abort to preserve their breasts.

Nukoro: When Queen Kauna of Nukoro lost her son, soon after she ordered all small boys to be killed so that her subjects would share her sorrow. Then, still not content, she ordered all pregnant women to abort.

Kadiveo: Women of the Kadiveo, a nomadic tribe, abort because they are afraid their husbands might leave them behind. This can boomerang, for sometimes a woman will become sick from the abortion and she will be left behind anyway.

Central Australia: In times of famine a woman in this region will abort to feed the fetus to the children already born.

Gilbert Islanders: The Gilbert Islanders abort because their soil is barren and cannot support a larger population.

Turkey: Turkish women abort after they have borne two children; a Turkish husband does not care to support more than two.

New Britain: Here a woman aborts in the early years of marriage so the couple can have more freedom together.

Buka: In Buka, jealous husbands require their adulterously pregnant wives to abort.

Tupinamba: Here if a mother is a prisoner of war of a cannibal tribe, she will abort to prevent her child from being eaten.

Victoria: Women of this region abort if they are angry with their husbands.

Fiji: A Fiji woman may abort to annoy her husband if she suspects infidelity.

Massawa: The Massawa father must hang his premaritally pregnant daughter because of shame.

## Techniques of Abortion in Other Cultures

The techniques to abort women in other cultures are shocking, usually highly ineffective, and sometimes very dangerous.

Aranda: Black beetles are collected by Aranda women, who roast them, reduce them to powder, and then rub the powder in their armpits and on their bellies and pubes.

Smith Sound Eskimo: Anthropological observers have characterized the abortion method of these people as "gross traumatization." The husbands will use a whip handle to smite his pregnant wife's abdomen several times a day.

Crow: The Crow employ another form of "gross traumatization." The pregnant woman reclines on the ground; a plank or platform is put across her abdomen, and then several members of the tribe pounce up and down on it until blood spurts from the vagina.

Bukaua: The Bakaua girl makes incisions on her belly, elbows, knuckles, and heels with a certain sharp grass.

Islam: Persian women have been known to place leeches on various regions of the body to drain blood out.

Masai: The Masai believe that frequent intercourse during pregnancy will induce abortion. It is said this method is popular among the men of the tribe.

Kalmuck: Hot coals are wrapped in old shoe soles and put on the girl's belly.

Pima: The Pima girl will attempt to abort by going on a near starvation diet. Another method employed by this tribe is to bury the pregnant girl up to her waist.

Ao Naga: Allegedly, a few days before birth, the woman feels for the infant's head through the abdominal wall and then strikes it sharply with a heavy stone.

Mohave: The Mohave women, so the story goes, knows how to reach inside herself and choke the baby—presumably meaning a violent manipulation of the cervix.

Menomini: The Menomini chop the tail hairs off the blacktail deer and administer it in bear fat, causing gastric irritation and thereby possibly also uterine contractions.

Navaho: The Navahos use a mule's rectum, boiled with certain plants, as a sterilizing substance. Also, goat dung is taken internally which causes nausea and vomiting.

Taulipang: The Taulipang rely on magical rites. A gourd is tossed upon a fire. If it bursts, they believe the fetus will also burst.

Arabic nomads: Foam from a camel's mouth is taken internally as an abortificient.

Miriam: The Miriam woman stands with her back against a tree while two men, holding a pole, run towards her and ram it into her abdomen.

# PART VI
# REVOLUTION IN SEX PATTERNS

*If an adult examines the Bond movies from the traditional moral-religious outlook, he most likely concludes that we are in the throes of a sexual revolution. He sees naked women, and he sees naked Bond, and he sees them both in bed. And there are children in the audience. The movie would have been considered scandalous a few decades ago.*
*Mark Gerzon*, The Whole World Is Watching
*(1969)*

# THE FALL OF
# THE VIRGIN IDEAL

## Changing Sexual Morality

The concept of sex as sin has a long and oppressive history. In part the belief was based on the ancient church doctrine of the perversity of the flesh. The central theme of this credo revolved around the morbid view that man's whole physical being was evil, and that only his soul could be pure. It depicted sexual conduct as a vile form of "giving in to the flesh." Sex was the source of original sin which cursed all succeeding generations.

The Church has had considerable influence in creating the ideal of premarital chastity, but the idea was initially born out of property considerations. Kinsey tells us: "The demand that the female be virgin at the time of her marriage was comparable to the demand that cattle or other goods he bought should be perfect . . . Our moral judgments of premarital coitus for the female are, however, still affected by this economic principle which developed among the Chaldeans and other ancient peoples, three or four thousand years ago."

In the age of the moral revolution, American society is no longer accepting the Christian dogma on sexual life—that premarital sex is wrong. French scholar Raymond Aron says: "We are still living in a society where the main religious creed is Christianity, and our private morality is primarily a revolt against Christian morality. Divorce is completely accepted, freedom of sexual intercourse between young men and young women is fully accepted. In sexuality, we are in revolt against Christianity."

The mass media have played an important role in shaping the new moral attitudes. In motion pictures premarital and in many cases extramarital sex are no longer accompanied by guilt. Try to recall a motion picture in the last twenty years where the girl has premarital intercourse and is overcome by shame. The Scarlet Letter does not exist anymore.

The greatest change in sexual morality is taking place among young women. The experts believe that teenage girls in particular seem to be less inhibited about sexual intercourse than in the past. Years ago, they say, only boys talked about sexual prowess. Now they report that college girls keep records, compare weekend affairs, even borrow birth control devices. Contraceptive pills are widely used, and some girls regard virginity as a nuisance. The incidence of venereal disease has skyrocketed in recent decades. In 1962 there were 400,000 cases reported. The number of illegitimate births has tripled since 1940. In 85 percent of all marriages in which both partners are high school students, the bride is pregnant. And in the entire fifteen-to-twenty-years age group, one bride out of four is already pregnant. All this substantiates the fact that premarital sex is more widely accepted today than it was a generation or two ago. Professor Lester Kirkendall of Oregon State University agrees: "Although the number of men who have had premarital relations is high . . . the proportion among women is rising. I think it is increasing very rapidly." Young people are breaking away from the counseling of parents and churches. They are experimenting to determine their own sexual morality.

The modern urban environment facilitates greater sexual activity. The sheer propinquity of people makes temptation almost a daily occurrence. On the subway, aboard a bus, in an elevator, one finds himself next to an attractive member of the opposite sex. For the frontier farmer, contact with people outside of his own family was very infrequent. The city also encourages sexual activity by virtue of the cover and anonymity it gives its citizens.

Harvard sociologist David Riesman, says: "Indeed the availability of girls in America is an omnipresent and inseparable part of our visual esthetic—built into the width of our ears, the reels of our movies, into the pages of our advertisements, and built into the girls themselves, I might add, in the way they carry themselves and dress."

Surveys on Sexual Freedom

Some observers believe the accounts of sexual permissiveness among the young are overblown and distorted by the media. They cite the recent Katz study (1967) of Stanford and the University of California at Berkeley students, which found that 60 percent of the males and 62 percent (Stanford) to 72 percent (Berkeley) of the females had not had sexual intercourse by the middle of their junior year. In addition the report revealed that 33 percent of the men and 25 percent of the girls did little or no dating at the end of the senior year. The new sexual revolution, this suggests, is not one of deed; the revolution is one of ideas, sexual values, and attitudes.

Other surveys, however, suggest that the sexual phase of the moral revolution is one of deed and not merely intellection. Stanford psychiatrist Donald Lunde reports that over the past twenty years there has been a substantial increase in the number of college-age women who engage in masturbation and intercourse. University of Minnesota sociologist Ira Reiss found in his survey that 40 percent of women are non-virgins by age twenty, and that 70 percent have had sex by the time they marry, which represents an astronomical increase over statistics from Grandma's day. A Gallup poll in 1970 showed that three out of four students are indifferent to virginity—or lack of it—in the person they marry. Says British gynecologist John Slore: "The kiss of the 1940s and 1950s has become the sexual intercourse of the 60s and 70s." Emancipated young women are getting rid of the notion that sex is something that men do to women.

Anthropologist George Murdock, in a worldwide survey of 250 cultures, discovered that 70 percent condone sexual freedom by the young before marriage. He says that the present trend in sexual laxity among youth, if social evolution is allowed to take its course, might be expected to produce a general social tolerance of such sex behavior in a couple of generations. On the other hand, he states that society, instead of passing through such a slow and distressing evolution, "can expedite the transition by converting a social evil into a positive social value by an act of social engineering." He argues that "lifting the taboo lessens the burden of guilt" accompanying prohibited sex behavior. In other words, premarital sex should be given society's blessings because restraint of a physical urge will frequently result in psychoneurosis. Under Christianity, repression of the sexual drive was virtue and expression evil. The neo-Freudians now say that repression is neurotic and expression healthy. Neo-Freudian psychiatry offers a new moral orthodoxy.

## Opposing Arguments

Professor Ray Baber of Pomona College rejects this reasoning. The facts do not fit such assumptions in his view. There are many physical urges which cannot be satisfied whenever desired and which must be and are controlled successfully. The view that it is a crime against oneself to deny satisfaction to any natural appetite and that anyone has the right to satisfy a natural appetite is socially fallacious. The life of men is enclosed within conditions which men never made and cannot unmake.

Other opponents of sex freedom contend that once the restraints are completely removed from sex, the quality of social life will deteriorate to gross mediocrity. All human energy will go into sex instead of creative accomplishment. Professor Unwin of Oxford, after studying eighty primitive societies, concluded that sex freedom often means social stagnation. In many societies outside the Western world, each adult member normally has sexual intercourse at least once in every twenty-four hours. Our rates are puny by comparison to the Aranda of Australia where allegedly it is not uncommon to copulate three to five times nightly; or the Thonga of Africa where it is a usual practice for a man to have sexual intercourse with each of three or four wives in one night; or the Chagga of Tanganyika where it is said that "intercourse ten times in a single night is not unusual." While such a preoccupation with sex would likely leave the individual with little energy for other pursuits, to grant sexual freedom does not necessarily or even probably mean that Americans are going to run sexually amuck. Common sense will immediately recognize one significant difference between primitive and civilized societies, which is the significantly greater number of choices in activities offered by the latter. It is not difficult to understand the frequent incidence of sex between a man and a woman staring at each other in a barren one-room hut.

Rollo May has criticized the new permissiveness as spiritually diminishing. Looking back at the Victorian Age he says we have gone from one extreme to the other, from "love without sex, to sex without love." Others see the new freedom as a spiritual gain. For the first time in thousands of years, we have sexual standards which tend to unify rather than divide men and women. For the first time, Western society is evolving sexual standards which will tend to make men and women better able to understand and live with each other.

# THE DECLINE OF CENSORSHIP

"We are in an era of revolt against censorship," says Edward Sagarin in *The Sexual Revolution*. Judge John H. Norton of Fairfield County, Connecticut observes: "There is a growing tendency in America toward the relaxation of standards of obscenity in all media of communication. . . . What was shocking twenty years ago is now dull and unexciting." Richard Gilman in the *New York Times* (1969) writes: "That we're in the presence these days of an unprecedented and steadily increasing range and intensity of public sexual expression is an observable fact . . . the distance we've come since 1930 when Dreiser's *An American Tragedy* was judicially held to be 'lewd and obscene' is quite extraordinary."

A report by the United States Senate Subcommittee to Investigate Juvenile Delinquency alleged that traffic in pornography in the 1960s increased by hundreds of millions of dollars. In 1962 the United States Post Office estimated that throughout the country there is "a five-hundred-million-dollar-a-year business in mail-order pornography alone—and the business is still growing." Large amounts of material defined by the establishment culture as immoral and outrageous are today being legally rather than surreptitiously published and distributed.

The courts, especially the Supreme Court, have steadily narrowed the legal definition of obscenity, in regard to both the written word and films, to a point where most of the prohibitions and prosecutions of earlier periods are unthinkable now. Critic Edmund Fuller comments: "Just about every possibility you can think of in sex has been boldly, frankly, and interminably explored." British critic Malcolm Muggeridge on a visit to this country in 1963 bemoaned the fact that he spent all his time trying "to dodge sex. You can't get away from it even for five minutes. Americans are balmy on sex."

Though censorship is declining, Richard Gilman says, "the thing has happened grudgingly, confined . . . to constitutional grounds, the central moral and intellectual issues never faced. The result is that protection for the erotic in art and entertainment rests on the shakiest of moral and philosophical foundations. . . ." Most judges have displayed a distinct aversion to the whole subject and have remained in entrenched moral positions even when they might be advancing legal ones. The following remarks by Pennsylvania Supreme Court Justice Michael Musmanno about *Tropic of Cancer* reflect the intransigent attitude:

"*Cancer* is not a book. It is a cesspool, an open sewer, a pit of putrefaction, a slimy gathering of all that is rotten in the debris of human depravity. And in the center of all this waste and stench, besmearing himself with its foulest defilements, splashes, leaps, cavorts, and wallows a bifurcated specimen that responds to the name of Henry Miller." To all such attacks Miller's consistent rejoinder has been as follows: "What is it that disturbs them so? Is it the existence, the prevalence of immoral, amoral, or unsocial behavior, such as is described in my works, or is it the exposure of such behavior in print?"

Some say that whatever is done today lay hidden in the repertoire of past generations, performed more covertly but not less frequently. Others insist that mores have undergone profound changes, with new attitudes being translated into new moral practices. One thing is certain: public expression pertaining to sexual matters is totally unlike what it was a few decades ago, and the indications are that the tide has not yet turned.

In the recent cornucopia of sexual expression, nudity has come to the centerfold of *Cosmopolitan*, and, on the stage, in the musicals *Hair* and *Oh! Calcutta*. Graphic description of sex in books has mushroomed. Imagine Norman Mailer having now to make his soldiers say "fug," as he did in 1948 to insure that *The Naked and the Dead* would get by? Edmund Wilson's *Memoirs of*

*Hecate County*, banned in 1945, reads like a nursery rhyme compared to the 1971 national best-seller, *The Sensuous Woman*, which is not only legally available in major bookstores but has become a subject of open discussion on television talk shows. Striptease shows in the 1940s ended with the girl in skimpy tights and pasties. The contemporary counterpart of such shows in numerous cities ends in total nudity. In Charlotte, North Carolina, the city council debating antiobscenity statutes heard a Chamber of Commerce spokesman complain that his home town, once known for its churchly atmosphere, now bore the reputation of "titty city" because of its nudie saloons. Several Los Angeles nightspots present young couples engaging in live intercourse on the stage. The more popular of these clubs invites audience participation. The city of Houston has topless shoe shine stands, topless bars, and there is talk of topless banks.

Not long ago the motion picture was regarded as the sanctuary of family entertainment. The film industry regulated itself with a strict moral code. The typical American couple was portrayed on the screen as almost sexless. They were shown either sleeping in twin beds or if in the same bed with both feet touching the floor. The code prohibited coarse language and controversial themes such as lesbianism. Moreover, the exposure of the complete male or female anatomy was completely forbidden.

Today, the trend of realism in movies recognizes no censorship boundaries. Law students at Yale recently tabulated a list of eighteen movies licensed for showing in New York. The theme in nine was listed as "illicit love," and the themes listed for the remaining nine were "illicit love and murder," "rape of a wife," "illicit love and prostitution," "rape and drugs," "bigamy," and "drugs and illicit love." In the 1970s the neighborhood theaters of America not only hosted scenes of lesbianism, group orgies, and sadomasochism, but also offered viewers the unprecedented spectacle of seeing well-known actresses such as Ann-Margret prance nude on screen.

An attempt has been made to exclude minors from sex heavy movies by the rating system. No one knows how well it has worked out, but many are skeptical, and there is one case reported where it created more harm than good. A fourteen-year-old girl asked her parents to take her to a film with them one evening, but they refused because it was rated X. After her parents left for the film, the girl invited her fourteen-year-old boy friend over who impregnated her that night.

Author Susan Sontag suggests that what many consider pornography will eventually be covered by the more respectable term, "art." And so a painter like Charles Stark, who calls his work erotic and not pornographic, has gone beyond nudes to curiously vivid drawings and oils of buttocks and genitals and predicts that several hundred years from now people will recognize and enjoy the personal quality of genitals and buttocks in art as they now do that of faces in portraits. (Miss Lee Wong, a Los Angeles doctoral candidate and part-time porno actress, told a college audience at Valley State that someday pornographic films will be beamed up at superpanoramic screens provided by clouds.)

Oregon enacted a new law in 1972 permitting the sale of pornography as long as it is not sold to minors. The *National Decency Reporter* (April 1972) reports that under the Oregon law: "There has been a tremendous increase in the number of outlets for pornographic books, magazines, and films, and even 'model studios' where men can pay to be masturbated by naked models—which, under the new criminal code, is not a crime!" In the city of Long Beach a new product has been introduced on the porno market, an inflatable female doll which is being sold to lonely servicemen for simulated intercourse.

When and where will it stop? The Silent Majority has been regrouping its forces, and the resistance is beginning to emerge. By the end of 1971 over two hundred pieces of obscenity legislation were pending in state legislatures all over the country. A brief was filed with the United States Supreme Court by a conservative group to support the Ohio Supreme Court's ruling that the motion picture *Vixen* is a public nuisance that should be abated. Courts in Los Angeles have been coming down hard with heavy sentences for obscenity violators. In one case the owner of a porno theater was sentenced to two years in the state prison. Undoubtedly, the pendulum of censorship will swing back with the recent Nixon appointments to the United States Supreme Court, but the mandates of the First Amendment guarantee of freedom of speech must still be respected. The inevitable legal response to the question of obscenity, however slow it may be coming, should be that censorship begins properly at home and in the private mind, not in the courts.

## Definitions of Obscenity

Definitions of "obscenity" and "pornography" are essential to any discussion of censorship. The problem is that, although many people and many courts have attempted to define these terms there has been very little agreement; what is clear is that people's conceptions of what is obscene vary from year to year, from place to place, and sometimes from sex to sex. In a 1972 West Virginia case, a mistrial was declared when a jury of six men and six women could not agree on whether a bottomless dance was obscene. Courtroom sources said the six men voted for acquittal and the six women for conviction.

*Webster's New Twentieth Century Dictionary* defines *obscene* as "(1) offensive to modesty and decency; (2) foul; filthy; repulsive; disgusting." It defines *pornography* as "writings, pictures intended to arouse sexual desire." *Roget's Thesaurus* lists a swarm of sixty synonyms for obscene—from common words "smut" and "ribaldry" to the exotic-sounding "fescenninity" and "coprophilia." The strongest synonyms given for *obscene* are probably "beastly," and "swinish" (one wonders why the innocent pigs get blamed for everything—as if they printed the 25,000 volumes of pornography held in custody at the Vatican). The etymology of *obscenity* is disputed and not very helpful. It is a Latin word derived possibly from "ob" (on account of) and "caenum" (filth). Havelock Ellis suggested that the word is a modification of "scena," and means literally what is "off the scene," and not normally presented on the stage of life. The term *pornography* comes from Greek and means "the writing of harlots."

Authorities in the literary world and social sciences have offered their own definitions of obscenity. D. H. Lawerence defines it "not as art which stimulates sexual desire but rather as art which contrives to make good sex ugly by excluding it and leading the observer away from sexual intercourse and toward masturbation." For Margaret Mead, obscenity is "daydream material calculated to feed the auto-erotic desires of the immature, perverted, and senile." Aldous Huxley says that "some day obscenity will be defined as motherhood." A Los Angeles judge ruling on a bottomless case declared "a nude dance is obscene if the girl dancing has an ugly body." In another bottomless case the alleged obscenity of nude dancing turned on how far apart the girls were spreading their legs during the performance. The presiding judge had a policeman get up on the stage and use a tape measure to determine the spread of a dancer's legs. Over twenty-six inches apart was considered obscene. United States Supreme Court Justice Potter Stewart, struggling with the problem of defining obscenity, has admitted that he cannot clearly put it down in words, but added the by-now classic definition: "I know it when I see it." In truth obscenity is impossible to define. It has no corresponding tangible object like nouns such as *table*, *chair*, *blackboard*, etc. It is the reaction of the human mind to a certain type of experience—both subjective and relative. A dramatic illustration of the relative nature of obscenity is the case of *Midnight Cowboy*. In most parts of the country this Academy Award-winning film was acclaimed as a brilliant artistic achievement, but in a small Texas town it was banned by the local courts as "obscene . . . vile and disgusting without any redeeming social value." D. H. Lawerence eternally capsulized the relativeness of obscenity in his remark: "What is pornography to one man is the laughter of genius to another." Obviously, the question of obscenity is not a black-and-white matter, but one involving many shades of gray. The resolution calls for as strict an examination of our present culture and morality as the words, pictures, and acts in question.

## History of Censorship

The earliest traces of what might today be defined as pornography are to be found in caves of prehistoric man. The first connection between sex and any kind of language appears to be in Egyptian hieroglyphics. One Egyptian papyrus illustrates fourteen different positions of sexual intercourse, indicating that erotic literature is not a "modern" phenomenon. Another papyrus, exhumed by Flinders Petrie, and dating back to about 1300 B.C., depicts homosexual activity between two of the gods, Horus and Set. The first evidence of extensive sexual literature was found in Greece. The Greeks produced an abundance of frank, unmistakably sensual material. Graphic illustrations of people performing sexual intercourse were common in homes and public places. On ceremonial days the populace sang erotic songs and listened to the bawdy stories recounted by poets. Greek drama frequently mirrored the lascivious and sexual, primarily because the Greeks accepted sex and all of its variations as an integral part of life without all of the negative connotations that it has in today's society. The best-known surviving example of erotic Greek drama is *Lysistrata* by Aristophanes. First performed in 411 B.C., *Lysistrata* was deemed obscene by the United States Post Office as late as 1955.

The Roman attitude toward erotica was similarly free of restraint. In the ruins of Pompeii, destroyed in A.D. 79 when Mount Vesuvius erupted, volcanic ash preserved a number of frescoes and mosaics which revealed every form of sexual intercourse in rooms fashioned for pagan orgies. (Guides will take only male tourists to these rooms. Women are not allowed to see them.) Numerous works of Roman erotica have survived to the present day. Among the most notorious are Ovid's *The Art of Love*, which in parts reads like a seduction manual, and Petronius' *Satyricon*, which

presents a blatantly hedonistic view of life. In these ancient
civilizations, censorship was aimed predominantly at political
attacks on the state. There is little evidence to suggest that any
social agency was in the slightest ruffled by public expressions of
sex, however pornographic those expressions might be. It is clear
that cultural attitudes are crucial in determining what and how
much censorship is to prevail. The Romans, free from the bonds of
puritanism, allowed great latitude in sexual matters but very little
in the way of political dissent. On the other hand, America
remains relatively uptight about the sexual currents running
through it but tolerant of political expression, largely because of
our First Amendment traditions.

The evidence of sexual material vanished, for all intents and
purposes, during the Middle Ages. The early Christian fathers,
inspired by the teachings of St. Paul, considered sex sinful. According to St. Paul, since man was conceived in Original Sin, sex
had to be inherently wicked. To promote the Christian virtue of
chastity the church went to extremes to mortify the flesh. With
religious fervor the Christians found a hundred ways to abuse their
bodies. Every stinging lash of a flogging was a small victory over
the Devil. The early Roman Christian historian Palladius described
a churchyard outside of Alexandria with three palm trees. On each
of the trees was a whip—one for the local citizens, one to punish
marauders, and one for casual passersby. The cult of flogging
continued through the Middle Ages. Krafft-Ebing relates the story
of St. Magdalene, a Carmelite nun of the sixteenth century who
pledged her life to chastity and virtue at the age of four. "It was
her greatest delight," he reports, "to have her hands bound by the
prioress behind her back, and her naked loins whipped in the
presence of the assembled sisters." As she was being beaten, she
would grow excited and then begin screaming: "Love! Love!
Enough! Fan no more the flame that consumes me. This is not the
death I long for; it comes with all too much pleasure."

Another method by which the church discouraged sexuality and
promoted chastity was to romanticize it. There grew up tales of
virtuous knights and virginal maids. Robert Irvine, in *An Illustrated History of Pornography*, writes: "This saccharine literature
was superseded by the more realistic writings of the Renaissance
which showed that what the knight really wanted to do with the
fair and beautiful maiden was rape her." This view is doubtless an
exaggeration but beneath their chivalry the knights surely had
healthy sexual inclinations. Sexual materials were not copious
during the Middle Ages, but they were in circulation and not

subject to zealous censorship. The church was more concerned with ferreting out heresy. The monks themselves wrote lewd riddles as evidenced by the *Exeter Book.*

During the Renaissance, to the dismay of the church, the printing press made possible the widespread dissemination of literature to a public which was increasingly literate. This included antichurch statements as well as works with clearly sexual overtones. One such work, Boccaccio's *Decameron*, published around 1350, may be considered the first piece of modern pornography. Geoffrey Chaucer's *Miller's Tale* written in 1388 is another Renaissance classic treating sex in a bawdy manner. A good deal of erotic writing was published in this period without restriction until 1526. At this time the Catholic Church, disturbed particularly at insults to its own membership, had a large number of books burned. In 1527 the Church issued a statement that no books could be printed or published without being approved by a special body, the Council of Ten of Venice. The edict was aimed primarily at works of heretical and seditious ideas, but a number of bawdy books were destroyed in the process. Exotic literature managed to flourish throughout the Renaissance in the capable hands of such people as Rabelais.

The upheaval of the church at the end of the Renaissance and the consequent rise to power of the Protestants effected a change in the moral atmosphere of Europe. Sensual pleasure was a primary target of the Puritans who won power in England during the English Civil War. However, when the Puritan reign of Oliver Cromwell ended and Charles II became king, stringent moral prohibitions ended and pornography once again flourished. But the Puritans had left their mark. During the Renaissance, sex and pornography were not inextricably linked to sin. Pornography resembled more closely the classical erotica which did not play upon the reader's sense of shame in order to shock. Under the reign of Charles II, pornography was specifically calculated to outrage one's sense of morality. It was a reaction against Puritanism, and in this respect is somewhat similar to pornography today.

By the early 1700s the English market was flooded with mass-produced pornographic literature. There were some prosecutions for obscenity, but for the most part authors wrote what they chose. The situation changed drastically in the late 1700s. Earlier, most of the education and all of the power resided in a sophisticated aristocracy. Toward the close of the century, with the advent of the Industrial Revolution, there emerged a large, vociferous, and newly literate middle class, which rejected the values of its old leaders and concerned itself greatly with the suppression of vice. Now that literature was available to the masses, it had to be suitable reading matter for the middle class. The Evangelicals set about substituting "good" reading matter for "bad." A new moral orthodoxy was introduced. Novels had to have a moral purpose. As the drawing room became the center of the middle-class family, books had to be sufficiently proper to lie on the drawing room table without offending the eyes of a young lady. The book became a symbol of taste and refinement.

Groups were formed to help suppress pornography, and by the mid-1800s Victorian censorship was in high gear. The Victorians did not limit their efforts to a mere self-defense against pornography. Their rabid drive to cleanse and purify literature resulted in a deep suspicion of all imaginative writing. When Thomas Bowdler censored portions of Shakespeare, his behavior was symptomatic of the era's morbid concern with human passions. Eventually, the movement reached neurotic proportions. Books by male and female authors were kept on separate shelves. Stories are told that piano legs were kept covered so as not to suggest female legs to the viewer. Even in marriage a good Victorian was not supposed to see his wife's body nude. Intercourse was carried out in the dark and, as a further precaution, the wife wore a petticoat. If she became pregnant, at the time of delivery she wore several petticoats to hide her body from the doctor.

In the United States in 1792, thirteen of the fourteen states that ratified the Constitution held that freedom of speech did not protect profanity or blasphemy. In 1842 Congress banned the importation of obscenity, and not long after placed legal sanctions on the use of the mails to convey obscene material. The first legal definition of obscenity was announced in 1868 in the famous Hicklin case. Material could be judged obscene merely by the effect of an isolated passage on a child. The standard of acceptable literature for this nation became the moral level of a child. Anthony Comstock, who founded the New York Society for the Suppression of Vice, set out to rid America of obscenity. His fanatical group suppressed everything with any imagination or mention of sex, from birth control literature to Walt Whitman's *Leaves of Grass*. Comstock personally was able to boast that he had destroyed more than 50 tons of indecent books, 28,425 pounds of printing plates, and nearly 4 million obscene pictures.

Federal customs officials banned the importation of such classics as Balzac's *Droll Stories*, the complete works of Rabelais,

Boccaccio's *Decameron*, Ovid's *Art of Love*, and Aristophanes' *Lysistrata.* The Post Office banned sex education materials. The police attempted to ban Shaw's *Mrs. Warren's Profession.* Shaw concluded that the excesses in censorship confirmed ". . . the deep-seated conviction of the Old World that America is a provincial place, a second-rate country-town civilization." Comstock countered by labeling Shaw an Irish smut peddler.

Victorianism wound down with the twentieth century. The family began to lose the place it had held in the mid-1800s. The drawing room and its reading habits were passing from existence, and a new generation of readers demanded the right to read what they liked—vice as well as virtue. Oscar Wilde said in his preface to *The Picture of Dorian Gray:* "Vice and virtue are to the artist material for his art. . . . There is no such thing as a moral or immoral book. Books are well written or badly written." Authors on both sides of the Atlantic—Frank Norris, Theodore Dreiser, Thomas Hardy, and James Joyce—broke away from the genteel tradition. They demanded the right to portray human passions.

The first major assault on the Hicklin Rule was made in 1913 in an opinion by Judge Learned Hand who said, "the rule as laid down, however consonant it may be with mid-Victorian morals, does not seem to me to answer the understanding and morality of the present. . . ." Before the pendulum could swing in the direction of a commonsense approach to obscenity cases, the censors had to reveal to the public and the courts just how far they intended to go in controlling the reading matter of a mature public.

In 1929 a censorship fever hit Boston, and when it was over sixty-eight books had been banned including such authors as Hemingway, Huxley, Lawrence, Dreiser, and Anderson. The United States Post Office added to the list Voltaire, Tolstoy, Maupassant, Dumas, Steinbeck, and Zola.

The high walls of censorship in the United States have been torn down in a span of thirty to forty years by a dozen key court decisions, especially Supreme Court decisions. The first major swipe was taken in 1933 in the *Ulysses* case, but it wasn't until the 1957 case of *U.S.* v. *Roth* that the vast bulk of legal barriers to sexual materials came crumbling down. Since *Roth*, we have seen almost a complete reversal of Victorianism. Bishop Sheen has commented that "the Victorians pretended that sex did not exist, but the moderns act as if nothing else does."

Though censorship has dramatically declined in recent decades, practices are not uniform in the United States. Censorship is complicated here because we have both federal and state judicial systems. There are federal as well as state laws governing obscenity and, in addition, there are county and city ordinances. Thus, there are hundreds of obscenity laws, administered by hundreds of law enforcement agencies and interpreted by many judicial systems. To the degree that uniformity is possible and desirable, it must come from the Supreme Court.

## Arguments For and Against Censorship

*Pro Censorship:* "The lesson should be clear to those that advocate 'freedom' for filth, smut, rebellion and a general climate of permissiveness. All these are direct stepping stones to the youthful riots and rebellion surging through our land, the spiraling rise of crime and drug addiction, the destruction of millions of dollars in properties and possessions, and the literal deaths of many of the youthful dissenters and police plus increasing numbers of innocent bystanders." Robert C. Meredith, in an article entitled "Permissiveness, Curse of Western Society" in *The Plain Truth Magazine*, is here expressing the fear of many people in the face of greater amounts of more blatant pornography being circulated in this country.

According to a recent Gallup poll, three-fourths of the American people favor tougher laws on pornography. They have a deep-rooted suspicion that the current flood of pornography is damaging our society. Their fears find scientific support in the research of Oxford Professor J. Unwin, whose extensive studies of eighty primitive and civilized societies reveal a correlation between increasing sexual freedom and social stagnation. The more sexually permissive a society becomes, Unwin contends, the less creative energy it exhibits and the slower its movement toward rationality, philosophical speculation, and advanced civilization. The noted psychoanalyst Bruno Bettelheim lends his influence to this point of view: "If a society does not taboo sex, children will grow up in relative sex freedom. But so far, history has shown that such a society cannot create culture or civilization; it remains primitive."

Paul Gebhard and his collaborators, in *Sex Offenders: An Analysis of Types*, claim pornography can be a factor in bringing some people to serious criminal acts. These writers state that of those sex offenders whose crimes included violence or duress, "between one-eighth and one-fifth reported arousal from sado-masochistic noncontact stimuli." While it is probable that in a few cases such stimuli triggered an offense, it seems reasonable to believe that they do not play an important role in the precipitation of sex offenses in general, and at most only a minor role in sex offenses involving violence. Among those most responsive to pornography were the aggressors against minors. Gebhard reports: "They seem in general a group of uninhibited young men who respond unthinkingly and violently to various stimuli. Their reaction to pornography is merely a part of their exaggerated reaction to almost everything."

Dr. Nicholas G. Frignito, chief neuropsychiatrist and medical director of the Philadelphia municipal courts, cites actual case histories which in his opinion prove that sexual arousal from "smutty" books leads to criminal behavior. In 1960 the late J. Edgar Hoover added his authority to this proposition. According to Hoover, "sex crimes and obscene vulgar literature often go hand in hand." The New York Academy of Medicine publicly announced in 1963 that reading salacious literature "encourages a morbid preoccupation with sex and interferes with the development of a healthy attitude and respect for the opposite sex." If young people are stimulated to experiment with forms of perversion before they understand their implications, traumatic experiences may occur which leave them psychologically scarred for life.

Some critics of pornography would like to see it banned on aesthetic grounds. Judicially, matters of aesthetics, taste, personal choice or preference are, at least outwardly, avoided by express disclaimers. Thousands of cases from all over the United States have arisen each year with reference to the nebulous area of aesthetics and to the notion that this is not a fit area for either the courts to dwell on or the legislatures to act upon. These cases touch all forms of human activity and enterprise and range from billboards, cemeteries, and clotheslines to zoning ordinances, junkyards, and obscenity.

This is not to say that aesthetics as a judicial or legislative devise is impotent and heedless. In the case of *City of Passaic* v. *Patterson Bill Posting Company*, the court held that: "Aesthetic considerations are a matter of luxury and indulgence rather than necessity and it is necessity alone which justifies the exercise of the police power."

However, in the more recent case of *People* v. *Stover*, the court considered a city ordinance which was clearly aimed at an individual whose method of protesting tax increases was to hang old rags on his clothesline. It was apparent that this form of protest was upsetting to the finer sensibilities of the city fathers and the court as well. For the court upheld the ordinance saying: "It is our opinion that the ordinance may be sustained as an attempt to preserve the residential appearance of the city and its property values. In other words the statute though based on aesthetic considerations proscribes conduct which offends the community and reduces real estate values." The court concluded with the comment that the defendants were not "privileged to violate (the ordinance) by choosing to express their views in the altogether bizarre manner which they did." Opponents of obscenity who consider it a blight on the social landscape would like to see the courts extend the above cause to outlaw "porno theaters, bottomless bars, smut bookshops, etc."

One of my students at UCLA argues that pornography should be suppressed simply because a majority of the population demands its suppression. She says:

> All of the major premises on which our society rests derive from the realm of intuition—the viscera. Can anyone prove that the family is a desirable institution? That higher education promotes human welfare? That technology makes men happier? That love is better than hate? That democracy is superior to dictatorship? None of these questions are subject to scientific proof. But this does not stop us from acting on our best judgment, knowing that all human judgment is fallible. If then, the regulation of pornography comes down to a matter of visceral hunches, why should not the majority of viscera prevail?
>
> Critics of censorship, are inclined to evaluate it by its failures, the banning of works of genuine merit. But it is unfair to exhibit the failures of censorship without considering the other side of the coin. If all of the loathsome materials which officials have confiscated and the law has discouraged were balanced against the mistakes, the overall results would look much less damning for censorship than many English professors would have us believe.

In 1971 a Los Angeles court introduced a new and novel assault against pornography. California courts in that year were dealing with the subject of nude dancing. The California Supreme Court has ruled that nude dancing is a form of communication. Hence, it is a form of speech and as such entitled to consideration under the First Amendment. It has further ruled that nudity per se is not obscene. Aware that in these bottomless (total nudity) cases, obscenity charges would be thrown out as unconstitutional by the

California Supreme Court, the lower court in *People* v. *Robinson* (1971) invoked the balancing doctrine. The major thrust of the balancing doctrine is that if, in any particular case, a court is presented with two or more conflicting interests, it must weigh them against one another, determine the most important interest and rule accordingly. Courts have claimed that although the state has an interest in protecting First Amendment rights of its citizens, it has the more important interest of protecting their health. In *People* v. *Robinson* the court declared that nude dancing was a health hazard because the nude body transmits germs to customers. Such reasoning is a transparent pretext for outlawing sexual behavior. If the court was seriously concerned about health, it would have outlawed cigarettes and alcohol before nude dancing, and perhaps environmental polluters before either of these.

The fact emerges that many people are afraid of sexual demonstrations. They fear that if the moral and legal restrictions imposed by society were to be loosened, civilization would degenerate into chaos. Sigmund Freud, in *Civilization and Its Discontents*, argues that the renunciation of instinctual drives is necessary to maintain civilization. If human beings gave free reign to their impulses, society would return to the bestial state of nature.

*Con Censorship:* The commission appointed by President Lyndon Johnson in 1968 to study pornography labored two years, expended $1.8 million, poured over millions of words of published data, and let more than forty research contracts. In its report, the commission claims that its investigations "do not indicate any causal relationship between exposure to or use of explicit sexual materials and such social or individual harms as crime, delinquency, sexual or nonsexual deviancy, or severe emotional disturbances." The commission recommended that adults be given legal access to pornographic materials, in part by repealing 114 state and federal laws forbidding importation, sale, and display of pornographic material for adults. The commission claimed "the right of each individual to determine for himself what books he wishes to read and what pictures or films he wishes to see." Also advocated was massive sex education programs because widespread failure to deal with the subject frankly leads to an unhealthy emphasis on sex and encourages clandestine channels of information. It also recommended that the laws should continue to protect children from exposure to sexually explicit materials. The reaction of the Nixon administration to the commission's findings, which were not made public until Johnson was long out of office, was to ignore or denounce them.

In Denmark since 1969 there has been no restriction on pornography except for purposes of protecting children and preventing blatant public displays. Up until 1967 Danish obscenity laws were quite restrictive, but Danish judges admitted that they were unable to come up with a clear-cut distinction between the obscene and the legitimately sexual. A conservative minister of justice, Knus Théstrup, appointed a committee of public officials to examine existing Danish pornography statutes. Following the committee's recommendations, in 1967 the Danish Parliament ended legal prohibition on the publication or sale of printed pornographic literature. With the legal barriers down, and no longer forbidden fruit, sales of such literature declined and there was a tremendous boom in the sales of still illegal pictorial pornography. Investigations were again made, this time by a parliamentary committee, which, after a year of public hearings, recommended that all restrictions on pornography be removed except for those on public displays and sale to children. Contrary to the fears of many, the liberalization of Danish law has not resulted in a rise in sex crimes, but has instead produced a decrease in those crimes. Psychiatrists speculating on his phenomenon contend that sex energy that before might have exploded in actual rape is now vicariously channeled off or sublimated through pornography. Many Danes feel that their country has performed a service to the world in proving that censorship is not necessary in order to prevent society from becoming barbarous and falling apart. Danish police officials are not impressed with the statistical decrease in sex crimes. They do not credit it to a lessening of antisocial impulses, but to the fact that there are less sex crimes now on the books since pornography and voyeurism are no longer offenses.

Hans Hesselund, a social psychologist at the University of Copenhagen, has praise for the decision to end censorship in his country. He claims that Danes are less afraid of sex than they used to be because they can discuss it more openly. Anne Theander, one of the top executives for Radox-Trading, a leading producer of Danish pornography, says that people were more interested in pornography when it was illegal, i.e., when it was forbidden fruit. She guesses that 10 percent of her firm's publications are purchased by Danes. The bulk of her sales are exports to taboo countries.

Another perspective is put forth by Justice Potter Stewart in his dissenting opinion in a 1966 obscenity case:

Censorship reflects a society's lack of confidence in itself. It is a hallmark of an authoritarian regime. Long ago those who wrote our First Amendment charted a different course. They believed a society can be truly strong only when it is truly free. In the realm of expression they put their faith, for better or for worse, in the enlightened choice of the people, free from the interference of a policeman's intrusive thumb or a judge's heavy hand. So it is that the Constitution protects coarse expression as well as refined, and vulgarity no less than elegance. A book worthless to me may convey something of value to my neighbor. In the free society to which our Constitution has committed us, it is for each of us to choose for himself.

Censorship in the form of attempts by individuals and groups to deny students access to books and periodicals thought to be objectionable ranks high among the many problems that beset public school teachers and officials. The problem is a national one, with attacks by amateur censors occurring in communities in every section of the nation. Individual self-appointed censors include citizens from every socio-economic level of the community.

What are the characteristics of the amateur censors? One is judgment of a book on a single aspect or episode, viewed out of context and without consideration of the intent of the complete work. Thus, Scarlet's immorality has been the basis for objections to *Gone with the Wind.* Fornication has been the grounds for protesting the availability to students of Leon Uris' *Exodus.* The liberal use of the word "goddam" in *Catcher in the Rye* has been labeled sacrilegious. Language may be alleged to be offensive because it is substandard, and students should not be exposed to "bad" or "incorrect" English. In this view, a novelist like Mark Twain has been attacked for corrupting students' language because of his use of dialect. The John Birch Society has sought to remove *Animal Farm* from school bookshelves, fearing it will incite "the masses to revolt." *A Bell for Adano* has been objected to because John Hersey is a "Russian author," and *Androcles and the Lion* because Shaw was an atheist. *Holiday* magazine has been censored by school administrators because it contains liquor ads—a librarian terminated the subscription. *Failsafe* was found objectionable because it "undermines America's confidence in its defense system." Scores of protestors sought removal of *The Ugly American* because it presented "critical pictures of Americans abroad." Objections to the jokes in *Wisconsin Engineer* were met by tearing out the jokes before placing the magazine on the racks.

In the 1960s promising approaches for alleviating the school censorship problem were put into effect. The National Council of Teachers of English published *The Students Right To Read*. The council proposed a two-step program of action by every school to meet the threat of censorship: (1) establishment of a committee of teachers to consider book selection and (2) a campaign in each community to enlist the cooperation of informed citizens in support of the freedom to read. Widely put into effect in the last decade was the reserved shelf or restricted circulation. Admittedly a compromise, the procedure at least makes the books in question accessible to the students aggressive enough to ask for them.

### Censorship and Children

One of the greatest fears of those who would like to see pornography banned, and even of those who are otherwise against censorship, is the fear that obscene material will fall into the hands of the young. We have seen this to be the case with members of the Supreme Court, with members of the President's Commission on Pornography, and also in Denmark. A somewhat typical view is expressed in *The Sex Age* by Howard Whitman who states that to those who are fairly well adjusted sexually, pornography will probably be no more than a bit unsettling. But he goes on to say, "Youth is tabula rasa. Youth's mind is clean. The possibilities of healthy mental emotional growth stretch out ahead. . . . But a youngster in his teens has the job of dealing with new, burgeoning urges which are strange to him . . . he needs all the help he can get." Even the more liberal tend to think that this "help" entails not allowing youth to see most sexual materials.

An argument is now being made by New Moralists that pornography should not be taboo to the young. They say the effect of preventing juveniles from seeing pornography is to make them want to see it more. Young people know that adults are trying to keep sex a secret from them. Keeping sex wrapped in an aura of mystery and sin, argue New Moralists, is not going to help anyone develop healthy sexual attitudes. The Danish Medical Legal-Council has stated that "it is inconceivable that coarse external influences such as pornography should be of any significance in the sexual development of children and adolescents. Conversations with sexual neurotics will almost invariably reveal that in their childhood, any mention of sexual subjects was tabooed in their homes. One gets the impression that they have been told too little about sex life and thought and that they have read too little rather than too much erotic literature." A contrary view is held by the United States Senate Subcommittee To Investigate Juvenile Delinquency, which reported that pornography dealers depend upon school children from their profits and that such pornography has been directly connected with juvenile sex offenses.

It is argued that objection to pornography is not that it deals with sex but that it deals with sex in a negative way. Pornography does in fact often present sex as something humiliating and sadistic, often something endured unwillingly by women. Simply because purveyors of such material are constantly looking for newer and greater perversities in order to sell more copy, there is justification in not wanting one's children to be confronted with material of this sort. But keeping children away from obscenity will not protect them from the negative sexual attitudes rampant in our society. When Howard Whitman says "Youth's mind is clean," he is perhaps saying that adults' minds are dirty. He is perhaps expressing the guilt of the average man about sex, the guilt that children cannot fail to miss. This is, at any rate, what a youth may assume if he is sent out of the room when sex is being discussed, or if he is commanded not to read a certain book or see a certain movie. It may be apparent to youth that their parents feel shame in connection with sex, and this general climate of sin and guilt surrounding sex is exactly the kind of climate in which pornography flourishes. These negative sexual attitudes are by no means the exclusive property of pornographers. Women can hardly be said to be more exploited by pornography than they are by frequent portrayals of them in the mass media.

Sexual maturity in the mass media is almost nonexistent, as can be seen in commercials such as those selling toothpaste by suggesting it will give our mouth sex appeal. All of us, including our children, are bombarded with these images to buy goods by virtue of sexual suggestion. What the media gives us in one sense is what we deserve for standing for it. Industry has found that sex does in fact sell their products. The media's level of sexual maturity is society's level of sexual maturity. We buy whatever they sell, be it products like beer, where the commercial tells us we can be like the virile guy on the tube; be it *Playboy* which strives so painfully to create the right image of "the man who reads *Playboy*"; or be it flavored lipstick that will have boy friends dying for a taste—we're buying what they're selling and they're selling sex.

While most of us may be agreed that the consciousness of

children ought not to be subjected to what it isn't prepared to deal with, viz., pornography, we should not organize our society's moral system on the basis of what only applies to children. We have to be allowed our adulthood with all its risks. Sexuality is a risk, and so is sexual expression. Restrict what children can choose to see, restrict also flagrant pornographic displays as Denmark has, but give adults the responsibility to choose for themselves. More than three hundred years ago Milton's *Areopagitica* enunciated this eternal point against censorship. "For those actions which enter into a man rather than issue out of him, God uses not to captivate under a general prescription, but trusts him with the gift of reason to be his own chooser."

## Supreme Court and Censorship

The way in which the United States Supreme Court becomes involved with censorship is through the First Amendment of the Constitution which says that Congress shall make no law abridging the freedom of speech. The Constitution says nothing about what the states can or cannot do in respect to this question, but in 1925 in *Gitlow* v. *New York* the Supreme Court held that the due process clause of the Fourteenth Amendment incorporated the First Amendment. Hence, it prohibits the states from making any law which abridges freedom of speech. The Court did, however, qualify its statement. Freedom of speech, it declared, is not an absolute right to speak or publish whatever one chooses. As Justice Holmes put it in *Schenck* v. *United States*, "The most stringent protection of free speech would not protect a man in falsely shouting fire in a theater and causing panic." Free speech is a relative right in the sense that it is limited by the coexistence of rights of others, and the needs and demands of national security.

In 1933 a federal court ruled that James Joyce's *Ulysses* was not obscene. The court established guidelines for censorship. The guidelines were: (1) only the dominant effect of a book is of concern in judging whether it is obscene; (2) concern is only with its effect on an average reader; (3) the purpose of the author must be taken into consideration; (4) the court must consider literary and artistic merit of a work in question; and (5) testimony by literary critics is admissible as evidence. This decision had limited effect as it was made by a lower federal court, but in ensuing years the Supreme Court came to adopt several of its principles.

In 1942 in *Chaplinsky* v. *New Hampshire* the Supreme Court held "there are well-defined and narrowly limited classes of speech the prevention and punishment of which have never been thought to raise any Constitutional problem. These include the lewd and obscene . . . It has been well observed that such utterances are no essential part of any exposition of ideas and are of such slight social value as a step to truth that any benefit that may be derived from them is clearly outweighed by the social interest in order and morality."

Justice Brennan in 1957, when he delivered the opinion of the Court in *Roth* v. *United States*, said that in light of previous American legal history it "is apparent that the unconditional phrasing of the First Amendment was not intended to protect every utterance." He also remarked that "All ideas having even the slightest redeeming social importance—unorthodox ideas, controversial ideas, even ideas hateful to the prevailing climate of opinion have the full protection of the guaranties. . . . But implicit in the history of the First Amendment is the rejection of obscenity as utterly without redeeming social importance."

But what about the question of what was obscene? It was necessary for the Court to find a legal test which would supplant the Hicklin test for obscenity, and which would fully protect the right to deal with sexual subjects. The test offered by the majority was "whether to the average person, applying contemporary community standards, the dominant theme of the material taken as a whole appeals to prurient interests." The improvements in this standard over Hicklin are obvious. It is the average person, not the susceptible person, whose morals are to be protected, and it is the dominant theme of the material taken as a whole as the basis for judgment, not isolated passages.

Justice Black and Justice Douglas both dissented and in the dissent written by Douglas he stated that, "when we sustain these convictions, we made the legality of a publication turn on the purity of thought which a book instills in the mind of the reader. I do not think we can approve that standard and be faithful to the command of the First Amendment. I reject too the implication that problems of freedom of speech and of the press are to be resolved by weighing against the values of free expression, the judgment of the court that a particular form of that expression has 'no redeeming social importance.' The First Amendment, its prohibition in terms absolute, was designed to preclude courts as well as legislatures from weighing the values of speech against silence. The First Amendment put free speech in the preferred position."

The presence on the Supreme Court of such conflicting opinions is illustrative of the general disagreement on the obscenity question. It also shows the court as being overall less hostile toward pornography than one might guess from reading only the majority opinion. The more "liberal" line of the minority was to some degree taken up in the cases which followed *Roth*. Although *Roth* had held obscenity to be prosecutable, it was still unclear as to what exactly constituted obscenity. From 1957 to 1960 the Court showed that it held the category of obscenity to be a narrow one, and it cited *Roth* in a number of cases where it reversed lower court decisions that had found publications obscene.

In 1959 the Supreme Court reversed the court of appeals of the State of New York decision in *Kingsley International Pictures Corp.* v. *Regents.* Here the Supreme Court made the distinction between obscene works and works which portray an idea hostile to conventional morality. The state of New York had refused a license to the film *Lady Chatterley's Lover* because it depicted adultery as a suitable form of behavior under certain circumstances. Justice Stewart stated in his opinion "the First Amendment's basic guarantee is of freedom to advocate ideas. The state, quite simply, has thus struck at the very heart of constitutionally protected liberty." Thus, the lower courts were overruled.

The next important step in limiting the obscenity concept, and thus decreasing the scope of censorship, was taken in *Manual Enterprises, Inc.* v. *Day* (1962), where Justice Harlan writing for the Court added another requirement. Not only did the matter in question have to appeal to "prurient interests," it also had to be of "patent offensiveness." On the basis of the patent offensiveness test, Harlan absolved *Manual* magazine of obscenity charges which were based on the fact that it contained photos intended to appeal to male homosexuals.

A third requirement, likewise narrowing the application of obscenity, and thereby reducing still further the scope of censorship, was put forth by Justice Brennan in *Jacobellis* v. *Ohio* (1964). In reversing a conviction for possessing and exhibiting an obscene film, Brennan announced that the film was not obscene within the terms enunciated in *Roth* v. *United States.* Building on a statement in the Roth case, he said obscenity is "utterly without redeeming social importance." If it is true that obscenity is "utterly without redeeming social importance," then it must be equally true that anything with redeeming social importance cannot be obscene.

The Court also rejected the argument that the "community standard" test of the Roth case meant that the film could be adjudged obscene on the basis of the standards of the community in which the film was exhibited. Instead, it stated that "the constitutional status on an allegedly obscene work must be determined on the basis of a national standard. It is, after all, a national constitution we are expounding." In the concurring opinion of Justices Black and Douglas it was stated that the reason for their advocation of reversal of the conviction was that they felt censorship to be in violation of the First Amendment right of free speech. Here again they enunciated what they had previously in their dissenting opinion of *Roth*. Justice Stewart's concurring opinion brought out the universal difficulty in defining obscenity. He said prosecutions should be limited to "hard-core pornography" and he added, "I shall not today attempt further to define the kinds of material I understand to be embraced within that short-hand description; and perhaps I could never succeed in intelligibly doing so. But I know it when I see it, and the motion picture involved in this case is not that."

The opinion of two or three dissenting justices further shows the complexity of the problem. Despite the fact that the opinion of the Court written by Brennan claimed to have found the film not obscene under the standard of the Roth case, Warren's dissent implies accusation of the majority over throwing out the Roth decision. Warren also argues that "community standards" means just that and not a national standard as claimed in Brennan's opinion.

In 1966 in the Fanny Hill case the Supreme Court integrated the principles espoused in the *Roth* line of cases. Justice Brennan wrote: "We defined obscenity (in *Roth* v. *United States*) in the following terms: 'Whether to the average person, applying contemporary community standards, the dominant theme of the material taken as a whole appeals to prurient interest.'" Under this definition, as elaborated in subsequent cases, three elements must coalesce; it must be established that (a) the dominant theme of the material taken as a whole appeals to a prurient interest in sex; (b) the material is patently offensive because it affronts community standards relating to the description or representation of sexual matters; and (c) the material is utterly without redeeming social value. The Supreme Court reversed a lower court decision in Fanny Hill as obscene by saying the lower court had misconstrued the *Roth* requirement of "redeeming social value" as reading requiring more than minimal social value, when in fact for a work to be obscene it had to be "utterly without redeeming social importance."

In 1966 in *Ginzberg* v. *United States*, the Supreme Court upheld a conviction of Ralph Ginzberg for mailing obscene material. What was different about this case was that the court did not claim the works to be utterly without social value. Instead it claimed that though the publications were not obscene in and of themselves, they were advertised in such a way as to appeal to the prurient interests of the prospective reader. The majority opinion stated: "The deliberate representation of petitioner's publications as erotically arousing, for example, stimulated the reader to accept them as prurient; he looks for titillation, not for saving intellectual content . . . and the circumstances of presentation and dissemination of material are equally relevant to determining whether social importance claimed for material in the courtroom was, in the circumstances, pretense or reality—whether it was the basis upon which it was traded in the marketplace or a spurious claim for litigation purposes."

Four of the justices dissented, including Justice Black who stated what may well have been the opinion of a good many other people in this country: "I think that the criteria declared by a majority of the court today as guidelines for a court or jury to determine whether Ginzberg or anyone else be punished as a common criminal for publishing or circulating obscene material are so vague and meaningless that they practically leave the fate of a person charged with violating censorship statutes to the unabridled discretions, whim and caprice of the judge or jury who tries him." Ginzberg had no way of knowing that otherwise unobscene material could be judged obscene because of his unorthodox methods.

The Supreme Court in 1968 (in *Ginzberg* v. *New York*) held that it is constitutional to accord minors under seventeen a more restricted right than that assured to adults by preventing them from purchasing material which is not considered to be obscene for adults. The majority opinion said that "the State has an independent interest in the well-being of its youth . . . an interest to protect the welfare of children" and to see that they are "safeguarded from abuses which might prevent their growth into free and independent well-developed men and citizens." The magazines which it was feared might inhibit this "growth" merely depicted uncovered female breasts and buttocks. In 1969 the Supreme Court without overruling the Roth case, held that under the First Amendment a man has a right to possess and read any obscene literature in his home.

The opinions of the Supreme Court have fluctuated somewhat

with the compositions of its members. With four conservative Nixon appointees it may be argued that pornography will be given a more difficult time in the future. However, the entire country has become more sophisticated over the years and one wonders whether the Court will feel the need to institute new and more stringent controls. There may be growing sympathy on the court with the position of Justice Harlan who favors giving local communities discretionary power to decide what is obscene. But some such as Brennan fear provincial extremism would ban many valid works of art as in the case of a Texas town that banned *Midnight Cowboy* as utterly without redeeming social value.

*Cohen* v. *California* dealt with the use of four-letter words in public places. Cohen had the words "Fuck the Draft" on the back of his Levi jacket. He was arrested for disturbing the peace and "offensive conduct." This case made a plain distinction between cases such as Cohen and those involving "erotica." Since this case is plainly not an "obscenity" case it is within the protections of the First and Fourteenth Amendments. The Court makes several comments about situations where one is confronted with socially unacceptable, but legal, speech: (1) ". . . so long as the means are peaceful, the communication need not meet the standards of acceptability"; (2) ". . . we are often captives outside the sanctuary of the home and subject to objectionable speech"; (3) ". . . if the particular word is not directed toward a particular 'hearer.' " (This is because the state does have the power to ban "fighting words" which are likely to provoke a violent reaction.)

## Censorship in Other Lands

Margaret Mead has commented that "every known human society exercises some explicit censorship over behavior relating to the human body especially as the behavior involves or may involve sex." The nations with the most stringent censorship controls are the newly developing Asian and African states and the communist bloc. It has been speculated that a young nation in the process of industrializing seeks to channel all energy into this task. It was during the Industrial Revolution in England that the Protestant ethic made a virtue out of hard work and a cardinal sin out of sex.

Denmark: On July 1, 1969, all legal restraints on pictorial pornography were removed. In October of that year the Danes held a "Pornography Fair," which was the greatest assemblage of sexual material ever displayed.

Italy: The Italian constitution deems "all which according to public sentiment offends public morals" to be obscene and censorable. This is evidently interpreted quite liberally if one is to judge from the great number of pornographic films made in Italy.

Great Britain: As in the United States, British censorship has loosened up over the past few decades. The Hicklin Rule, still in effect, is very liberally enforced. In 1959 in the Obscenity Publications Act, literary and educational value were made legal defenses against the charge of obscenity.

Germany: According to a social psychologist recently retained by the West German government, that country will be the next to remove all legal bars to pornography. At this point censors in that country are being circumvented in part by the use of educational formats to provide a defense to charges of obscenity, as they did in the case of the film *Helga*.

Belgium: Censorship of films has never existed for adults. The law regulates only what children may be allowed to view.

India: Kissing is permitted on the screen only if it is crucial to the story; in every other instance kissing is prohibited. Censorship of sex materials is exceedingly strict.

Sweden: Censorship is more directed at scenes of violence and killing than sex. If portions of a film are expurgated, it will be more often because of objectionable violence than frank sexuality.

Soviet Union: The state places a heavy lid on sex material. Censorship is rampant and severe.

# HOMOSEXUALS "OUT OF THE CLOSET"

## Homosexual Revolution

It would be a gross misrepresentation to contend that the American homosexual is on the threshold of social acceptance. The truth is that forty-five states still outlaw the private, adult consensual acts of homosexuals; that in seven states life imprisonment is the maximum penalty for such acts; and that in thirty-five states the maximum sentence is at least ten years. During debate, Sir Cyril Osborne, Conservative member of Parliament, thundered: "I am rather tired of democracy being made safe for the pimps, the prostitutes, the spivs, the pansies, and now, the queers." In England he may have spoken for a minority (a 1967 Gallup poll in England showed 60 percent of those polled favored homosexual law reform), but he probably mirrors a majority of American opinion, though most would not be as vitriolic.

But the trend is clear. Opposition to homosexual law reform is noticeably declining. The majority of European nations have legalized homosexual acts between consenting adults. Since 1961 five states in American have done the same. Britain's Wolfenden Report in 1957 reflects a widening attitude on the issue. A government committee headed by Sir John Wolfenden said at the conclusion of a three-year study of homosexuality: "We do not think that it is proper for the law to concern itself with what a man does in private unless it can be shown to be so contrary to the public good that the law ought to intervene." The committee recommended that homosexual behavior between consenting adults no longer be considered a criminal offense. A similar recommendation has been included in the American Law Institute's Model Penal Code.

But the true progress of the homosexual movement cannot be solely measured by statutory changes, although these changes are the primary goals. Equally important at this time are developments within the churches and within the homophile organizations themselves. The churches are especially important because much of the hostility directed toward homosexuals is the product of religious dogma which brands it sinful. Therefore, if the revolution of the homosexual is to prevail, it must reach the churches. This it seems to be doing.

The Methodist Conference and the Congregational Union have endorsed the conclusions of the Wolfenden Report, and a meeting of Episcopal clergymen concluded publicly that homosexuality might, under certain circumstances, be adjudged "good." In 1971, the Reverend Troy Perry, a Pentecostal preacher based in Los Angeles, created a national federation of churches for male and female homosexuals. Called the Universal Fellowship of Metropolitan Community Churches, the nation's newest denomination claims a total membership of three thousand. The Reverend Perry has performed dozens of marriage services for homosexuals. California law recognizes all marriages between partners who can show a certificate from an ordained minister proving that their marriage has been solemnized in a church ceremony. This law does not stipulate that the partners must be a man and a woman, only a "husband" and a "wife."

As to homophile organizations themselves, they are not only existent and growing, but are becoming more vocal and aggressive. There are presently at least forty such organizations in this country. They are no longer content to provide social services and mutual consolation; they are evolving into political action and propaganda agencies. Homophile organizations have picketed the State Department, Pentagon, White House, and Independence Hall. In fact, picketing Independence Hall has become an annual affair. A survey taken by and of the Florida Mattachine Society, a homophile organization, indicated 82 percent of those questioned favored public picketing by homosexuals. On the campuses of

Cornell, Columbia, Stanford, and New York University, among others, accredited homophile organizations have been formed for students. In 1968 the New School for Social Research inaugurated a full semester course entitled "Understanding the Homosexual."

The media have vigorously assisted the homosexual movement. In 1968 a New York station WBAI ran a sixteen-program series on the subject of homosexuals. National magazines such as *Life* and *Time* have carried major articles on the homosexual movement. The stage and film have focused on the homosexual in such works as *A Taste of Honey*, *The Boys in the Band*, and *The Killing of Sister George*. Even major television variety shows feel free now to tell homosexual jokes, which is a sign of growing public tolerance.

Attitudes of law enforcement officers and prosecutors yield further evidence of a new tolerance toward homosexuality. There is an unmistakable tendency today to allow homosexuals to plead guilty to a lesser charge than that for which they were arrested. Moreover, when they are convicted of a homosexual offense, the courts now tend to sentence leniently. The United States Supreme Court has facilitated the creation and distribution of homosexual materials by ruling that male nudes are not, ipso facto, obscene. These developments reinforce the conclusion that we are living in an age of moral revolution.

## Statistical Survey of Homosexual Activity

Estimates on the number of homosexuals in the United States have ranged from one to six million, with the majority estimate around two million. Kinsey, in his 1948 research on the homosexual male, taking as his standard "physical contact to the point of orgasm," concluded that 37 percent of the male population of the United States had had some homosexual experience between the beginning of adolescence and old age; 25 percent of the male population had had more than incidental homosexual experience or reactions for at least three years between the ages of sixteen and fifty-five; 10 percent of the males were more or less exclusively homosexual for at least three years between the ages of sixteen and fifty-five; 8 percent of the males were exclusively homosexual for at least three years within these age limits; and 4 percent of them were exclusively homosexual throughout their lives after the onset of adolescence. Kinsey's figures are accepted as relatively accurate, and, in the absence of any other statistical research, he is quoted frequently; however, there are social scientists. who have taken issue with his methods of selecting random samples.

Kinsey reached a number of conclusions regarding the homosexual population. He found that homosexual activity occurs in every level of society. Other factors being equal, rural groups are less inclined toward homosexuality than urban groups. There is less homosexual activity among highly religious groups such as devout Catholics, Orthodox Jews and religious Protestants, and homosexual activity is less prevalent among women than men. According to Kinsey homosexual responses "had occurred in about half as many females as males, and contacts which had proceeded to orgasm had occurred in about a third as many females as males. Moreover, compared with males, there were only about a half to a third as many of the females who were, in any age period, primarily or exclusively homosexual. . . ."

### On the Causes of Homosexuality

Not many social scientists have ventured to explain why there is less homosexuality among women than men. Women who prefer not to have intimate relations with the opposite sex often become frigid and marry despite their frigidity, or else remain celibate; males who prefer not to have sexual relations with women more often become homosexuals.

Some psychiatrists believe that there is more male homosexuality because the male role in American society is particularly demanding. Pressure to conform with the masculine ideal may cause severe difficulties, particularly in young boys. The male child is expected to restrict his activities to "masculine" pastimes when he is only in kindergarten, whereas a girl may assume the female role less hurriedly. Parents expect their little girls to engage in male activities. Girls are allowed to play ball or cowboys, but parents are usually upset if their sons want to play with dolls. Pressure from parents and others often causes boys to fear being caught engaging in any activity that could possibly be construed as unmanly, and this pressure sometimes leads boys to develop a hostility toward anything feminine including females themselves.

The causes of homosexuality however, have been the subject of extremely divergent opinion. There was a time when homosexuality was thought to be the result of excessive debauchery, a predisposition activated by onanistic practices, the placement of a male soul in a female body, or vice versa. Later some ascribed it to a congenital abnormality, and still others believed it to be the result of a physiological imperfection such as hormonal imbalance; but most contemporary opinion on the subject considers homosexuality to be psychologically induced. Freud was among the first to focus on the sexual life of the infant as a prime determinant in the orientation of the sex drive in a homosexual direction. He claimed that all people are born with a sexual duality: the capacity to experience pleasure homosexually or heterosexually, and that only through training and identifying with one's own sex does one learn to repress all but the culturally acceptable modes of expression. He attributed failure of some people to make this heterosexual adjustment to an inability to resolve the Oedipus Complex.

Contemporary psychiatrists like Dr. Clara Thompson recognize homosexuality as a sympton of more general personality difficulties, instead of being the basic problem in a given case. It is but one of the manifestations of a character problem and tends to disappear when the more general character disturbance is resolved. Many psychiatrists claim that there is no particular situation where homosexuality always occurs. It is a symptom found in people of diverse types with diverse difficulties. It may express such differing problems as fear of the opposite sex, extreme guilt feelings toward sex acquired from parents, a need to defy authority, an inability to accept adult responsibility, an inability to cope with competition with one's own sex, a tendency toward destructiveness toward oneself or others, a diminished capacity for meaningful relationships with others, or it may be an expression of one's feelings of worthlessness.

People who have been intimidated or who are lacking in self-confidence, and thus have difficulties in dealing with others, often find themselves more comfortable with members of their own sex. A person's own sex is less frightening because it is familiar. Homosexuality appeals to people who fear intimacy with others and yet are afraid of loneliness. Homosexual relations often look less permanent, less entrapping, as if one could more easily escape when and if one chooses. People are also influenced by the fact that relationships with the other sex often make greater demands. Men are expected to support women, and women are expected to have children. People lacking in self-confidence may fear an inability to attract members of the opposite sex. Any of the above conditions may lead to homosexuality, yet millions of people with similar problems manage to marry and lead heterosexual lives. Why some do and some do not is largely a matter of speculation.

Psychiatrists tend to see homosexuality in one of two ways. Either they view it as a disease that must be "cured," or they feel that the therapist should determine on the basis of the patient's feelings about himself whether he should be helped to accept himself and adjust to being a homosexual, or whether an attempt should be made to lead the patient in a heterosexual direction.

The chief proponent of the view that homosexuality is a disease is psychoanalyst Irving Bieber. Central to his school of thought is the characteristic homosexual-producing mother, who is overly intimate with her son. This mother is very much afraid of losing her son and so is extremely possessive, resulting, according to Bieber, in a demasculinization of the child. The mother favors this particular son over the other children, even over the husband, encouraging an alliance against the father, thus further alienating the son from masculine identification. The mother is often frigid, yet her closeness stimulates the son, who suffers conflicting feelings of arousal and guilt. In Bieber's view this feeling later leads to the child's difficulty in responding to other women and is mainly due to an unconscious attempt on the part of the mother to extinguish her son's heterosexuality to thus prevent losing him to other women.

Comparing the case histories of 106 male homosexuals and 100 heterosexuals under psychoanalysis, Bieber concludes homosexuality is a disease. The flagrant shortcoming in his work is the fact that every homosexual in his study had been under psychiatric care. Therefore, it seems quite natural that he would find these persons exhibiting symptoms of mental illness. In response to Bieber's study, psychoanalyst Earnest van der Haag sneered, "I am reminded of a colleague who reiterated 'all my homosexual patients are quite sick'—to which I finally replied 'so are all my heterosexual patients . . .' "

Dr. Evelyn Hooker, one of the leading scientific authorities on homosexuality, in her own examination of a group of thirty homosexuals, found no obvious differences in general psychological adjustment from her control group of thirty heterosexuals. She claims, "homosexuals may be very ordinary individuals indistinguishable, except in sexual pattern, from ordinary individuals that are heterosexual or . . . that some may be quite superior individuals not only devoid of pathology, but also functioning at a superior level." She also criticizes Bieber's work as inadequate due to his selection of a test group drawn entirely from a patient population.

## Sexual Roles and Society

More and more men in the therapist's office voice the fear of homosexuality in themselves or in their sons. Myron Brenton, author of *The American Male,* claims a great many neuroses in males are the result of an inability to meet role expectations, often without loss of potency but always with "fear, hostility and flight from the female." There is no way of ascertaining whether the incidence of homosexuality is on the rise, but many authorities insist it is, and it seems a reasonable assumption in view of the threat posed by the shifting relationship between the sexes, the increased economic and psychological demands on family men, the heightened sexual competitiveness existing in our culture, and the other anxiety-provoking aspects of modern life—all of which act to precipitate a flight from women by men so predisposed. There is also the problem American men have in trying to reconcile the sedentary, overrefined present, which is marked by an extreme lack of physical challenges, with the age-old image of the male as hunter, builder, warrior, hewer of wood—a male who, in short, establishes a primitive contact between himself and his surroundings. Equally stressing is the problem of reconciling the democratic present, with its emphasis on equal rights for women with the age-old image of the male as provider, protector, and possessor—a male who, in short, is given unquestioned sanction to exercise his patriarchal duties and prerogatives.

In America the association of money and sexual potency has become notorious. The man who is not an economic success finds it increasingly difficult to retain self-confidence. Dr. Abram Kardiner, Professor of Psychiatry at Columbia University observes that "In a society where there is freedom of mobility in the social scale, the attainment of success has become more obligatory while the ability to make plans and fulfill expectations has become more difficult and uncertain." Between the changing role of the woman and the uncertainties of reaching preconceived goals, the male has lost some of his prestige and confidence in his ability to meet the roles of husband and father.

According to Kardiner, hatred of females is a constant concomitant of social stress. He contends that "Homosexuality is part of the price exacted by the pressures of Western civilization today and it cannot be treated as a local excrescence."

There seems to be a tremendous amount of irrational hatred directed against homosexuals. Some people appear to be threatened by the mere fact that homosexuality exists. Psychiatrists sometimes attribute this to the fact that, consciously or unconsciously, such people fear sexual inadequacy in themselves. The advertising media, quick to note our weaknesses, actually exploits fear of homosexuality to sell everything from shaving cream to cigarettes. The media always seems to be asking: "Are you man enough for our product?" Or, "Are you sure you aren't homosexual?"

An example of the irrational fear engendered in some people by homosexuality can be seen in the case of Dr. Carl McIntire, president of the International Council of Christian Churches. McIntire, in speaking about a small community called Alpine County where a large number of homosexuals wanted to move in order to become a voting majority, said that Alpine County could well become America's first Communist county.

In considering the case of Dr. McIntire and the cases of others who consider their objection to homosexuality to be its immorality, one should take into account the words of W. T. Stace in his *Concept of Morals:*

> I should maintain that sexual perversion is not, as such, immoral. In itself it has nothing to do with ethics, and is not a moral problem at all. Why, then, has it been thought immoral? The answer is that this is a perfect illustration of the principle that the popular consciousness tends to label as immoral anything which it deeply dislikes, although the grounds of its dislike may have nothing whatever to do with morality. It is a perfect example of the confusion of moral aversion with other kinds of aversion.

Any extreme human abnormality, whether physical or mental, tends to cause feelings of disgust in normal observers. The sight of a withered limb is to many people so repulsive that they have difficulty in forcing themselves to associate freely with the victim of the limb. And to persons of normal sexual appetites the very thought of homosexuality is loathsome. For Stace what is involved in society's aversion to homosexuality is nothing more than physical disgust. It is not in kind fundamentally different from nausea. "This physical disgust is mistaken by most people for moral repulsion."

The Civil Service Commission in its *Manual of Regulations* states that "immoral conduct" is a reason for disqualification. It defines immoral conduct as "action not within the sphere of conformity with the generally accepted standards of the community." Thus, homosexuals are excluded from employment by the federal government. Congress also decided in the 1950s that servicemen who were found to be homosexuals were not entitled to the privileges of other veterans. No G.I. rights to education, housing, loans, or other benefits are available to homosexuals.

Huey Newton, leader of the Black Panthers, once said, "I know through reading and through my life experience that homosexuals are not given freedom and liberty by anyone in this society. They might be the most oppressed people in the society." This is quite a statement, coming from Huey Newton!

## History of Western Law and Morals on Homosexuality

The contemporary immoral and illegal status of homosexual acts can be traced back to the Old and New Testaments. Scholars like to cite the Lot story in Genesis as being responsible for traditional abhorrence of homosexual conduct. The conventional interpretation of the story is that the men of Sodom demanded intercourse with the two angels who were guests of Lot, and that the city was destroyed for this attempted sacrilege. Besides this mention in Genesis, homosexual acts are condemned in Leviticus: "Thou shalt not lie with mankind, as with womankind, it is abomination." (Lev. 18:22)

Leviticus prescribed death by stoning as punishment for such transgressions; however, there is no evidence that this penalty was ever imposed. One interesting fact is that female homosexuality was barely punished. Women who engaged in such practices were simply not allowed to marry priests.

In the New Testament the most unequivocal and best-known condemnation of homosexual practice is made by St. Paul in his Epistle to Romans. Referring to the sins of the heathen he wrote, ". . . and likewise also the men, leaving the natural use of the woman, burned in their lust one toward another; men with men working that which is unseemly, and receiving in themselves that recompense of their error which was meet." (Rom. 1:26-27).

Tertullian in the Epistle of Jude denounces homosexuality, not as a sin, but as a monstrosity. St. Augustine in his Confessions declared that the sins which are against nature, "like those of the men of Sodom, are in all times and places to be detested and punished. Even if all nations committed such sins, they should all alike be held guilty by God's law which did not make men so that they should use each other thus. The friendship which should be between God and us is violated when nature—whose author He is—is polluted by so perverted a lust."

Denunciations such as the aforementioned naturally influenced ecclesiastical law and also the secular law when the Roman Empire became Christian. It should be noted, however, that laws punishing homosexuality had been in existence for years, though they were simply not enforced under the pagan empire, where homosexuality was widely practiced.

Church councils and synods imposed extreme penalties on sodomists. In 314 the Council of Ancyra passed two canons condemning homosexual practices and prescribing the death penalty. In 650 the king of Spain outlawed sodomy and ordered castration as punishment. In 693 the Council of Toledo ordered whipping and banishment as penalties for homosexual acts and to these, castration was later added by royal order.

During the Middle Ages clerics claimed homosexual acts were contrary to reason and the natural order of things. St. Thomas indicated that the purpose of sex is to provide children, and homosexuality frustrates this purpose. By perverting the purpose of procreation, the homosexual was violating the moral order.

Early English legal treatises prescribe various punishments for homosexual conduct. Fleta, dating from 1290, suggests burying alive and another treatise written soon after suggests burning. In 1533 in the preamble to the sodomy statute of Henry VIII, it was claimed that there was not yet sufficient punishment for the forbidden acts. Apparently the ecclesiastical courts were not enforcing their responsibility for dealing with sodomy. Eventually Henry transferred to his own royal judiciary the power of punishing homosexual offenders. Henry's law remained on the books for about 275 years, although it appears to have been sporadically enforced. English legal scholars deplored the law's inconsistency in punishing sodomists. Lord Coke denounced sodomy as a "detestable and abominable sin . . . and one of the sins crying out to heaven for vengeance." Until around 1830, most of those who were convicted of sodomy were hanged. Not until 1861 was the death penalty abolished and replaced by a term of servitude from ten years to life.

The Criminal Law Amendment Act passed in England in 1885 provided that any male person, guilty of committing or procuring or attempting to procure an act of gross indecency with another male in public or private, would be guilty of a disdemeanor punishable with a maximum term of two years in prison with or without hard labor. The House of Lords rejected a bill in 1921 that would have made female homosexual acts illegal. In 1954 a parliamentary committee was appointed to be chaired by Sir John Wolfenden to study the problem of homosexuality. The report was published in 1957 but was not discussed by Parliament until three years later; at that time the committee's recommendation that homosexual acts between consenting adults in private be legalized was rejected.

However, ten years after the publication of the recommendations of the Wolfenden Report, Parliament repealed, in the Sexual
Offenses Act of 1967, all criminal penalties for homosexual acts
committed in private by consenting adults. The committee had
considered the reasons why some felt that such acts should be
forbidden by the state. Some of these reasons were that homosexuality deprives society of children, that homosexuality creates
nervous undependable persons, that it menaces the health of
society, that it threatens the family, and that homosexuals may
molest minors. The committee answered these objections to
legalized consensual adult homosexuality by claiming that society
didn't need children but rather was threatened by overpopulation.
It said that homosexuals were nervous only because the law made
them so. The committee also said that homosexuality threatened
the family no more than adultery, premarital sex, or prostitution
(all of which are legal in England). And it also said that by
allowing consenting adults to engage in homosexual acts it would
discourage overtures to minors because that alone would remain
illegal.

The majority of European countries do not punish homosexual
acts between consenting adults. Only Germany and Austria punish
such offenses. In Norway, though homosexual behavior is tech-
nically illegal, the law is not enforced. In England, Denmark,
Sweden, France, Italy, Spain, Greece, Switzerland, and the Netherlands, homosexual acts between consenting adults is not illegal.

American law derives directly from English law (but we have
not in recent years followed in the steps of England by removing
criminal sanctions from adult homosexual activity). However,
under English law a clearly graded order of penalties existed for
homosexual offenses, with sodomy receiving the harshest
penalties. American law is much less uniform with penalties
varying greatly from state to state. In California sodomy is an
"infamous crime against nature" under penal code section 286 and
is a felony punishable by not less than one year in prison. Lesbian
acts are illegal but are never prosecuted. Solicitation of anyone in
a public place to engage in lewd conduct is a misdemeanor under
California penal code section 647, and is the provision most often
invoked against homosexuals.

In recent years there has been some change in this country in
the direction of liberalization of statutes dealing with homosexuality. Illinois in 1961 legalized private consensual homosexual
acts between adults. Four years later North Carolina eliminated a
punishment of not less than five nor more than sixty years and
substituted a fine or imprisonment to be left to the discretion of

the court. The following year, 1966, New York attempted to do the same thing but at the last minute the bill was amended and consensual adult homosexual activity became a misdemeanor, In 1969 Connecticut made legal consensual adult homosexual acts. Other states such as Colorado have reduced the maximum penalty from life to fourteen years.

The American Law Institute in its Model Penal Code recommended that private consensual homosexual acts between adults be legalized. Its reasons were very similar to those of the Wolfenden Committee: lack of harm to the community, inability to enforce the criminal law, opportunities created for blackmail, unsuitability of prison for offenders, undue strain on limited police resources, and the undesirability of encroachment of the law into the private lives of the community.

When research for the Wolfenden report was being done the opinions of various religious groups toward change in the law regarding homosexuality were solicited. The Moral Welfare Council of the Church of England issued a report in which it said:

> In no other department of life does the State hold itself competent to interfere with the private actions of consenting adults. A man and a woman may commit the grave sin of fornication (nonmarital sex) with legal impunity, but a corresponding act between man and man is liable to life imprisonment, and not infrequently is punished by very long sentences, five, ten, or even more years.
>
> Such interference would only be warranted if there were proof that homosexual practices between males gravely affect society. Even if this is true, it could with justice be maintained that fornication and adultery threaten the well being of society still more seriously than homosexual practices. With fornication there is the risk—and the common result—of the birth of illegitimate children who may be deprived of the security of a home and the love of a father and a mother. Adultery undermines the unit of society, the home and family.
>
> Yet no legal penalty is now imposed for either fornication or adultery as such. The latter is only a ground for civil damages or divorce at the insistence of the person aggrieved. Formerly (by an Act of 1650) adultery was punishable—like homosexuality—with death.

The council also argued that penalties be eliminated for homosexual crimes for humanitarian reasons. It noted that there are persons who have committed suicide as a result of public disclosure at criminal trials, and it also mentioned the particular susceptibility of inverts to blackmailers. The committee also stated that there is reason to believe that older homosexuals seduce young boys because they are afraid of getting involved with other adults who might blackmail them.

The council further stated that "It is against the British conception of sociological principle to use the law in such a way as to create an aggrieved and self-conscious minority which becomes the center of dissatisfaction and ferment." Finally, the council argued that repealing criminal sanctions against homosexuality would "put an end to an unsavory type of police action," of using police as provocateurs in order to trap homosexuals into disclosing themselves.

The British Roman Catholic Advisory Committee on Prostitution and Homosexual Offenses claimed:

> Crime as such is a social concept not a moral one and therefore is a problem to be tackled by the State . . . Sin as such is not the concern of the State but affects the relations between the souls and God . . . Attempts by the State to enlarge its authority and invade the individual's conscience, however high-minded, always fail and frequently cause positive harm. The Volstead Act in the United States affords the best illustration of this principle. It should accordingly be clearly stated that penal sanctions are not justified for the purpose of attempting to restrain sins against sexual morality committed in private by responsible adults. They are, as later appears, at present employed for this purpose in this country and should be discontinued because; (a) they are ineffectual; (b) they are inequitable in their incidence; (c) they involve severities disproportionate to the offense committed; (d) they undoubtedly give scope for blackmail and other forms of corruption.

## Anthropological Perspectives

Clellan S. Ford and Frank A. Beach, in their book *Patterns of Sexual Behavior*, discuss the relationship between homosexuality in this and other societies. They claim that in forty-nine of the seventy-six societies (64 percent) for which information is available, homosexual activity of some kind is considered normal and socially acceptable for certain members of the community. In the other twenty-seven societies homosexual activity between adults is reported to be totally absent, rare, or carried on only in secret. It is to be expected, however, that this figure, which would run considerably below actual incidence as sexual expression in a society in which it is condemned, is not likely to become public fact. In some cultures it is clear that homosexual behavior is inhibited by severe childhood discipline. In several societies youngsters caught engaging in anything resembling homosexual play are whipped or beaten. For all societies in which homosexuality is rare or absent there is some social pressure directed against the forbidden behavior, whether it be a lesser pressure such as public ridicule or a greater one which in extreme cases may be the threat of death. According to Ford and Beach, "the cross-cultural and cross-species comparisons . . . combine to suggest that a biological tendency for inversion of sexual behavior is inherent in most if not all mammals including the human species," although homosexual behavior is never the predominant type of sexual activity for adults in any society or in any animal species.

The inherent mammalian capacity for sexual conversion tends to be obscured in societies susch as our own which condemn such behavior and relegate it to the level of the unnatural. In such societies, social forces impinge on the developing psyche from infancy onward and tend to inhibit receptivity to homosexual stimuli. But even in societies such as this which attempt to restrict homosexual tendencies, numerous individuals engage in homosexual activity—a great many more individuals than might be indicated by our cultural values and taboos.

## Social Sciences Debate Legalization

Kinsey, in *Sexual Behavior in the Human Male*, argues:

In view of the data which we now have on the incidence and frequency of the homosexual, and in particular on its co-existence with the heterosexual in the lives of a considerable portion of the male population, it is difficult to maintain the view that psychosexual relations between individuals of the same sex are rare and therefore abnormal or unnatural, or that they constitute within themselves evidence of neuroses or even psychoses.

If homosexual activity persists on as large a scale as it does, in the face of the very considerable public sentiment against it and in spite of the severity of the penalties that our Anglo-American culture has placed upon it through the centuries, there seems some reason for believing that such activity would appear in the histories of a much larger portion of the population if there were no social restraints. The very general occurrence of the homosexual in ancient Greece . . . and its widespread occurrence in some cultures in which such activity is not as taboo as it is in our own, suggests that the capacity of an individual to respond erotically to any sort of stimulus, whether it is provided by another person of the same sex or of the opposite sex, is basic in the species.

Kinsey claims that the idea that homosexual behavior is in itself evidence of psychopathic personality seems questionable when one is confronted with frequency data. He says that of the 40 to 50 percent of the male population which has some homosexual experience, certainly most would not be considered psychopathic on the basis of anything else in their histories.

Kinsey goes on to say that a judge who is considering the case of a male who has been arrested on homosexual charges would do well to keep in mind the fact that nearly 40 percent of all the other males in the town could be arrested at some time in their lives for similar behavior.

Dr. Karl Menninger, says that "Kinsey repudiates the concept of normality as beneath scientific contempt but by implication he substitutes for it the use of two other concepts, that of naturalness and that of prevalence (i.e., high relative incidence)." Menninger says that Kinsey is claiming homosexuality as a natural form of sexuality, like any other, because it is common in human beings and because animals also practice it. This puts Kinsey, according to Menninger, in the position of establishing inappropriate norms and setting up the worship of the factuality of fact, its material physicality, and its numerical strength. This has the effect of preventing consideration of social consequences of behavior by implying that certain behavior is social, valid, or justified merely because it exists in large portions of the population.

Louis B. Schwartz in his book review of *Sexual Behavior in the Human Male*, argues that the mere existence of widespread homosexuality does not necessarily mean that such behavior should be legal. If the forbidden conduct is in fact undesirable, evidence of promiscuous violation would more logically support an increase in penalties and more rigorous enforcement. Schwartz claims the validity of a criminal law does not reside in its correlation with actual behavior, but in its correspondence to behavior ideals and its ability to promote those ideals.

Kinsey's study itself clearly indicates that people who engage in illicit homosexuality nevertheless subscribe to the law and morality which condemn their conduct. Schwartz maintains that this is not hypocrisy, although hypocritical people may take such positions, but that it is only a recognition that there may be a better way of life than one is personally able to follow. Overt homosexuality is an isolated or transitory experience in the lives of a very large proportion of the 37 percent who have engaged in such behavior. "Even in the age of greatest frequency of sexuality in animals—only one percent of total sexual outlet takes this form." If the effectiveness of criminal law is to be tested by conformity and nonconformity, says Schwartz, one would have to say there was more evidence here of success than of failure. He goes on to say that the function of most of our criminal statutes is deterrence. Considering the number of sexual violations, there are relatively few people in jail on that account; but he maintains the efficacy of the law in deterring some people. Of course, he admits that difficulty may arise if infrequent enforcement leads to a cynical attitude toward the law. But this, says Schwartz, is less likely to happen in the case of sex violations since most of them occur in private. The public is, for the most part, unaware of the "glaring inconsistency between our ideals and our deeds." The revelations of Kinsey on the prevalence of homosexuality may in fact generate the very cynicism regarding the law which might not have followed from the undocumented and unpublicized fact that our sex lives do not conform to our moral professions. Schwartz does not question the desirability of keeping people in the dark.

In the book *Family, Socialization and Interaction Process* by Talcott Parsons and Robert Bales, it is claimed that the homosexual taboo is nearly as great a sociological universal as the incest taboo. The authors tell us that Freud made us aware of the presumably universal possibility of homosexual attraction, and they suggest the differentiation of sex roles. From the point of view of society they claim that it serves to prevent competing personal solidarities from arising which could undermine the motivation to marriage and the establishment of families. Basically the authors argue that homosexuality is a mode of structuring human relationships which is radically in conflict with the role of the nuclear family and its socialization of children, at least as these things exist in our society today.

Of course, legalizing private homosexual acts between consenting adults is not equivalent to removing the societal taboo on homosexuality, and certainly one could not simply assume that Parsons or Bales would be against such legalization. Homosexual activity has been legal in many European countries for a number of years, but generally speaking the taboo still remains. There appears to be no more widespread homosexuality in Europe than here. Nor has there been any difficulty in maintaining sex roles or in keeping together the nuclear family. In Connecticut where legal sanctions against consensual adult homosexual acts have been removed, the prevailing climate of opinion appears to be no more favorable toward the homosexual nor much more likely to produce homosexuals than any other state. In the *Connecticut Sunday Herald* (June 13, 1971), an editorial written about a recent legally executed "gay march" in the city stated:

> This newspaper does not understand . . . why perverted people such as homosexuals of either sex should be allowed to flaunt their immorality and their abnormalities before the eyes of decent people . . . This sort of public behavior has to be brought to an end and these people should be arrested for public display of what, in many cities is still a crime, and should be in all cities.

It is quite clear that in this instance, legalizing homosexuality has done little to remove the stigma generally associated with such behavior.

There are, however, a number of people who feel that homosexuality might be much more prevalent than it is. But even people like Kinsey, who believe that there are homosexual tendencies in most if not all humans, acknowledge the fact that heterosexual relations are more prevalent than homosexual ones in all animal species and in all human societies, even in those societies where such relations are not taboo. Homosexual urges appear quite clearly to be of lesser strength than heterosexual urges in the human species as a whole. There is no particular reason to believe that legalizing or removing the taboo from homosexuality would endanger the family. In other societies where such relations are accepted, the majority of people choose heterosexuality and have families. But even if this were not to be the case and if in fact besides the law being changed, the taboo on homosexuality was somehow lifted and people chose to indulge more frequently in homosexual activity (with a resultant blurring of the sex roles and decrease in the number of families and children), it would only be because these people had found something more satisfying. There appear to be no experts, no psychologists, sociologists, or anthropologists who feel that homosexual relations would ever preclude heterosexual ones. And most experts feel that although humans are capable of homosexual responses the majority of humans would, in a situation where there were no sexual inhibitions of any kind, more often choose heterosexual relations because anatomically speaking they would afford the most and the easiest gratification. If the nuclear family is the most desirable means of socialization,we should have no reason to fear it being discarded in favor of a less desirable one. If there were no taboo on homosexual activity it would merely give people the option of choosing one more type of behavior; and, if they did choose it, it would only be because it afforded them a better way of life.

### Lesbianism

The phenomenon of female homosexuality seems to be of much less interest to writers and researchers in the field of sexual inversion than male homosexuality. The fact that there is less female homosexuality does not go far in explaining the relative lack of interest in the subject. Most books (this one included) that contain a chapter on homosexuality devote themselves almost exclusively to a discussion of male homosexuality and manage to dispose of female homosexuality in a paragraph or two at the end. This seems to be a parallel phenomenon to that in our Western legal system where for years female homosexuals have been generally ignored by the forces of justice while male homosexuals have been known to have been put to death. In England female homosexual acts have never been illegal. In the United States they are illegal in a few states but enforcement of the law against female homosexuals seems to be so rare as to be of no social importance. Some psychologists think this may be the result of what they call psychic annullment: the male ego is simply not capable of accepting the fact that females can get sexual gratification without a male.

There are, of course, other explanations. Women in general are permitted greater physical intimacy with each other without social disapproval than is the case for men. Kissing and hugging are acceptable forms of friendly expression between women. In America a father is often too self-conscious to kiss his own son. According to psychiatrist Clara Thompson, "compulsive hetero-sexuality is one outgrowth of the taboo on even close friendship with one's own sex." It is obvious that in the case of women there is a much more permissive attitude toward friendship with one's own sex and also toward overt homosexuality. Women may be content with the relatively generous amount of physical intimacy that they may legitimately share whereas men seeking much less physical contact (outside of sports) with other men must expect to be labeled homosexual. One might even hypothesize that females are less apt to choose homosexuality because it is much easier for them to do so. Males may find homosexuality an effective way of deriving masochistic pleasure from society's con-tempt and hatred whereas women seeking to punish themselves might do better finding another type of antisocial behavior.

# THE CONTRACEPTIVE EXPLOSION

In the early years of the twentieth century Margaret Sanger began her one-woman crusade for birth control. Today, birth control has become a worldwide movement. In the United States, the courts, the legislatures, and the pronouncements of public officials on local, state, national and international levels, increasingly reflect the change in birth control from the status of moral taboo to an approved imperative. Over 90 percent of the American people exercise the right to limit their families. Dr. James Bryant Conant, former president of Harvard University, speaking to the American Chemical Society in 1951, predicted that

> . . . by 1961 bio-chemists will have made available cheap and harmless anti-fertility compounds to be added as one saw fit to the diet . . . as the twentieth century draws to a close, the attitude of religious leaders of the world will have completely altered on this subject, without any diminution of religious feeling.

With an estimated seven million women in the United States now on the pill, Dr. Conant's prophecy is fast becoming a reality.

More and more inexpensive, and highly effective contraceptives are being developed in both chemical and mechanical forms. The majority of the medical profession is now in support of birth control. An overwhelming section of the church community also recognizes birth control as a civil liberty and a moral right, and a necessary prerequisite to the solution of poverty and population growth.

Dr. Alan Guttmacher, author of *Birth Control and Love*, reviewing the contraceptive picture in America, calls it

> One of the most remarkable sociomedical changes in history; in just five decades, effective fertility control, once available only to affluent couples, has come within the reach of Americans of modest and even low incomes ... the changes since the introduction of new methods in 1960 have been perhaps even more remarkable. In five years, the pill became the single most popular contraceptive method ... By 1965, one-fourth of all United States contraceptive users already had used the pill and it was estimated that this proportion would soon increase to nearly half. Medical historians can recall few other recently developed health procedures which have been adopted so quickly, so widely—and with such enthusiasm.

In a Gallup poll released in January 1965, 81 percent of Americans favored giving contraception to anyone who desired it; 78 percent of Catholics polled shared this view. The most comprehensive studies on contraceptive practice have been done by GAF Studies, which stands for Growth of American Families. They involved extensive interviews with nationwide samples. According to their findings, 95 percent of all Jewish couples practice birth control. Among Protestants the proportions were 84 percent of all couples and 92 percent of fully fertile couples. The latest study in 1965 showed 78 percent of all Catholics using birth control (53 percent using a means other than the rhythm method). Thus, it appears that Catholics respond only a little less readily than other Americans in general to the idea of family limitations.

## History of Birth Control

From prehistoric times man has attempted to control conception. Anthropologists have established that primitive tribes employ a variety of rational, magical, and sometimes crude methods for birth control. These methods include infanticide, abstinence, and abortion, as well as chemical, mechanical, and surgical devices. It has been reported that the Negro women of Guiana use a diluted lemon juice as a douche solution, a practice medically approved as an effective spermicide. Numerous kinds of pessaries, supposi-tories, and condoms are recorded from the ancient civilizations. Plato wished to restrict all procreation by law, confining it to men between the ages of thirty and thirty-five, and women aged twenty to forty. During the Middle Ages, Islamic contraceptive medicine made progress, but in Europe the Church impeded such research. In the sixteenth century an Italian, Gabriel Fallopio, recom-mended use of a linen condom for antisyphilitic protection. The condom became prevalent in Europe during the eighteenth century, being used in brothels and sold in city shops. As the evangelical movement got underway in the 1780s, however, con-traceptives were vehemently denounced as immoral and sinful; the Victorians associated birth control material with obscenity.

A Surrey curate, Thomas Malthus, was the unwitting founder of the modern birth control movement by means of his famous *Essay on the Principle of Population*, published in 1798. Malthus lived at a time when improved hygiene and midwifery were greatly re-ducing child mortality, and thereby increasing the size of the family. Malthus theorized that both population and food supplies tend to increase but since population increases faster than means of subsistence, the majority of the human race is doomed to perpetual poverty and malnutrition. Disease and war serve as natural checks and thus prevent a worldwide cataclysm. The only avenue of escape from this dilemma, argued Malthus, was by the widespread adoption of "moral restraint," by which he meant the deferred marriage of those who could not afford a normal family. He did not recommend any form of restraint within marriage, and expressly assailed recourse to "improper arts."

The pessimistic message in Malthus's doctrine provoked an angry reaction in socialist and radical circles. Generally accepted, it would dampen hope for all social programs aimed at improving the human condition. It was imperative to find a solution to the Malthusian problem, otherwise humanity would have to resign itself to unending war and famine. Surely population could be held in check by some other means. In 1822, Francis Place in *Illustrations and Proofs of the Principle of Population* suggested that the answer to the population problem lay in the use of artificial contraception. He wrote: "Once clearly understood that it was not disreputable for married persons to avail themselves of such precautionary means as would, without being injurious to health or destructive of female delicacy, prevent conception, a sufficient check might at once be given to the increase of population . . ." Place distributed handbills among the working classes detailing a particular method of contraception—the use of a sponge and attached ribbon. Though condemned as "diabolical" the handbills were not legally suppressed.

The writings of Place influenced Robert Knowlton, who in 1832 published the first American book on contraception, *The Fruits of Philosophy*. Knowlton prescribed a solution of alum as a postcoital contraceptive douche to "which a little spirits is added," to prevent it from freezing. For his pioneering efforts he was sentenced to three months at hard labor in jail. In England the British Society for the Suppression of Vice was in a fury against contraceptive books. The solicitor general, reflecting the society's view, told an English court: "I say that this is a dirty, filthy book, and the test of it is that no human being would allow that book to lie on his table, no decently educated English husband would allow even his wife to have it." In 1873, Anthony Comstock induced Congress to pass the Comstock Law which classified birth control information with obscenity and made its dissemination by mail illegal. The Tariff Act of 1890 barred the importation of all literature on birth control.

There were socioeconomic forces in motion, however, in the nineteenth century which were generating pressures in favor of birth control. The Industrial Revolution and the fall in the death rate had resulted in a vastly increased population; the great depression of 1873 to 1896 led to widespread dislocation in agriculture and industry; women were becoming more emancipated and unwilling to bear the burden of unrestricted families; legislation forbidding child employment had reduced the value of children as income earning assets. Shortly after the Bradlaugh-Besant trial in 1880, education for the first time was made compulsory, and this further increased the financial burden of large families. Despite these socioeconomic developments, contraception was a long way from general social acceptance. In 1916 Margaret Sanger opened the first birth control clinic in Brooklyn. She was arrested and sentenced to thirty days in jail for "maintaining a public nuisance." The Lambert Conference of 1920 issued a solemn warning against "the use of unnatural means for the avoidance of conception," and stressed that the primary purpose of marriage was procreation.

The tide was given a chance to turn with several court decisions legalizing the prescription of birth control for health reasons. In 1921 the American Birth Control League was formed, which embodied a number of birth control clinics from different areas of the nation. In 1942 this organization escalated into the Planned Parenthood Federation of America with offices in virtually every state of the nation. The Planned Parenthood Federation provided birth control assistance and education to parents and enlightenment to legislatures. In 1958 the Lambert Conference, reversing its earlier position, gave unanimous approval of contraception. It passed a resolution in the following terms:

> The Conference believes that the responsibility for deciding upon the number and frequency of children has been laid by God upon the consciences of parents everywhere . . . responsible parenthood, built on obedience to all the duties of marriage, requires a wise stewardship of the resources and abilities of the family as well as a thoughtful consideration of the varying population needs and problems of society and the claims of future generations.

In 1965, the Supreme Court removed essentially all legal barriers to contraception by striking down a Connecticut anti-contraceptive statute as unconstitutional.

Recently, the Zero Population Growth organization has moved to the forefront in this area, with branches all across the nation. It recognizes that its greatest weapon in averting potential population crises is widespread and readily available contraceptive use and information, especially for the poor. It is a tragic irony that those who can least afford, and often least want, children are those who remain most ignorant of the benefits of birth control. Accordingly, ZPG devotes much of its energy to the establishment of birth control clinics.

## Means of Birth Control

*The Rhythm Method:* The rhythm method is predicated on the fact that conception can occur only at a certain time during the monthly cycle. Intercourse can be avoided during the time when ovulation takes place. Regrettably, the time of ovulation cannot be predicted with sufficient accuracy. A slight change in temperature is taken as a sign that the egg has begun to descend, i.e., about fifteen days before the start of the next period. When the temperature remains at about 98 degrees for several days in the middle of the cycle this is viewed as an indicator that ovulation has taken place. In effect it restricts intercourse to a few days after menstruation has ceased and some days before ovulation is anticipated. Since the human body does not behave with clockwork regularity, this method is far from reliable.

Dr. Eustace Chesser believes there is something ridiculous in the idea that a man and a wife should read the thermometer and make calculations from the calendar before deciding to have intercourse. Moreover, it is beyond the understanding of the illiterate millions in underdeveloped countries such as India which are bursting with people. Attempts have been made to help these unfortunate women avoid bearing children by supplying them with beads to count instead of a calendar. The story is told that many of these women counted the beads at night, believing they had some magical contraceptive power, and then had intercourse with their husbands.

*The Pill:* The most effective means of birth control available today and the one coming into greater and greater use is the pill. The pill contains hormonelike materials which enter the blood stream and prevent the release of the egg. Instead of killing the sperm, or interposing a blockade between it and the egg, it ensures that there is no egg available. If there is no egg there can be no fertilization—which makes the pill virtually 100 percent effective. A doctor's prescription is necessary in order to obtain birth control pills, but they are available at any public health clinic or hospital clinic. The pill can be injurious to the health of a woman and should be taken under medical supervision. Side effects such as nausea, headaches, and menstrual disturbance have been recorded. While the pill is being used successfully by millions of women in the world, it does not suit everyone in all circumstances.

*Temporary Sterilization:* There is now in the testing stage a new contraceptive in the form of a monthly injection for both males and females which supplies thirty days of sterilization. Another prospect being pursued is a pill taken by the man which would prevent the release of the sperm.

*Vasectomy:* This is a surprisingly simple operation performed on the male organ which simply removes the capacity for transferring sperm to the woman. It has the advantage of simplicity—one quick operation provides infallible contraception for good; on the other hand, it allows no subsequent change of mind, for it is of permanent effect. Obviously, it is suitable only for those who have definitely made up their minds that no more children are wanted under any circumstances.

*Intrauterine Devices:* Another relatively new and highly effective method of birth control is the use of intrauterine contraceptives— the plastic coil or the stainless steel ring which are placed inside the uterus. Once the ring or coil is in place it can be left for a year or more. The woman has no awareness of it. It has been charged that the intrauterine devices endanger health, but there is not the slightest evidence to support such a charge. In 1930 Dr. Frederick J. McCann, president of the League of National Life, (an organization formed to combat the spread of birth control), claimed to have discovered a serious condition brought about by the use of contraception; he called the condition Malthusian uterus, which was characterized by an overly large womb. The medical profession quickly rejected this claim as nonsense.

The stainless steel ring is much more reliable than the plastic coil; however it is more expensive and there are only a limited number of doctors skilled in its technique.

*The Condom:* No doubt the oldest method of birth control is interposing a barrier, either of rubber or plastic, generally categorized as the condom. There are many kinds of condoms on the market. Some are made of thick rubber and can be washed and used again. Naturally, the thickness diminishes the pleasure, but it is economical. Condoms which are used only once are made of a thinner material.

### Religious Views on Contraception

*Roman Catholic:* The Catholic church condemns contraception as contrary to natural law. The nub of the Catholic position is contained in canon law where it is stated that the primary purpose of marriage is the procreation and education of children. The Catholic natural law tradition accepts as self-evident that the primary purpose of sexual intercourse is procreation, and relegates as secondary such ends as festering mutual love, and perfecting the personalities of the spouses.

Contraception, maintain some Catholic thinkers, not only violates natural law but also corrupts the individual since it reduces self-control and its employment in the majority of cases will be for selfish reasons. Marriage will be degraded to a legalized form of prostitution. Moreover, contraceptives undermine public morality, removing the fear of pregnancy, which is a powerful deterrent against promiscuous intercourse.

Pope Paul, in his encyclical *Humana Vitae* (Of Human Life) reaffirmed the traditional Catholic opposition to all forms of contraception except the rhythm method. Birth control by chemical or mechanical means would frustrate the primary purpose of marriage, procreation, and hence offend natural law. Catholics are permitted to use the rhythm method if there are serious reasons, "such as those often provided in the so-called 'indications' of the medical, eugenical, economic, and social order." As examples of these indications, Monsignor George A. Kelly, in his book *The Catholic Marriage Manual*, states that medical reasons include cases in which a woman lacks the strength to carry a child, or in which her life would be endangered by another pregnancy. A eugenic reason is one in which there is a great probability the couple would give birth to a defective child. An economic reason would be to enable the couple to have only "as many children as they can support reasonably."

A significant number of Catholic theologians question whether the rhythm method is the only moral means of family planning. Some argue that birth control pills are inherently different from mechanical contraceptives, and can be morally used by Catholics, since they simply postpone ovulation without interfering with the sexual act. In 1958, Pope Pius XII had approved use of the pills for the treatment of disease, but condemned their use for prevention of conception. This was broadly interpreted by some moralists to mean the pill could be used for curing a neurotic fear of pregnancy. Others wanted to extend it beyond therapeutic limits.

In 1967 the Third World Lay Catholic Congress almost unanimously approved a resolution on "The Anguishing Problem of Demographic Expansion." It called for "a clear statement of the church concentrated on the fundamental moral and spiritual values, without themselves proposing scientific or technical solutions to achieve responsible parenthood." The resolution left "the choice of the means to the conscience of parents in conformity with their Christian faith . . ." Also, a group of more than two hundred American priests announced their opposition to the papal position. Led by Father Charles Curran of Catholic University in Washington, they declared, "Spouses may responsibly decide according to their conscience that artificial contraception in some circumstances is permissible and indeed necessary to preserve and foster the values and sacredness of marriage." Meanwhile in Europe, the Catholic bishops of France and the Netherlands viewed the papal pronouncement as but "one of the many factors" to be considered by husbands and wives in making decisions on child spacing and family size.

*Protestant:* Virtually all Protestant churches are now in favor of birth control. In 1961, the National Council of Churches of Christ, representing some forty million parishioners, declared that birth control is morally permissible for married couples. The Protestant position is based on the Protestant view of the basic purposes of marriage. These purposes include not only parenthood, but equally important, the growth of mutual love and companionship, and family service to society. When a couple believes that a pregnancy would undermine any of these important purposes, it is permissible to use birth control to prevent procreation. The council pointed out: "Most Protestant churches hold contraceptives and periodic continence to be morally right when the motives are right. They believe that couples are free to use the gifts of science for conscientious family limitation, provided the means are mutually acceptable, non-injurious to health, and appropriate to the degree of effectiveness required in the specific situation."

*Jewish:* Endorsement of birth control among Jewish groups has become the established position except for extreme Orthodox Jews. In 1960, the Central Conference of American Rabbis stated the acceptance of birth control for the Reform sect of Judaism. "We hold that apart from its procreative function, the sex relation in marriage serves positive spiritual values. Parents have the right to determine the number and to space the births of their children in accordance with what they believe to be the best interests of their families." In the next year, the Rabbinical Assembly of America, spokesman for the Conservative sect of Judaism, said: "There is precedent in Jewish law for sanctioning birth control. The vocation of parenthood fulfills its God-endowed mission when it is rendered consistent with the requisites of life and health of all the constituent members of the family."

This reaffirmed the Assembly's earlier statement in 1934 that "We regard it as legitimate and completely in consonance with the spirit of Jewish tradition, to permit the use of contraceptives on economic grounds as well, when the earning capacity of the family makes the postponement of childbearing or the limitation of the number of children socially wise and necessary . . . Proper education in contraception and birth control will not destroy, but rather enhance, the spiritual values in the family and will make for the advancement of human happiness and welfare." Orthodox doctrine, which represents a numerical minority, prohibits birth control unless "the health of the female is jeopardized."

## The Law and Contraceptives

The use of birth control is now legal in every state, as a result of the U.S. Supreme Court decision in 1965 holding the Connecticut anticontraceptive statute unconstitutional. In 1966, Massachusetts repealed the last restrictive statute on the American legal scene. Doctors are now free to prescribe contraception anywhere in the United States.

The pill has been influential in producing the sexual revolution, but judging by the spiraling rate of unwanted pregnancies, its impact may be overestimated. University of Michigan psychologist Judith Bardwick suggests another unanticipated side-effect: Instead of liberating women to enjoy sex, the pill has replaced fear of pregnancy with fear of being used. "Far from giving young women the sexual license that men have so long enjoyed, the pill has caused some women to resent male freedom even more. Far from alleviating anxiety over sexual use of the body, the pill has exacerbated it."

In summation, sexual freedom is the present reality, but it has proven to be not so simple a reality. Just as restrictions proved burdensome in the past, new freedoms are proving equally difficult to handle for some. It remains to be seen what styles and preference will evolve in the future.

# APPENDIX

# REFORMED ABORTION LAWS IN THE UNITED STATES

The following is a listing of laws in the United States permitting abortion on request or for reasons of health as of 1971.

*Alaska*
1. On request. (Restricted to "nonviable" fetus, that is, a fetus unable to survive outside mother's body. In practical terms this means that a woman should be no more than twenty to twenty-four weeks pregnant.)
2. Unmarried woman under eighteen years of age needs consent from parent.
3. Thirty-day residency requirement.
4. Must be performed by physician in a hospital or other facility approved for the purpose by the Department of Health and Welfare or a hospital operated by the federal government or an agency of the federal government.

*Arkansas*
1. May be performed to protect the life or health of the woman.
2. May be performed in cases of fetal deformity, incest, or forcible rape.
3. Four-month residency required.
4. Must be performed by a physician in a hospital with approval of three consultants.

*California*
1. May be performed to protect the life or the physical or mental health of the woman up to the twentieth week of pregnancy.
2. May be performed in cases of incest, forcible rape, or statutory rape (under age fifteen).
3. Must be performed by a physician in a hospital, with approval of a two-member therapeutic abortion board through the twelfth week of pregnancy, a three-member board thereafter.

*Colorado*
1. May be performed to protect the life or physical or mental health of the woman.
2. May be performed in cases of fetal deformity; within first sixteen weeks in cases of forcible rape, incest, or statutory rape (under age sixteen).
3. Must be performed by a physician in a hospital with approval of a three-member board.

*Delaware*
1. May be performed to protect the life or the physical or mental health of the woman through the twentieth week of pregnancy. After twenty weeks a pregnancy may be terminated to preserve the woman's life or where the fetus is dead.
2. May be performed in cases of fetal deformity, incest or forcible rape.
3. Four-month residency required, unless the woman or her husband works in Delaware or she has previously been a patient of a Delaware physician or her life is in danger.
4. Must be performed by a physician in a hospital with approval of one consultant and a hospital review authority.

*District of Columbia*
To protect the life or health of the woman.

*Georgia*
1. May be performed to protect the life or health of the woman.
2. May be performed in cases of fetal deformity, forcible rape, or statutory rape (under age fourteen).
3. State residency required.
4. Must be performed by a physician in a hospital with approval of two consultants and a three-member board.

*Hawaii*
1. On request. (Restricted to nonviable fetus.)
2. Ninety-day residency required.
3. Must be performed by a physician in a hospital.

*Kansas*
1. May be performed to protect the life or the physical or mental health of the woman.
2. May be performed in cases of fetal deformity, incest, forcible rape, or statutory rape (under age sixteen).
3. Must be performed by a physician in a hospital "or other place as may be designated by law" with approval of three consultants.

*Maryland*
1. May be performed to protect the life or the physical or mental health of the woman through the twenty-sixth week of pregnancy. After the twenty-sixth week to preserve maternal life or when the fetus is dead.
2. May be performed in cases of fetal deformity or forcible rape.
3. Must be performed by a physician in a hospital with approval of hospital review authority.

*New Mexico*
1. May be performed to protect the life or the physical or mental health of the woman.
2. May be performed in cases of fetal deformity, incest, forcible rape (under age sixteen).
3. Must be performed by a physician in a hospital with approval of a two-member board.

*New York*
1. On request, through twenty-fourth week of pregnancy. After twenty-four weeks pregnancy may be terminated to preserve

maternal life.
2. Must be performed by a physician.

*North Carolina*
1. May be performed to protect the life or health of the woman.
2. May be performed in cases of fetal deformity, incest, or forcible rape.
3. Four-month residency required.
4. Must be performed by a physician in a hospital with approval of three consultants.

*Oregon*
1. May be performed to protect the life or the physical or mental health of the woman. ("In determining whether or not there is substantial risk [to her physical or mental health], account may be taken of the mother's total environment, actual or reasonably foreseeable.")
2. May be performed only until 150th day of pregnancy, except in cases of danger to life.
3. May be performed in cases of fetal deformity, incest, forcible rape, or statutory rape (under age sixteen).
4. State residency required.
5. Must be performed by a physician in a hospital with approval of one consultant.

*South Carolina*
1. May be performed to protect the life or the physical or mental health of the woman.
2. May be performed in cases of fetal deformity, incest, or forcible rape.
3. Ninety-day residency required.
4. Must be performed by a physician in a hospital with approval of three consultants.

*Virginia*
1. May be performed to protect the life or the physical or mental health of the woman.
2. May be performed in cases of fetal deformity, incest, or forcible rape.
3. One-hundred-and-twenty-day residency required, provable by affidavit.
4. Must be performed by a physician in a hospital with approval of board.

*Washington*
1. On request through seventeenth week.
2. Ninety-day residency required.
3. Must be performed by a physician in a hospital "or other place as may be designated by law." If married and residing with husband or unmarried and under the age of eighteen years, with prior consent of husband or legal guardian respectively.

*Wisconsin*
On request. No restrictions.

# TABLE OF CASES

Rex v. Bourne 1 K.B. 687 (1939)
Roth v. United States 354 U.S. 476 (1957)
Schenck v. United States 249 U.S. 47 (1919)
Skinner v. Oklahoma 315 U.S. 789 (1942)
Stanley v. Georgia 394 U.S. 557 (1969)
State v. Sander 48 *Mich. Law Review* 1197 (1950)
United States v. One Book *Ulysses* 72 F.2d 705 (1934)
Winters v. New York 333 U.S. 510 (1948)

# REFERENCES AND
# SUGGESTED READING

American Law Institute. *Model Penal Code*, p. 276, Draft No. 4, 1955.

Amos, Sheldon. *A Comparative Survey of Laws in Force for the Prohibition, Regulation, and Licensing of Vice in England and Other Countries.* London: Stevens and Sons, 1877.

Anslinger, H. J. *The Murderers: The Story of the Narcotic Gangs.* New York: Farrar, Straus, 1960.

―――― and Cooper, C. R. "Marijuana: Assassin of Youth." *American Magazine*, 1937.

Ansbacher, Heinz. *The Individual Psychology of Alfred Adler.* New York: Harper Press, 1956.

Atkinson, Maxwell J. *Images of Deviance.* Great Britain: Penguin Books, 1971.

Bacon, Francis. *New Atlantis.* London, 1614.

Bartell, Gilbert. *Group Sex: A Scientist's Eyewitness Report on the American Way of Swinging.* New York: Peter H. Wyden, 1971.

Barzun, J. "In Favor of Capital Punishment." *Crime and Delinquency*, Vol. 15, January 1969.

Bauer, Bernhard. *Woman and Love.* New York: Liveright, 1971.

Beach, Frank and Ford, Clellan. *Patterns of Sexual Behavior.* New York: Harper & Row, 1970.

Becker, Dr. Howard, "Marijuana: A Sociological Overview." *The Marijuana Papers.* New York: Bobbs-Merrill, 1966. Edited by David Solomon.

Bedau, Hugo. *Death Penalty in America.* Chicago: Aldine, 1968.

Beiber, Irving. *Homosexuality: A Psychoanalytic Study.* New York: Basic Books, 1962.

Bergsma, Daniel. Symposium on Intrauterine Diagnosis, in *Birth Defects: Original Article Series.* Vol. 7, No. 5, April 1971.

Blackstone, William. *Commentaries.* Oxford, 1775.

Borroughs, William S. "Sedative and Consciousness-Expanding Drugs." *The Marijuana Papers.* New York: Bobbs-Merrill, 1966.

Bowman, Karl, and Engle, Bernice. "A Psychiatric Evaluation of Laws of Homosexuality." *Temple Law Quarterly.* 29:273, Spring 1956.

Boyko, E. P., and M. W. Rotberg, "Constitutional Objections to California Marijuana Possession Statute." *UCLA Law Review,* Vol. 14 (March 1967).

Brenton, Myron. *The American Male.* New York: Coward-McCann, 1966.

Buckley, William F. "How to Protest Abortion." *National Review,* XXIII (April 20, 1971), 445.

Butterfield, Herbert. *Christianity and History.* New York: Scribner, 1950.

Cairns and Wishner. "Sex Censorship: The Assumptions of Anti-Obscenity Laws and the Empirical Evidence." Vol. 46, *Minnesota Law Review* (1962).

Cannon, William P. "The Right to Die." *Houston Law Review* 7:654, May, 1970.

Camus, Albert. *The Myth of Sisyphus.* New York: Random House, 1955.

Carter, M. "Death Penalty in California." *Crime and Delinquency,* Vol. 15, January 1969.

Chamberlin, Anne. "Marriage Is Easy, if You Can Survive the Wedding." *McCalls* (May, 1971), pp. 86-88.

Chesser, Eustace. *Love and the Married Woman.* New York: Signet, 1969.

Clor, Harry. *Obscenity and Public Morality: Censorship in a Liberal Society.* Chicago: Chicago Press, 1969.

Collier, James. *The Hypocritical American.* New York: Bobbs-Merrill, 1964.

Comfort, Alex. *The Anxiety Makers.* London: Nelson, 1967.

———. *Sex in Society.* New York: Citadel, 1966.

Cory, D. W. *The Homosexual in America.* Philadelphia: Chiltor, 1959.

Cowles, "University of Jurisdiction Over War Crimes." *California Law Review*, Vol. 33 (1945).

Cox, Claire. "Marital Ceremony Gets Personal Look." *Daily Breeze.* October 11, 1971.

D'Apolito, Rose M. "My Lai: Jurisdiction over the Guilty Civilians." *New England Law Review*, Vol. 6 (Fall 1970).

Despert, J. Louise, M. D. *Children of Divorce.* Garden City, N.Y.: Doubleday Co., 1962.

Dickson, Ruth. *Marriage Is a Bad Habit.* Los Angeles: Sherbourne Press, 1968.

Donelsen, K. and I. "Twenty-year Fracture: Long Term Marriages." *Harvest Years.* February, 1970.

Downing, A. B. *Euthanasia and the Right to Death.* London: Peter Owen, 1969.

Draper, Elizabeth. *Birth Control in the Modern World.* London: Pelican, 1965.

Durant, Will. *The Pleasures of Philosophy.* New York: Simon and Schuster, 1953.

Durkheim, Emile. *Suicide.* New York: The Free Press, 1951.

Edmiston, Susan. "A Report on the Abortion Capital of the Country." *The New York Times Magazine* (April 11, 1971) pp. 10-47.

Eich, W. F. "From Ulysses to Portnoy: a pornography primer." *Marquette Law Review*, Vol. 53 (Summer 1970).

Elias, E. A. "Sex Publications and Moral Corruption: the Supreme Court Dilemma." *William and Mary Law Review*, Vol. 9 (Winter 1967).

Ellis, Albert. *Sex Without Guilt.* New York: Lyle Stuart, 1958.

Emerson, Thomas I. "Toward a General Theory of the First Amendment." *Yale Law Journal*, Vol. 72 (April 1963).

Engdahl, David E. "Requiem for Roth: Obscenity Doctrine is Changing." *Michigan Law Review*, Vol. 68 (December 1969).

Eysenck, Hans J. "Introverts, Extraverts and Sex." *Psychology Today*, January 1971.

Falk, Gerhard. "The Roth Decision in the Light of Sociological Knowledge." *American Bar Association Journal*, Vol. 54 (March 1968).

Farberow, Norman L., and Edwin S. Shneidman. *The Cry for Help.* New York: McGraw-Hill, 1961.

Filas, Francis. *Sex Education in the Family.* New Jersey: Prentice-Hall, 1966.

Finnis, J. J. "Reason and Passion: The Constitutional Dialectic of Free Speech and Obscenity." *University of Pennsylvania Law Review*, Vol. 116 (December 1967).

Fletcher, Joseph. *Morals and Medicine*. Princeton: Princeton University Press, 1964.

Ford, Clellan S., and Beach, Frank A. *Patterns of Sexual Behavior*. New York: Harper and Row, 1951.

Frankl, Dr. Victor E. *Man's Search for Meaning*. New York: Washington Square Press, 1963.

Freud, Sigmund. *Civilization and Its Discontents*, translated by James Strachey. New York: Norton, 1962.

Friedan, Betty. *The Feminine Mystique*. New York: Norton, 1963.

Friedman, Theodore. "Prenatal Diagnosis of Genetic Disease." *Scientific American*, November 1971.

Gagnon, John H., and William Simon. *Sexual Deviance*. New York: Harper and Row, 1967.

Garfinkle, Ann, Carol Lefcourt, and Diane Schulder. "Women's Servitude Under Law." *Law Against People:Essays To Demystify Law, Order, and the Courts*. New York: Vintage Books, 1971. Robert Lefcourt, Editor.

Gebhard, Paul H., Gagnon, John H., and Pomeroy, Wardell B. *Sex Offenders: An Analysis of Types*. New York: Harper and Row, 1965.

Gerzon, Mark. *The Whole World Is Watching*. New York: Viking, 1969.

Gillam, Jerry. "Assembly to Take Up Ban on Death Penalty." *Los Angeles Times*, April 7, 1963. Part I, p. 13.

Gilman, Richard. "Pornography and Obscenity." *New York Times Magazine*, September 8, 1968, p. 79.

Ginsberg, Allen. "The Great Marijuana Hoax: First Manifesto to End the Bringdown." *The Atlantic*, November, 1966.

Girvetz, Harry, et al. *Science, Folklore and Philosophy*. New York: Harper and Row, 1966.

Gold, Edwin M., et al. "Therapeutic Abortions in New York City: A Twenty-Year Review." *American Journal of Public Health*. LV (July, 1965), pp. 964-965.

Goldberg and Dershowitz. "Declaring the Death Penalty Unconstitutional." *Harvard Law Review*, Vol. 83, June 1970.

Goldstein, Joseph and Gitter, Max. "Divorce without Blame." *The Humanist*. May/June 1970, p. 12.

Gottlieb, G. H. "Capital Punishment." *Crime and Delinquency*. Vol. 15, January 1969.

Greer, Germaine. *The Female Eunuch.* New York: McGraw-Hill, 1971.

Guttmacher, Alan F., M. D., W. Best, and F. Jaffe. *Planning Your Family.* New York: MacMillan Co., 1964.

———. *Birth Control and Love.* New York: MacMillan Co., 1961.

Guyon, Rene. *Sex Life and Sex Ethics.* London: John Lane, The Bodley Head, 1933.

Hadden, Jeffrey K., and Marie L. Borgatta. *Marriage and the Family: A Comprehensive Reader.* Itasca, Ill.: F. E. Peacock, 1969.

Hadden, Samuel B. "A Way Out for Homosexuals." *Harper's Magazine.* March 1967.

Hale, M. *Pleas of the Crown.* London, 1678.

Hardin, Garrett. *Population, Evolution, and Birth Control.* San Francisco: Freeman, 1964.

Harper, Robert A. (ed). "Premaritan Sex Relations: The Facts and the Counselor's Role in Relation to the Facts." *Marriage and Family Living,* XIV (August, 1952), 229-38.

Hartung, Frank. "Cultural Relativity and Moral Judgments." *Philosophy of Science.* II (April, 1954), 118-26.

Hays, H. R. *The Dangerous Sex: The Myth of Feminine Evil.* New York: G. P. Putnam's Sons, 1964.

Henkin, "Morals and the Constitution: The Sin of Obscenity." *Columbia Law Review,* Vol. 63 (1963).

Hill, Reuben. *Families under Stress.* New York: Harper and Brothers, 1949.

Hillman, James. *Suicide and the Soul.* Great Britain: Hodder and Stoughton, 1964.

Hiltner, Seward. "Suicidal Reflections." *Pastoral Psychology.* (December, 1953), pp. 33-41.

———. *Sex Ethics and the Kinsey Reports.* New York: Association Press, 1953.

Himelhoch, Jerome, and Silvia Fava (eds.). *Sexual Behavior in American Society.* New York: Norton, 1955.

Himes, Norman E. *Medical History of Contraception.* Baltimore: Williams and Wilkins Co., 1936.

Hirschfeld, Magnus. *Sexual Anomalies: The Origins, Nature, and Treatment of Sexual Disorders.* New York: Emerson Books, 1956.

Hochkammer, W. O. "Capital Punishment Controversy." *Journal of Criminal Law.* Vol. 60, September 1969.

Hoffman, Martin. *The Gay World.* New York: Basic Books, 1968.

Holbrook, Clyde A. *Faith and Community.* New York: Harper and Brothers, 1959.

Hooker, Evelyn. "A Preliminary Analysis of Group Behavior of Homosexuals." *J. Pscyh.* 42: 217-225, 1956.

———. "The Adjustment of the Male Overt Homosexual." *J. Proj. Tech.,* 1957.

———. "Male Homosexuality in the Rorschach." *J. Proj. Tech.,* 1958.

Hoult, Thomas F. *The Sociology of Religion.* New York: Dryden Press, 1958. Hunt, Morton M. *The Affair: A Portrait of Extra-Marital Love In Contemporary America.* Cleveland: The World Publishing Co., 1969.

Hunt, Morton. "Future of Marriage." *Playboy Magazine,* 1971.

———. *The Natural History of Love.* New York: Alfred A. Knopf, 1959.

Huxley, Aldous. *Brave New World.* New York: Harper and Brothers, 1950.

Jacobson, Paul H. *American Marriage and Divorce.* New York: Rinehart and Co., 1959.

Janov, Arthur. *The Primal Scream.* New York: Dell Publishing Co., 1970.

Jensen, Oliver. *The Revolt of American Women.* New York: Harcourt, Brace and Co., 1952.

Johnson, Cecil E. *Sex and Human Relationships.* Columbus, Ohio: Charles E. Merrill Publishing Co., 1970.

Johnson, Gerald W. "Dynamic Victoria Woodhull." *American Heritage,* VII (June, 1956); 44-47, 86-91.

Kamisar, Yale. "Some non-religious views against proposed 'mercy-killing' legislation." *Minnesota Law Review,* 42:16 (May 1958).

Kaplan, John. *Marijuana: The New Prohibition.* New York: Simon and Schuster, 1971.

Kardiner, Abram. *Sex and Morality.* Indianapolis: Bobbs-Merrill, 1954.

Karpman, Benjamin. "Sex Life in Prison." *Journal of the Institute of Criminal Law.* January-February 1948.

Katz, A. "Free Discussion v. Final Decision: Moral and Artistic Controversy and the *Tropic of Cancer* Trials." *Yale Law Journal,* Vol. 79 (December 1969).

Kaufman, Walter. *Existentialism from Dostoevesky to Sartre.* Cleveland: The World Publishing Co., 1956.

Kelly, Father Gerald. "The Morality of Artifical Fecundation." *The Ecclesiastical Review,* 1939.

Kelly, Monsignor George A. *The Catholic Marriage Manual.* New York: Random House, 1958.

Kinsey, Alfred Charles. *Sexual Behavior in the Human Male.* London: Saunders Co., 1948.

Kirkendall, Lester A. and Robert N. Whitehurst. *The New Sexual Revolution.* New York: Brown, Inc., 1971.

Krich, A. M. *The Homosexuals, As Seen by Themselves and Thirty Authorities.* New York: Citadel Press, 1954.

Kuh, Richard H. *Foolish Fig Leaves? Pornography in—and out of—Court.* New York: MacMillan, 1967.

Kutner, Luis. "Due Process of Euthanasia: The Living Will, a Proposal." *Indiana Law Journal* 44:539, Summer 1969.

LaFarge, John, S. J. *Reflections on Growing Old.* Garden City, N.Y.: Doubleday and Co., 1963.

Landis, Judson T. and Mary G. Landis (eds.). *Readings in Marriage and the Family.* Englewood Cliffs, N.J.: Prentice-Hall, 1952.

Lang, Irving. "The President's Crime Commission Task Force Report on Narcotics and Drug Abuse: A Critique of the Apologia." *Notre Dame Lawyer*, Vol. 43, 1968.

Lasagna, Louis. *Life, Death and the Doctor.* New York: Alfred A. Knopf, 1968.

Laughlin, Harry H. *The Legal Status of Eugenical Sterilization.* Municipal Court of Chicago, 1929.

Laughlin, Stanley K. "A Requiem for Requiems: The Supreme Court at the Bar of Reality." Vol. 68, *Michigan Law Review*, 1970.

Leach, Gerald. *The Biocrats.* New York: McGraw-Hill, 1970.

LeShan, Eda. *Mates and Roommates: New Styles in Young Marriages.* New York: Public Affairs Committee, 1971.

Leuba, Clarence James. *Man: A General Psychology.* New York: Holt, Rinehart and Winston, 1961.

Lipton, Lawrence. *The Erotic Revolution.* Los Angeles: Sherbourne Press, 1965.

Lynch, T. C. "California Narcotic Addict Rehabilitation Law." *New York Law Forum*, Vol. 12 (Fall 1968).

Machover, Karen Alper. *Personality Projection.* Springfield Ill.: Charles Thomas, 1968.

Mann, K. W. *Deadline for Survival.* New York: Seabury Press, 1970.

Marmor, Judd. *Sexual Inversion: the Multiple Roots of Homosexuality.* New York: Basic Books, 1965.

Matheney, Ruth Virginia. *Psychiatric Nursing.* St. Louis, Mo.: C. V. Mosby Co., 1953.

Meerloo, Joost A. M. *Suicide and Mass Suicide.* New York: Dutton, Inc. 1968.

Menninger, Karl. *Man Against Himself.* New York: Harcourt Brace, 1938.

Meredith, Robert C. "Permissiveness, Curse of Western Society." *The Plain Truth Magazine,* 1971.

Meyers, David W. *The Human Body and the Law.* Chicago: Aldine Publishing Co., 1970.

Millet, Kate. *Sexual Politics.* New York: Avon, 1969.

Morgan, Robin (ed.). *Sisterhood is Powerful.* New York: Vintage Books, 1969.

Morreale, J. P. "Obscenity: an Analysis and Statutory Proposal." *Wisconsin Law Review,* Vol. 1969 (1969).

Murtagh, John M., and Sara Harris. *Cast the First Stone.* New York: McGraw-Hill, 1957.

Myrdal, Gunnar. *An American Dilemma.* New York: Harper and Brothers, 1944.

National Manpower Council. *Womanpower.* New York: Columbia University Press, 1957.

Newcomb, Theodore. "Recent Changes in Attitudes Toward Sex and Marriage." *American Sociological Review,* II (December, 1937) 659-67.

Ogburn, William F. *On Culture and Social Change: Selected Papers.* Chicago: University of Chicago Press, 1964.

Olsen, Arthur R., Emily H. Mudd and Hugo Bourdeau (eds.). *Readings on Marriage and Family Relations.* Harrisburg, Pa.: The Stackpole Co., 1953.

O'Neil, Eugene. *Anna Christie.* New York: Boni and Liveright, 1923.

Otto, Herbert A. "Communes: The Alternative Life-Style." *Saturday Review.* April 24, 1971; pg. 17.

———. *The Family in Search of a Future.* New York: Appleton-Century-Crofts, 1970.

Parsons, Talcott and Robert Bales. *Family, Socialization and Interaction Process.* Glencoe, Ill.: The Free Press, 1955.

Poe, D. A. "Capital Punishment Statutes in the Wake of United States v. Jackson: Some unresolved questions." *George Washington Law Review,* Vol. 37, May 1969.

Pohlman, E. *The Psychology of Birth Planning.* Cambridge, Mass.: Schenkman, 1969.

Pollak, Otto and Alfred S. Friedman. (eds.). *Family Dynamics and Female Sexual Delinquency.* Palo Alto: Science and Behavior Books Inc., 1969.

President's Commission. *Report of the Commission on Obscenity and Pornography.* New York: Random House, 1971.

Ratner, L. G. "Social Importance of Prurient Interest—Obscenity Regulation v. Through-Privacy." *Southern California Law Review*, Vol. 42 (1969).

Rees, J. Tudo and Harley v. Usill. "The Homosexual and Christian Morals," in *They Stand Apart*, symposium, New York, 1955.

Reich, Charles A. *The Greening of America.* New York: Random House, 1971.

Reiss, I. L. *Premarital Sexual Standards in America.* New York: The Free Press, 1960.

Resner, Robert G. *Show Me the Good Parts: The Reader's Guide to Sex in Literature.* New York: Citadel, 1964.

Reuben, Dr. David. *Everything You Always Wanted to Know about Sex and Were Afraid to Ask.* New York: McKay, 1969.

Riley, John W. and Matilda W. Riley. "The Use of Various Methods of Contraception." *American Sociological Review*, v. (December, 1940).

Rimmer, Robert H. *The Harrad Experiment.* Los Angeles: Sherbourne Press, 1966.

———. *The Rebellion of Yale Marratt.* New York: New American Library, 1968.

Rosenfeld, Albert. "Eighty Million Earthlings Watched Their World Shrink." *Life*, 66:50-52A, May 30, 1969.

———. "Science, Sex and Morality; Adaptation of the Second Genesis." *Life*, 66:37-40. June 13, 1969.

Rougemont, Denis De. *Love in the Western World.* New York: Harcourt Brace, 1950.

Rubin, Isadore. *Sexual Life after Sixty.* New York: Basic Books, 1965.

Rubin, Isadore and Lester A. Kirkendall (eds.). *Sex in the Adolescent Years.* New York: Association Press, 1968.

Ruitenbeck, Rendrick. *The Problem of Homosexuality in Modern Society.* New York: Dutton, 1963.

Russell, Bertrand. *Marriage and Morals.* New York: Liveright, 1929.

Sagarin, Edward and Donald E. J. MacNamara. *Problems of Sex Behavior.* New York: Thomas Y. Crowell Co., 1968.

Saltman, Jules. *Marijuana and Your Child.* Ed. by Thetis Powers. New York: Grosset and Dunlap, 1970.

Schofield, M. *The Sexual Behavior of Your People.* London: Longmans, Green, 1965.

Sellin, Thorsten. *Capital Punishment.* Edited by Donald Cressey, New York: Harper and Row, 1969.

Shapiro, Harry L. (ed.). *Man, Culture and Society.* New York: Oxford University Press, 1956.

Sheckley, Robert. *Untouched by Human Hands.* New York: Ballantine Books, 1954.

Sherif, Muzafer, and Carolyn W. Muzafer. *Reference Groups.* New York: Harper and Row, 1964.

Shneidman, Edwin S. *Essays in Self-Destruction.* New York: Science House, 1967.

———, and Norman L. Farberow. *Clues to Suicide.* New York: McGraw-Hill, 1957.

———, and Robert E. Litman. *The Psychology of Suicide.* New York: Science House, 1970.

Simpson, George Gaylord. *The Meaning of Evolution.* New Haven: Yale University Press, 1951.

Skidmore, Rex, and Anthon Cannon. *Building Your Marriage.* New York: Harper and Brothers, 1951.

Smuts, Robert W. *Women and Work in America.* New York: Columbia University Press, 1959.

Solnit, Albert. "Wear and Tear in the Communes." *Nation.* April 27, 1971, pp. 524.

Sprey, Jetse. "On the Institutionalization of Sexuality." *Journal of Marriage and the Family.* 31 (August 1969) pp. 432-440.

Stace, W. T. *The Concept of Morals.* New York: Macmillan, 1962.

Stengel, Erwin. *Suicide and Attempted Suicide.* Great Britain: Penguin Books, 1964.

Stephens, William N. *The Family in Cross-Cultural Perspective.* New York: Holt, Rinehart and Winston, 1963.

St. John-Stevas, Norman. *Life, Death and the Law.* New York: Meridian 1964.

Stocking, Susan. "Purpose of Book on Death to Help Living Face Inevitable." *The Los Angeles Times,* December 14, 1971; VI, 7.

Taylor, Gordon Rattray. *The Biological Time Bomb.* New York: The World Publishing Co., 1968.

Taylor, Howard C., Jr. *The Abortion Problem.* Baltimore: Williams and Wilkins Co., 1944.

Thompson, Clara. "Changing Concepts of Homosexuality." Mullany, Patrick II, (ed.). *A Study of Interpersonal Relations.* New York: Hermitage Press, 1949.

———. *Interpersonal Psychoanalysis.* Maurice R. Green (ed.). New York: Basic Books, 1964.

Thompson, Warren S. *Population Problems.* New York: McGraw-Hill, 1953.

Thomson, George. *The Foreseeable Future.* New York: Viking, 1960.

Todd, Richard. "Alternatives." *The Atlantic.* 226:112+ November, 1970.

Toffler, Alvin. *Future Shock.* New York: Random House, 1971.

Tucher, E. W. "Law of Obscenity—Where Has It Gone?" *University of Florida Law Review,* Vol. 22 (Spring-Summer 1970).

Udry, J. Richard. *The Social Context of Marriage.* New York: J. B. Lippincott, 1966.

Van Den Haag, J. "On Deterence and the Death Penalty." *Journal of Criminal Law,* Vol. 60, June 1969.

Vaux, Kenneth, (ed.). *Who Shall Live?* Philadelphia: Fortress Press, 1970.

Walker, Brooks R. *The New Immorality.* New York: Doubleday, 1968.

Weininger, Otto. *Sex and Character.* New York: Putnam, no date.

Westermarck, Edward. *A Short History of Marriage.* New York: Humanities Press, 1968.

Whitman, Howard. *The Sex Age.* New York: Bobbs-Merrill, 1962.

Williams, Glanville. *The Sanctity of Life and the Criminal Law.* New York: Alfred A. Knopf, 1957.

Winch, Robert F., and Robert McGinnis (eds.). *Selected Studies in Marriage and the Family.* New York: Henry Holt and Co., 1953.

———. *Mate Selection.* New York: Harper and Brothers, 1958.

Winter, Walter T. *Divorce and You.* New York: Crowell-Collier Publishing Co., 1963.

Wood, Frederick C., Jr. *Sex and the New Morality.* New York: Association Press, 1968.

# INDEX

3  5282  00351  0206